The GIRLS of SUMMER

THE
GIRLS
OF
SUMMER

THE U.S. WOMEN'S SOCCER TEAM
AND HOW IT CHANGED THE WORLD

Jere Longman

HarperCollins*Publishers*

FIRST EDITION

Printed on acid-free paper

Designed by Elliott Beard

Library of Congress Cataloging-in-Publication Data has been applied for.

ISBN 0-06-019657-2

00 01 02 03 04 ❖/RRD 10 9 8 7 6 5 4 3 2

To Deborah and Julie-Ann, and to my parents

CONTENTS

Contents

The GIRLS of SUMMER

1

The List

BENCHES HAVE ALWAYS seemed comically out of place on a soccer field, the scooped Plexiglas roofing resembling a bus stop, the nervous, hunched coaches smoking and checking their watches as if waiting impatiently for public transportation. Lauren Gregg, who does not smoke and sometimes seemed too busy even to inhale a breath, instead held a marker in her hand on the American sideline. She was going nowhere anytime soon. The assistant coach wrote 10 names on a borrowed piece of paper this blistering July afternoon, the San Gabriel mountains doing a smog-shimmy above the lip of the Rose Bowl, the United States and China having played to near collapse under an interrogating, bare-bulb sun.

Through two hours of regulation and overtime neither team had mustered a goal in the final of the 1999 Women's World Cup, and so the game would be decided by the most tense and capricious arbiter— penalty kicks. The ball would be placed 12 yards from goal on a white dot, an oversized cue ball set on green felt lushness. Five players from each team would shoot and the goalkeepers would face worse odds than a carnival game, lucky to stop one attempt out of five. Hope for the keeper offered only three slim options—to guess beforehand and make a desperate lunge left or right, to maintain itchy patience and react after the ball was struck, or to read the shooter's body language on the approach and hope that the hip or knee or foot would betray some accidental intent. This is what Tony DiCicco, the American head coach, preferred. Reading. Not the splayed, mortar-wound dive of guessing, or the zero intolerance of reacting, but the bar-code scan of a shooter's form for some inadvertent signal. Maybe there would be no signal, but a faint impression would emerge, a feeling, a premonition, a detection of insecurity in the sag of the head or the droop of the shoulders. The best goalkeepers, DiCicco believed, could sense the electrical hum of distress like a shark.

As the 90 minutes of regulation moved into two 15-minute periods of fallow overtime, Gregg began to make her list. The first five on the list were guaranteed to shoot, alternating with Chinese players. If the penalty-kick phase remained tied, six through 10 would be on alert for the roulette of sudden death. During preparation for the Women's World Cup, Gregg had logged nearly every penalty kick taken by the American players in practice over six months, noting whether the kick was accurate, whether it missed, whether it was placed high or low and to the left or the right, whether it was launched confidently or struck with leaky assurance. The essence of soccer was spontaneity and improvisation, and Gregg realized that it was a player's game, but she believed that almost nothing should be left to chance. She was the team's tactical analyst, head scout, video expert. At 39, she abhorred passivity. Seven years earlier, she had broken her back, and doctors told her she might never walk again. Having recovered her health enough to scrimmage with the national team, she worked with obsessive diligence of those who lived life as a second chance. She logged the rehearsed penalty kicks in a notebook, on scraps of paper, whatever she could find, sometimes relying on another person to write while she called out hits and misses like a firing-range instructor.

After the second overtime, the American players walked and jogged to the sideline in relieved exhaustion. They had escaped disaster in the first extra period with a headed ball saved off the goal line. They drank water from bottles, poured it over their heads, draped themselves in icy towels, and lay on the verdant turf to have their flatlining legs resuscitated by massage. The temperature on the field had reached 105 degrees. The coaches gave the players a few quiet minutes to rest, to rehydrate, to spritz each other with the small chatter of reassurance.

"This is ours."

"This is what we've been working for six months."

"They are not going to take it from us."

There was a jaw-set composure, an inevitability, about the Americans as they waited for the penalty kicks. Some of them sat up on the turf, legs spread, a teammate pushing on their backs to make their tired muscles limber and responsive. Sweat, mixed with dousings of water, beaded and dribbled from their faces.

On this seething afternoon of July 10, women's sport had reached its apotheosis after a century of forbidden participation, neglect, dismissal, grudging acceptance, and at least in the United States, eventual legal and public embrace after the passage in 1972 of Title IX, which prohibited discrimination on the basis of gender at educational institutions receiving federal aid.

Women's team sports reached a critical mass of public and corporate interest in the mid-1990s. Connecticut won the national collegiate basketball championship in 1995 with an undefeated season and with a nearness to a New York media market that gave the team widespread, legitimizing coverage. At the 1996 Atlanta Olympics, American women won gold medals in basketball, soccer and softball, and followed with a victory in hockey at the 1998 Winter Games in Nagano, Japan. Professional leagues formed in both basketball and softball and plans were being drawn for a women's soccer league to begin play in 2001.

A women's sporting event had never been played on such a grand stage as the World Cup, out from behind the curtain of the Olympics, able to breathe its own air, cast its own light. For the final in the Rose Bowl, 90,185 fans crammed into a football stadium for women's soccer, the largest crowd ever to watch a women's sporting event in the United States and, presumably, the world. President Clinton munched on popcorn in a luxury suite, "so far on the edge of my seat," he would say later, "I actually almost fell out of the skybox."

An official of FIFA, soccer's Swiss-based world governing body, approached Gregg and asked for the roster of American penalty kickers. Any reasonably athletic person could make a penalty kick, could elude a goalie and shoot a ball into a goal that stood eight yards wide and eight feet tall. A goalkeeper had to defend an area the size of a two-car garage. But the pressure of a filled stadium, the stovetop boil of national expectation, could work like plaque in the bloodstream, constricting reliability, causing arteriosclerosis in a shooter's confidence. In this very same Rose Bowl, Italy's Roberto Baggio, the Divine Ponytail, considered the world's top player, ballooned a penalty kick in the final of the 1994 men's World Cup against Brazil. He had done the unforgivable, missing the goal entirely, and his head dropped like a guillotine.

The ability to make a penalty kick reveals little about a person's general skill at soccer, just as kicking a field goal confirms nothing about competence at football. What is required is composure in static moments, decisiveness and accuracy in the stationary instant when time slows and stretches like taffy, noise disappears as if a window has been shut, and vision and perception narrow into a tunneling aloneness. Penalty kicks are tormenting, and universally dreaded by players who take them, but there is nothing like the captivating agony they bring. Five players on each team, 10 kicks, nothing to be judged or reviewed, the ball goes into the net or it does not, a point goes on the scoreboard or it does not, no muddled conclusion, the whole body of the shooter launched in ecstatic release or convulsed in inconsolable despair. In these untethered seconds, the handrail of teamwork is ungraspable. All eyes and pressure fall to the shooter. No one else can share the praise or deflect the blame.

China won the coin toss and, given no option, would take the first penalty kick. The shootout would proceed like a baseball game reduced to five urgent at-bats instead of nine leisurely innings. The first shooter was in many ways the most vital. It was her job to score emphatically and to send a ripple of calm through her teammates. A miss could drag a team into a psychological undertow. Michelle Akers would have been the natural choice to lead off for the United States. At 5-foot-10, 150 pounds, she was known as Mufasa by her teammates because of her Lion King mane of brown curls. Playing through repeated injury and the sapping limits of chronic fatigue syndrome, she possessed a confidence that straddled recklessness, sending teammates and opponents sprawling like bowling pins. When the Americans were awarded a penalty kick late in the semifinals of the 1996 Olympic tournament, Akers turned toward the coaches and demanded with her insistent look to take it. She did and the Americans won. In the semifinals of the 1999 World Cup, the United States held to a tenuous 1–0 lead over Brazil with 10 minutes remaining when another penalty kick was granted. Akers volunteered again, *Yeah, baby, give me that,* and she stood over the ball, head down like a placekicker, waiting, waiting, waiting, until the tension seemed to spot-weld the Brazilian keeper to the goal line. Akers had scored with an authoritative stroke, but she was unavailable now for penalty kicks in the final, having been inadvertently punched in the head by goalkeeper Briana Scurry. Akers had played herself to such exhaustion after regulation that her jersey had to be cut off with a pair of scissors.

The absence of Akers meant that Carla Overbeck, the team captain, would shoot first for the Americans. Her place on the defensive line had seemed tenuous before the World Cup began. At 31, Overbeck lacked the speed of her teammates, and sometimes she played with a risky caution. Gregg had considered it one of her most important successes to keep Overbeck in the lineup. In truth, it was difficult to imagine the Americans succeeding without her. She was the leader of the team and in many ways its most vital player. Having grown up in suburban Dallas, a fan of Roger Staubach and his fourth-quarter rescues of the Dallas Cowboys, Overbeck possessed the same unruffled composure and impatience with mediocrity. Everything about her, her angular face, the way she talked, even the way she spit through her front teeth, suggested confidence and reliability. She set such a demanding tone for physical fitness that she lifted weights the day before her one-year-old son, Jackson, was born. In the opening World Cup match against Denmark, a game official had told the married American women to remove their wedding rings to avoid possible slashing injuries. It seemed an unreasonable request, considering that male soccer players wore more jewelry than home-shopping models. "These don't come off," Overbeck said bluntly, and the official relented. In the final, she had played the game of her life, allowing none of China's speedy forwards behind her or around her. And now it was Overbeck's job to score the first penalty kick, to assure her teammates that their own shots would be just as accurate and unstoppable.

Second up for the Americans would be Joy Fawcett, the elegant defender who had assisted on the winning goal against China in the gold-medal game of the 1996 Summer Olympics. It was Fawcett, too, who scored the winning goal off a corner kick against Germany in the 1999 World Cup quarterfinals. She had sustained her soccer career through the birth of two daughters, playing with a pickpocket's stealthy grace. DiCicco long considered her the team's most consistent player and the best defender in the world. In February, four months before the World Cup began, the coach was stunned when Fawcett approached him and asked if she were going to be cut from the team. He would have laughed if he had not realized that she was serious. She might have seemed an unlikely choice to take a penalty kick. But, intermittently, Gregg approached the American players during the spring, telling them that she was considering them for penalty kicks in the World Cup, gauging their reactions. Fawcett seemed eager.

At the inaugural Women's World Cup, played in China in 1991, the Americans were so unnerved about the possibility of penalty kicks that the coaches made them rehearse at one practice without balls in an elaborate pantomime. Each player walked to the penalty spot with an imaginary ball, pretended to set it down, backed up several steps then ran forward and feigned a kick while the goalie made an illusory dive. After each kick, the shooter ran back to midfield and joined her teammates in mock celebration. The Chinese spectators looked quizzically at this fanciful exercise, as if to say, "What the hell are these Americans doing?" Then, DiCicco remembered, they began to smile as if they, too, were in on the joke. Fawcett had been among the reluctant players in 1991, but, eight years later, when Gregg said to her at practice, "I'd have you in my five," Fawcett replied, "I would want one."

"That showed the evolution of the psyche of the team," said Gregg.

"Every one of them can kick the ball between the goal posts. That's not the issue. The psychological element is the number one variable."

Third on the list was Kristine Lilly, the most experienced international player in the world, man or woman. She had made 186 appearances for the United States, and she could swing effortlessly between midfield and forward. She had joined the national team in 1987 at age 16, so young that she had to ask her parents for permission to take a trip to China. Twelve years later, she played with such quiet efficiency that she often seemed invisible around her more flamboyant teammates. After the World Cup, a Colorado woman would feel so secure with Lilly's low profile that she would attempt to impersonate her at a soccer match. No one was in better shape on the team, or played more minutes, than Lilly, and no one could match her brilliance for the routine. In the first overtime of the World Cup final, Lilly slid two yards from the left goal post after a corner kick, as she had done hundreds of times and headed away a shot that saved the game, an ordinary maneuver in an extraordinary moment. "Just doing my job," she said in typical understatement.

Number four on the list was Mia Hamm, the sport's all-time leading scorer with 111 international goals, 34 more than even the great Pelé of Brazil. She was an unselfish superstar, a ferocious defender, always willing to pass the ball, along with credit for her success, to her teammates. But Hamm was also a player of fragile confidence, insecure, punishingly self-critical. When she went without a goal for eight exhibition games as the Americans prepared for the World Cup, Hamm had a meeting with DiCicco and appeared distraught to the point of tears.

"I've lost a step," she told him.

"No you haven't," he told her, taking Hamm through a checklist of her skills and convincing her that her game needed only a tuneup, not an overhaul.

With her scoring and passing, Hamm had dominated the first two matches of the World Cup, against Denmark and Nigeria, but now she had gone four games without a goal and, always searingly honest about her frailties, had admitted queasiness about taking a penalty kick.

"Penalty kicks are not about technique, it's about confidence,"

Hamm said after the semifinal victory over Brazil. "You have this one opportunity to put your team ahead or tie. You have to be completely focused and completely confident. I'm still not at that level."

But DiCicco had insisted that she be included among the first five shooters if the final was to be resolved by the vagary of penalty kicks. He had begun to question himself about removing Hamm from the third game of the World Cup, a meaningless round-robin match against North Korea, knowing that when her scoring came to a halt, it did not start again so easily. Perhaps she should have played every minute of every game, he told himself. Maybe the goals would have kept coming and her confidence would not have flickered. But he hadn't, and now the World Cup would be resolved as much by chance as by skill. By his way of thinking, Hamm, however nervously, had to take one of the kicks. If the Americans lost, she would question herself for not being involved in the decisive moment. And he would be forever second-guessed by the media, by the fans, by other coaches, and he would forever second-guess himself.

"Can you imagine not putting in the world's greatest scorer?" he said.

In the fifth spot on her list, Gregg wrote two names. One was Julie Foudy, the American co-captain, and the other was Brandi Chastain. This could be the decisive kick, one that would secure the dog-pile celebration of victory or the stunned, gallows-walk of defeat, and Gregg wrestled with her decision. At one time, Chastain would have been the obvious choice. She was a theatrical player, nicknamed Hollywood for her ornate style and her sense of the dramatic. Since she was nine or 10 and heard a stadium crowd cheer for a goal she scored during a halftime exhibition, she had been drawn to florid, climactic moments like this. "Brandi would have preferred to hear the national anthem before she kicked," DiCicco joked. "Or a drum roll."

From 1996 until early 1999, DiCicco could not remember Chastain missing a single penalty kick. But she had struggled with consistency in recent months, missing as many shots in practice as she made. Three months before the World Cup, in a tournament in Portugal, she had become intimidated by the Chinese goalie and had ricocheted a shot off the crossbar. The Americans had lost. Taking penalty kicks with her right foot, Chastain had become predictable, shooting to the goal-keeper's right, and if the Americans had decoded this pattern, no doubt the Chinese had, too.

"Talk to Brandi," DiCicco told Gregg. "See if she'll take one left-footed."

It is one thing to be a switch hitter in baseball, but it is far rarer to find a soccer player as comfortable with one foot as with the other. Few women, or men, can shoot left or right with equal precision, especially in the crucible of a World Cup. Chastain was one of them. Her father had coached her when she was young, and after having blown out his own right knee while taking up soccer in his mid–thirties, he brought his daughter to a park down the street in San Jose, California, and made her pass and shoot with her left foot, day after day, week after week. If the wiring in one leg became unraveled, she could always rely on the other.

As Gregg walked up to her, Chastain lay facedown on the Rose Bowl turf, eyes closed, her shoulders covered by a towel, so exhausted that she felt she could not control her legs, telling herself just to relax, to breathe easily. Her legs had begun to cramp in the second overtime, and now she worried for a fleeting moment whether she would be able to take a penalty kick without another seizure in her calves. And yet, outwardly, she appeared as calm as if she had been tanning in a quiet park, her hair pulled into a California-blond ponytail, her ears decorated with a pair of diamond earrings that her husband had given her as an anniversary present.

"Do you want a kick?" Gregg asked.

The question caught Chastain off-guard. Was there any doubt? Of course, she wanted a kick.

"Yes," she nodded.

"Are you going to make it?"

"Yes."

"Kick it with your left foot."

"Okay."

The first five kickers were set. Foudy would be sixth, followed by Tisha Venturini, Shannon MacMillan, Sara Whalen and Kate Sobrero. If the score remained tied after 10 kicks, Scurry, the American goal-keeper, would take her chance. This is how the women's game gained legitimacy in Germany. In 1989, the goalkeeper Marion Isbert scored the decisive goal in a penalty kick shootout against Italy in the semifinals of the European championship. Her picture made the front page of Germany's largest-selling newspaper and she became a national hero. The most protracted shootout is said to have occurred in 1989 in Buenos Aires, when the male club teams, Argentinos Juniors and Racing, resolved a draw after 44 penalty kicks.

"It was a world record for penalties," the Uruguayan author, Eduardo Galeano, wrote in his book *Soccer in Sun and Shadow*. "In the stadium, no one was left to celebrate and no one even knew which side won."

The Americans and Chinese were certain to come to a quicker, more definitive resolution. As the American players gathered around the coaches, slapping high-fives, placing arms on each other's shoulders for support, Gregg read off the names with the crisp matter-of-factness of a grocery list. In this moment of exhaustion and distraction, though, there was confusion about the order of the penalty kicks.

"Which kick are you taking?" Hamm asked MacMillan, who possessed the hardest shot on the team.

"I don't have one," MacMillan responded, meaning in the top five.

"Do you want one?" Hamm asked.

"Yeah, sure."

Hamm approached Gregg. She was adamant. She did not want to take a kick.

"Why isn't Mac taking one?" Hamm said. "Mac should be taking one."

The holder of a master's degree in consulting psychology from Harvard, Gregg knew that she could not allow any waver of authority in her voice, any quiver of doubt in Hamm. Three days earlier, while practicing before a crowd of 3,000 spectators, Hamm had seemed precarious with her penalty kicks, firing shot after shot over the crossbar, but she had worked through her nervousness, readjusting her aim, and she had begun to put the ball into the net. In previous years, the coaches believed, she had not wanted the responsibility of carrying the American team, or if she wanted the responsibility, she was not prepared to risk the consequences of failure. She was a player of great emotion, and sometimes her emotions worked against her. When she wasn't scoring, her whole game once seemed to suffer. She didn't chase down balls as enthusiastically, or work as relentlessly on defense. But Gregg had sensed in Hamm a new completeness, a willingness to lead, to be the fulcrum on which the team pivoted. Intense, shy, Hamm now seemed to be more vocal in encouraging other players, in sensing their needs, in giving them instruction.

"Mia you're taking one," Gregg told her.

"Why?" Hamm asked.

"Because I've already turned in the list."

There was nothing left to argue, no time to alter the order.

"You'll be fine," Gregg said.

"I know," Hamm replied.

As the 10 American players gathered at midfield to begin the penalty-kick phase, Chastain remembered a suddenly emboldened Hamm saying, "We're going to win this."

"I think she even surprised herself," Chastain said. "It's not like her to say something like that."

Before leaving the sideline, Lilly walked over to Scurry, the American goalkeeper, who was sitting on the ground, drinking water, a baleful stare of concentration on her face that she described as the look of death. Lilly and Scurry slapped hands.

"Catlike reflexes," Lilly told Scurry. "Catlike reflexes."

"You're going to get one," Lilly said.

"I'll get one, you guys do the rest," Scurry replied.

On the sideline, dressed in a white polo shirt, blue shorts and sunglasses, Gregg felt the burden of her decision. Six months of training, of logging every kick in practice, a whole career of judgment and instinct, the entire World Cup, maybe even the future of a women's professional league, came down to this, 10 names submitted on a piece of paper.

Shit, she told herself. *I hope I didn't make a mistake.*

2

"I Will Have Two Fillings"

FOUR HOURS BEFORE the Americans and the Chinese appeared on the field, the ant-picnic of sport utility vehicles clogged roads dipping into the canyon of the Rose Bowl, bumper-to-bumper suburban anticipation. Inside, girls wore their Title IX grease-paint, their faces laminated red, white and blue like some Betsy Ross Halloween, Mia Hamm's No. 9 and her name scrawled on their arms as gender-equity tattoos. College boys wrapped themselves in flag sarongs, while young boys joined young girls in wearing Hamm's jersey, swept up in this acceptable moment of cultural cross-dressing. The families of the players sat in scattered groups, hopeful, scared, the natural worry of parents and friends and the haunt of possible defeat muting their cheeriness as spectators. The governor of California joined the president in luxury-box comfort. Pockets of Chinese fans proudly, defiantly waved their red and yellow star flags, little Alamos of resistance.

Up the California coast, a writer named Caroline Fletcher watched the match in a sports bar in the North Beach section of San Francisco. During the game, a municipal bus would push a pickup truck on top of her car. And when an inspector would come to assess the damage, she would be so riveted to the game that she would refuse to leave the bar. "A pickup is on your car, what can you do?" she said. She kept putting the inspector off, saying, "I'll be there in a minute," until he would give up and join her to watch the taut conclusion of the match.

In West Haven, Connecticut, Carl Guarneri, whose daughter attended Tony DiCicco's soccer camp, would hurry into a suit for a family wedding as he watched the match. With five minutes remaining, he would leave for the wedding, glancing at a portable television as he drove, missing the beginning of the ceremony as he watched the penalty kicks in the church parking lot. Later, on the way home from the reception, he would complain to his wife that his suit was too tight, that he was gaining weight and needed to start working out. Only when he undressed did he realize that, engrossed by the game, he had hoisted his suit pants over a pair of Bermuda shorts.

The American soccer team produced old-fashioned nationalism of the unprecedented, of transatlantic flights and moon walks, putting 90,000 spectators in the stands for the championship game and drawing 40 million more on American television, generating a higher rating than for the finals of professional hockey and basketball. Shattered was any lingering belief that no one would pay to watch women play soccer. Attendance reached 658,167 for the three-week World Cup, more than doubling the attendance of 300,527 for the 1999 women's NCAA basketball tournament, previously the largest sporting event held for women in this country. Some dismissed the attendance as America's infatuation with the big event, but the glow of the American team would linger long after the tournament. On Labor Day weekend, the women would draw 30,000 for a doubleheader match against Ireland in Foxboro, Massachusetts, doubling the usual attendance of the New England Revolution men's team in Major League Soccer. Three months after the World Cup final, the United

States women would attract more than 94,000 fans for three matches of a tournament played in the Midwest.

In the swarm of adulation during the World Cup, girls rode the elevators in team hotels and knocked on the players doors and followed Akers into the bathroom in public places. She would close the door and see the waiting of little feet. Professional autograph seekers hung in lobbies—"breathers" Kate Sobrero called them—and players took to registering under assumed names like Pig Farmer and Elvis. But pseudonyms provided only a thin shield of privacy. After a match against Nigeria at Soldier Field in Chicago, as Sobrero spoke by cell phone to a college friend in the parking lot, a man offered the friend money if she would let his daughter speak with a World Cup player. As the team left the stadium, a teenage girl began chasing the bus, arms raised, screaming, for a quarter mile, a half mile, so blind with delirium that she nearly ran into a parked car. Finally, worried that the girl might hurt herself, the players stopped the bus and Chastain gave her a pair of autographed shoes.

Soccer is best experienced as sport cloaked in spectacle and secular religion, and for the first time, Americans on a large scale felt—if only fleetingly, in a sanitized, hooligan-free, sample-sized container—the rosary-clutch, the chest ache, that makes this game the athletic heartbeat of nearly every other country of the world. At the 1990 men's World Cup in Italy, the red, white and green national flag was hung out daily on clotheslines with the laundry. Wine was furtively placed in bottles of mineral water to subvert laws governing drinking near the stadiums. Diners were left to chew on conversation while waiters and chefs clustered around televisions in the kitchen, watching the Azzurri, the Blues, in tense hope and, ultimately, in gathered betrayal. Four years later, as France won the 1998 men's World Cup, the collective indifference of Paris melted into the city's largest celebration since the end of World War II, the team's open-air victory bus turning a corner into the corpuscle-choke of the Champs-Elysées and being swallowed by the arterial pulse of a million people gathering in unexpected triumph.

Sustained interest in the 1999 Women's World Cup built gradually in the United States, like the word of mouth for books and movies that have escaped the Big Bang of critical approval. The timing for the final could not have been more exquisite, slotted in the test-pattern weeks between the end of professional basketball and the beginning of football. History, like a carpenter's level, requires a bubble of meticulous placement. Seven days later, and the national attention span would have been elsewhere. Exactly one week after the championship game, John F. Kennedy Jr.'s plane would fall off a radar screen. The open-mouthed, hugging, leaping, ponytail whip of exult on magazine covers, the "Girls Rule!" and "What a Kick!" celebrations, the muscular jubilance of Chastain in her sports bra, her famous abdominal muscles as grooved and ridged and seemingly hard as the carapace of a turtle, all of this would fall from the public radar, too, replaced by a media cortege of grief, a nation returning a bereaved salute that a boy had given his slain father three decades earlier.

"If this game had happened a week later, it would have been on ESPN2," said Jim Moorhouse, director of communications for the United States Soccer Federation.

This was America's new, cable-wired, online nationalism, honeycombed lives intersecting during collective agony, the knee-pad titillation of Oval Office sex, the rubbernecking of celebrity violence. Until the Women's World Cup, the two biggest sports-related stories of the 1990s were the murder trial of O. J. Simpson and the knee-whacking shatter of figure skating's porcelain myth. Fans cheer for professional city teams and alma maters, but there is no grand, cumulative rooting in the United States except for the disposable novelty of the Olympics. With rare exception the Super Bowl is background noise, commercials interrupted by a flabby game, the Coca-Cola bears more engaging than the Chicago Bears.

Not since the 1980 Olympic victory of the United States hockey team over the former Soviet Union had there been this kind of shared athletic excitement. But that hockey game carried the arousal of Cold War politics and the lithium rescue from national malaise. It occurred during the worst recession since the Great Depression. The Women's World Cup was a boom-time celebration of gender opportunity that occurred during a summer when Elizabeth Dole became the first serious female candidate for president, First Lady Hillary Rodham Clinton explored a run for the U.S. Senate and Carly S. Fiorina of Hewlett-Packard became the first female CEO of a mega-corporation. It was also the summer when the Miss America pageant explored the possibility of allowing contestants who had been divorced or had an abortion. A season when Eileen M. Collins became the first female Space Shuttle commander, Tori Murden of Louisville, Kentucky, became the first American to row across the Atlantic Ocean and Margaret MacGregor of suburban Seattle prepared for the first sanctioned boxing match between a woman and a man. There could be no doubt that the United States women's soccer team put the most visible crack in the glass ceiling.

"They were among the first generation of a large volume of female athletes taking us to a new place—the financial support of colleges, families flocking to a sporting event, a message of what used to be in sport, of passion, inspiration, fulfilling dreams, hero-epic kinds of things," said Donna Lopiano, executive director of the Women's Sports Foundation, a national non-profit organization dedicated to expanding sports opportunities for girls and women. "They demonstrated economic viability, which is what you have to do in a capitalistic society, first and foremost, to be respected. They got significant television ratings. As Billie Jean King demonstrated against Bobby Riggs in 1973, the biggest stereotype they had to overcome was that women fold under pressure. This team put that idea away. And they carried a different value system and popularized it. They abhorred violence. I can think of a moment in the championship game when someone took out Mia Hamm. They were looking to do it, and Mia immediately went to the ball for her free kick, put her hand up to the Chinese player like, 'I don't want to hear about it,' and went on with the game. I don't think that would have been the male reaction."

Baseball may be called the national pastime, but it survives on the sentimentality of middle-age men who wistfully dream of playing catch with their fathers and sons. Football, with its dull stoppages, lost its military-industrial relevance with the end of the Cold War, and has become as tired and predictable in performance as it is in political metaphor. The professional game floats on an ocean of gambling, the players' steroid-laced bodies having outgrown their muscular and skeletal carriages. Biceps rip from their moorings, ankles break on simple pivots, Achilles' tendons shrivel like slugs doused with salt. Soccer and basketball are the only mainstream sports that truly plug into the modem-pulse of a dot-com society. Soccer is perfectly suited for a country of the hamster-treadmill pace, the remote-control zap and the national attention deficit—two 45-minute halves, the clock never stops, no commercial interruptions, the final whistle blows in less than two hours. It is a fluid game of systemized chaos that, no matter how tightly scripted by coaches, cannot be regulated any more than information can be truly controlled on the Internet.

Like representative government, soccer has been imported from England and democratized in the United States. It has become the great social and athletic equalizer for suburban America. From kindergarten, girls are placed on equal footing with boys. In the fall, weekend soccer games are as prevalent in suburbia as yard sales. Girls have their own leagues, or they play with boys, and they suffer from no tradition that says that women will grow up professionally to be less successful than men.

"In the United States, not only are girls on equal footing, but the perception now is that American women can be better than American men," said Donna Shalala, the Secretary of Health and Human Services. "That's a turning point, a huge breakthrough in perception."

Soccer has become the fastest growing sport in the country in both high school and college. From 1981 through 1999, the number of women's collegiate soccer teams grew from 77 to 818, propelled by Title IX. There are now 93 more women's teams than men's teams at the university level. Soccer was serious enough now as a sport that coaches were fired for poor performance, the big football schools were showing increased interest and a few of the top women's collegiate programs now used private planes for recruiting. Chris Petrucelli, who won a national championship at Notre Dame, was lured to Texas in early 1999 by a contract worth $180,000 annually and by a $28 million soccer and track facility.

On the high school level, there were 257,586 girls registered to play soccer in 1998–1999, compared with 11,534 in 1976–1977. Of the 18 million registered soccer players in the United States, 7.5 million, or 40 percent, were girls and women, according to the Soccer Industry Council of America.

"My son, who is 10, took girls to a match," said Donna de Varona, chairwoman of the Women's World Cup and an Olympic champion swimmer. "When he goes to a dance, he feels awkward. But they were fine about soccer. It's a very comfortable relationship between males and females about competition, about sharing a passion for competing. It's a new language, a nonthreatening language, directed elsewhere rather than at each other. My son looked around at the stadium and said, 'Will they do this for guys some day?'"

At the World Cup level, American men are decades behind the rest of the world in terms of development and achievement. Until 1990, the men had gone 40 years without qualifying for soccer's world championship, and at the 1998 World Cup in France, the United States finished 32nd out of 32 teams, sinking in the quicksand of ego and ineptitude. Plenty of Americans have never even seen a topflight men's game, so there is little preconception that women put forth a subordinate effort.

"I think it is really important that this country doesn't have a tradition of seeing soccer as the epitome of masculinity as it is in Europe and Latin America," said Allen Guttmann, a sports historian and professor of American studies at Amherst College who has written extensively on women in sports. "Women don't have to struggle in that tradition."

Women's soccer is much newer, and the United States caught an early international wave when the sport began to swell in the mid–1980s. It would become fashionable in some places to dismiss the American women, to say they won simply because they held a cultural advantage over women from other countries. Yes, they did hold a cultural edge. The North Korean team, from a totalitarian nation wracked by international isolation and famine, arrived to play the Americans without so much as reliable dental care. After one player complained of a toothache, and received free care from FIFA, soccer's world governing body, a number of the players began complaining of dental problems so they could also get free treatment, said Brett Lashbrook, a spokesman for the Women's World Cup. But to attribute the American success only to a cultural advantage is an argument as specious as dismissing the New York Yankees because they have the highest payroll in major league baseball. In countries from Scandinavia to Iran, women began playing soccer before the Americans did. The games must still be played, and won or lost, the shots made and saved, and teams such as China, Brazil, Norway and Germany are quickly catching up.

The American women did not have the same strength and speed as male players, and they routinely were defeated by 18-year-old boys during scrimmages prior to the World Cup. But the World Cup itself was a competition among women, and in that respect, it was as unfair and meaningless to compare them disadvantageously to men as it was to compare boxers in different weight classes. The United States reached the final by playing an attractive, selfless, joyous, attacking style that, at a slower speed, brought a certain clarity to its game, which celebrated rudimentary brilliance and a reliance on the group rather than the individual. Female basketball players are often marginalized because they do not have the size or jumping ability of male players, because they do not dunk and play above the rim. But, in soccer, a lack of size is an advantage, not a disadvantage, in moving expertly in tight spaces. The prized skills of passing and dribbling are no less evident in women, and in fact, are a more essential part of a game based on fundamental collaboration.

Speaking of Mia Hamm, the coach of the Mexican women's team, Leo Cuellar, said, "Her quickness off the ball, her passing, dribbling, cutting, are up to the level of high-class men in the world."

Playing for the equivalent of minimum wage for professional athletes, Hamm and her teammates were unfailingly successful, having previously won the 1991 Women's World Cup and the 1996 Summer Olympics and having taken a bronze medal at the 1995 World Cup. They played fiercely and powerfully, and they were so well-conditioned that they would not surrender a goal in the second half of any of their six games in the 1999 World Cup. All of them had college degrees or were working toward degrees. They were smart, funny, gracious, attractive, accessible to fans and reporters. Their passion for playing was evident in the way they smiled and hugged and celebrated on the field, and their sense of responsibility was evident in the way they stayed around after games, autographing posters, jerseys, soccer balls, the foreheads of awestruck girls. Most importantly, they played as a team, which was hammered home by the self-parodying wink of advertising. When one player went on a date, they all went on a date. When one had dental work, they all had dental work. "I Will Have Two Fillings" became the password for cooperation, dependability, solidarity, consensus. Given a free night several days before the final, the players chose to spend it, not with their families, but with each other in a Mexican restaurant.

"We are not accustomed to seeing women work together," wrote Bonnie DeSimone, who covered the Women's World Cup for the *Chicago Tribune.* "Hollywood bombards us daily with images of women competing with each other for men and prestige. Women are supposed to connive, gossip, backstab. Women are supposed to climb the corporate ladder and kick it out from underneath their sisters. Women are not supposed to be seen in the same dress at the same party, so it is novel to see these players walking the same walk, talking the same talk, wearing the same warm-ups."

Images of American female athletes have been captured mostly in fleeting snapshots from the Olympics, where individuals have been more often celebrated than teams. There was no Olympic soccer for women until 1996, and, even with the home country playing, NBC reduced the women's gold-medal match to highlight footage. Often, the most visible and enduring image is of impossibly flexible figure skaters and gymnasts whose international careers blossom and wither in their teenage years. Little girls in pretty boxes, as the author Joan Ryan refers to them. In these sports, maturity is seen as a hindrance to performance, the appearance of breasts and hips causing an unfortunate realignment of the body's center of gravity and providing an impeding wobble to the human gyroscope.

The American soccer team, by contrast, offered women who were playing elite sports at a high international level into their late twenties and early thirties. They were single, married, two had had young children. They came in all shapes and sizes and their bodies were as appreciated for how they performed as for how they looked. "Heroin chic is out," said Kate Sobrero, the young American defender. "People have begun to respect women who are in shape and take care of their bodies." The Americans formed a team that likely will never be seen again in this transitory age of free agency in professional sports. Seven of the 20 American players had been together for 11 years. Among each other, they found their best friends, they vacationed in groups, they attended each other's weddings, baby-sat for each other's children and, like British-invasion rockers, they even wore identical pantsuits for public appearances. When Michelle Akers suffered her most excruciating attacks of chronic fatigue syndrome, her teammates drove her home from practice. When Tiffeny Milbrett lost a necklace during practice, play was halted and the entire team walked the field in search of the missing jewelry. When Tisha Venturini fell into a post-Olympic depression in 1996, losing considerable weight and strength, her teammates intervened and helped to restore her resolve and her career.

No team is without its internal tensions, and the American women had distinct groupings of age and alma mater, but private cliques never became public nuisances. Perhaps the team's most urgent accomplishment away from soccer was to remain unified in purpose after a potentially divisive sexual harassment suit was filed in the summer of 1998 by one of their teammates against their former coach.

"We ended up seeing a different story unfold than the traditional male plot that includes individual heroes," said Mariah Burton Nelson, an author who has written extensively on the sociology of women in sports. "Several stars emerged. Little girls could see successful women athletes as role models. Little boys could see how talented the women were and how they were taken seriously by other adults. All of that makes a huge impression. Boys wearing jerseys of female players, having female athletic role models, that's new, in the last 10 years. It changes how boys think about women. It will change their relationships with women."

"Feminism is about increasing opportunity and respect for girls and women, and that's what female athletes are doing," said Burton Nelson, a former professional basketball player. "They call it role models. It's really radical what they are doing, changing opinions of women. I think female athletes are in the forefront of the feminist movement, although almost none of them use the word. They demonstrate strength, courage and freedom and they are going where no women have gone before. It is very exciting and has a huge impact on our culture."

Male athletes enter mainstream sports and follow safe, familiar tributaries, their secure careers flowing from the headwaters of long tradition, from Abner Doubleday's mythic invention of baseball to the peach-basket origins of basketball. But the women on the American soccer team were faced with all the Spindletop possibility and stock-market risk of speculators. They were pioneers, they made their own tradition. They began the team in anonymity, and, now, they had not only to play the game, but they had to build the World Cup's public awareness and to secure its financial viability. If they failed, not only the team, but the World Cup and the professional viability of the sport, might fail. This responsibility, this stepping onto a ledge of chance and venture and precarious gamble brought great pressure, but it also invested the American women with a vigorous sense of purpose, trust, reliance and competitive resolve.

"These are the most competitive women I've ever met," Brandi Chastain said. "You just don't want to let them down."

Everything became a competition for this team, especially for the nucleus of players that had been together for more than a decade. Colleen Hacker, the team's sports psychologist, remembers blood being drawn during a card game in which players had to reach forward and grab spoons, lest they be eliminated as in musical chairs. At a tournament in Portugal before the World Cup, the hunt for clues during a scavenger hunt became so raucous, with players hip-checking each other in the hotel hallway, that Tony DiCicco had to caution his players against injury, according to the reserve goalkeeper Saskia Webber. The team was in Chattanooga, Tennessee, during Halloween of 1997, when a pumpkin-carving contest turned into gourd warfare.

"They were hiding their pumpkins because they didn't want people stealing their ideas," said Aaron Heifetz, the team spokesman. "I've never seen anything so competitive."

This familiarity and common purpose also meant the players could challenge and demand of each other unceasingly, knock each other down in training, slide into each other's ankles, infuriate each other, with the confidence and respect that any practice blowups would not linger in their personal relationships.

Before the 1996 Summer Olympics, Shannon MacMillan fouled Hamm hard in practice one day, and Hamm, who was recovering from a knee injury, responded by pushing her. DiCicco screamed at Hamm, "If you don't want any contact, go play tennis. Get off the field." As DiCicco recalled, MacMillan took up for Hamm, saying, "It's okay, coach, I think I fouled her." It was exactly the response DiCicco had been seeking.

"I wanted the players pissed at me, not at each other," he said. "The best thing I could have done by coming down hard was to be the villain. You don't want that going on between teammates."

The Women's World Cup arrived at a time when women served as president of baseball's Milwaukee Brewers and basketball's Washington Wizards, and general manager of the San Jose Clash of Major League Soccer. Two NBA teams also had women running their financial operations. A few months after the World Cup, North Carolina and Notre Dame would draw a record crowd of 14,410 for the championship match of women's collegiate soccer, and Connecticut and Tennessee would draw 23,385 fans for a women's college basketball game.

"The mass popularity, the excitement of the final game, to me means we are moving toward unlimited possibility for women in sport after the World Cup," said Richard Lapchick, director of the Center for the Study of Sport in Society at Northeastern University. "I think women are going to break through barriers as leaders and players. We are not thinking of limitations anymore. We are thinking of who is best for the position, as well as where we might play games. We don't need to schedule a game in a small campus stadium if we can draw 23,000. If we market correctly and the team is good enough and we spend money to develop better players, we can see the unlimited possibilities."

While the American soccer team did provide an inviting peek forward, it also afforded a nostalgic glance backward by a public that does not begrudge actors and rock stars their astronomical incomes but wants a more familiar connection with its athlete-entertainers. Forget the fact that the American women were professionals and played for little money only because they were severely underpaid by the United States Soccer

Federation and had no league to boost their salaries. There was still a backyard quality to their enthusiasm that elicited a national embrace.

"People still long for the days when athletes were like them," said Mechelle Voepel, assistant sports editor of the *Kansas City Star.* "The days when baseball players used to ride the subway and had jobs in the offseason like everybody else. People still have that longing for that. When they saw the soccer team, they saw people they knew."

At the turn of the century, American fans had come to feel great confusion, resentment, dislocation toward sports and the athletes who played them. Players jumped from team to team, teams jumped from city to city, college athletes left school early, high school athletes sometimes skipped college and went directly to the pros. "Not knowing whether the player you like best will be in town next year, or whether the team will be in town next year, has the fan so disoriented," Lapchick said.

Further disillusionment was caused by the increased sharing in the headlines of scoring records with arrest records. As the millennium arrived, baseball's all-time leader in hits, Pete Rose, was disgraced because of gambling. Mark McGwire, the home run champion, had a body that appeared inflated for the Macy's Thanksgiving Parade and built his record with a steroid that was banned by other sports. Of the great running backs in history, O. J. Simpson had been convicted publicly, if not legally, of murdering his wife, and Jim Brown was appealing a jail sentence for vandalizing his wife's car in a domestic violence incident. Magic Johnson, the greatest basketball player of his generation, suffered from HIV, the virus that causes AIDS, from years of admittedly reckless sex. Diego Maradona of Argentina, second only to Pelé in the majesty of his soccer skills, was hospitalized with a serious heart condition and a cocaine addiction. Ben Johnson, the world's fastest man, had been stripped of his gold medal because of steroid propulsion, and Florence Griffith-Joyner, the world's fastest woman, had died in her sleep, never able to shake the suspicion that she also had achieved her speed through better chemistry. The two institutions that professed to be purer than all others—the Olympics and Notre Dame football—had been exposed for their hypocrisy, the Olympics tainted by corruption and unchecked drug use and Notre Dame sanctioned for rules violations. Eugene Robinson of the Atlanta Falcons, the NFL's civic man of the year in 1998, was arrested before the 1999 Super Bowl for allegedly soliciting prostitution from an undercover police officer. Peter Warrick of Florida State, the leading Heisman Trophy candidate in 1999, lost his bid when he faced a charge of grand theft. Two NFL players had been jailed on murder charges. Marty McSorley of the Boston Bruins faced a criminal assault charge for a vicious attack with his hockey stick. And the knee-whacking of Nancy Kerrigan by associates of Tonya Harding had raised the chilling prospect that one athlete would harm another for sporting gain.

Even with McGwire and Sammy Sosa chasing the home run record and with the New York Yankees winning more games than any baseball team had ever won, the 1998 World Series received its lowest television ratings ever. The 1999 World Series ratings were the second-lowest ever. The 1999 NCAA men's basketball tournament also reached a television nadir. In the NBA, there were troubling drop-offs, post–Michael Jordan, in television and spectator interest. Having difficulty determining what was real, Americans embraced what they knew to be fake, professional wrestling, which grabbed the largest audiences on cable television. In wrestling, there was no difficulty telling the heroes from the villains, the players didn't change teams and uniforms, and they illustrated the drift in sport from competition to celebrity and entertainment. The women's soccer team was the antithesis of this coarsening of American sport. The World Cup was something fresh and new. The competition was authentic, unsullied by the complications of big money. The players were having fun, they played as a team and there was no chance that they would spit on an umpire or choke their coach.

"ESPN is like turning on to *Eyewitness News*," said Webber, the reserve American goalkeeper. "Sports has become so negative. You can't watch without finding out that someone has been suspended, someone is facing laundering charges, someone has been picked up for soliciting and drug use. I think the public is tired of that, tired of seeing people being paid so much money to be so immature. I think they're tired of seeing people say, 'I'm not a role model.' That's ridiculous. Here comes a female team that could be your daughter, literally your daughter, that played rec soccer, that played in the backyard, that went to high school and college. You're not going to pick up the paper tomorrow and see one of us in it for money laundering or cocaine use or soliciting. You come to practice, you know your chances of getting an autograph are pretty high. If a kid says, 'Hey, let's take a picture,' I'm not going to say, 'Give me 20 bucks.' All of us want to be role models, want to be ambassadors. I'm not saying I'm some clean-cut kid who's home at 10 at night and sits in bed and drinks milk. I'm 28, I love to go out to the clubs, but I'm responsible, I'm intelligent, I know what's good and right to do."

3

Babe City

W ITH PRESIDENT CLINTON in attendance, security was unusually tight at the bank of elevators beneath the Rose Bowl press box. German shepherds sniffed the bags in which reporters carried their computers. Kelly Whiteside of *Newsday*, the Long Island newspaper, hurried into a closing elevator, only to find herself surrounded by security officials who were wearing black and carrying what appeared to be automatic weapons. "They were not amused," she said. "I was forcibly removed."

More than 500 reporters covered the final match of a tournament that had begun in the tire-ad anonymity of many daily sports sections, consigned by sports editors who were largely white and male and rubber-cemented to obsolete game stories, the dull football-baseball-basketball monopoly and numbing statistical pages, ignored by columnists who were uninformed and threatened by a game in which the ball was played with the feet and not the hands. In some ways, the

Women's World Cup would be the last great sporting event driven more by the print media than the broadcast media. *USA Today* and the large urban dailies in New York, Los Angeles, Chicago, Washington, Philadelphia, Dallas, the Bay Area and San Diego caught on early, determining that the largest event in the history of women's sports deserved serious, professional coverage. But never has the mainstream sporting media been so irrelevant to the making of a major sporting event. Important regional newspapers did not send staff writers to the tournament, citing financial concerns, staffing shortages, the inability to obtain credentials at the last minute. Papers in Houston, the nation's fifth-largest media market; in Denver, site of the country's last great newspaper war; in Minneapolis, the hometown paper of Briana Scurry, the American goalkeeper. Michelle Kaufman of the *Miami Herald* had to pay her own way to cover the championship game, and was only reimbursed later, "once editors realized what a big deal it was and decided to run giant front-page stories and photos. Just took them a while to catch on."

"We blew it on that one," said Glen Crevier, an assistant managing editor in charge of sports at the *Minneapolis Star Tribune*. "It's a major blunder at this point. If I had known how big it was going to be, we would have covered it."

The Women's World Cup built itself without any of the usual starmaker machinery, as the extreme sports such as snowboarding and skateboarding previously had, sidestepping the disinterest of the mainstream media. Kids and parents on the orange-slice fields of suburbia were alerted to the potential volcanic upthrust of the World Cup, while most sports pages and corporate boardrooms detected no seismic tremor of popularity beforehand. The World Cup provoked, imperiled, stunned male dominion. Mitch Albom of the *Detroit Free Press*, who is regularly voted the top sports columnist in the country by sports editors, accused the media of behaving "shamefully" and "irresponsibly" in leading the American bandwagon. In fact, the only irresponsible behavior was in ignoring the Women's World Cup. And there was no media bandwagon. The tournament earned legitimacy by building its own momentum. "There were no elaborate pregame shows, no special newspaper sections," wrote Christine Brennan of *USA Today*. "Just games. And sellouts. The minivan revolution ignored by the mainstream sports media for years was going on whether anyone paid attention or not." The word spread initially through nontraditional methods, through grassroots mailings, clever advertising, late-night television, the Internet, through daughters and fathers looking for shared sporting experiences.

"What the World Cup proved and the WNBA proved is that women's sports can survive in the big time even without a traditional male fan base," said Mary Jo Kane, a sports sociologist and director of the University of Minnesota's Tucker Center for Research on Women in Sport. "What is amazing is that this interest developed in the midst of a media blackout. Imagine what would happen if the media gave women one 50th of the coverage they give men. I won't say we can't use the media, but I won't say that lack of media coverage is a deathknell anymore, either."

At a time when newspapers were generally losing circulation, and were desperately looking to attract new readers, many sports sections were still not seriously cultivating half of their potential audience. Women make up 50 percent of the television viewership during the Olympics. Their interest in sports is undeniable. Two of the biggest sports stories of the decade involved women—the Nancy Kerrigan-Tonya Harding affair, and the Women's World Cup—yet the majority of American newspapers were unprepared to cover either one. Figure skating regularly grabbed higher television ratings than any sport but the NFL, and the American women's soccer team mirrored perfectly the suburban readership of most papers. But many sports departments remain in denial and confusion about what appeals to readers at a time when interest in sports is as splintered as interest in television. There remains a resistance to women's sports in general, and soccer in particular.

"Some people still don't get it," wrote Ann Killion of the *San Jose Mercury News*. "They still don't get that so many sports fans feel completely disenfranchised from professional sports, from the ticket prices, from the athletes' demeanor, from the corporate environment. They don't get that the moms and dads and kids who love sports don't have events they can attend together. Most professional sports are too expensive. Most aren't kid-friendly. They don't get that most Americans have

no problem these days rooting for female athletes. They don't get that
there is a huge and still growing fan base for soccer. That when the
product is presented well and the quality of play is high—male or
female—people want to see it. These mere notions threaten some people—media members and fans—who view sports as their personal
arena. They don't like a lot of enthusiastic kids, or women, or soccer
players, getting a piece of the pie. Or the sports page. Or the air time.
They've all been proven wrong in the summer of 1999. No one can ever
say again that nobody cares about women's sports."

The media were not the only ones slow to catch on. Major League
Soccer, the men's professional league, showed marginal interest. The
Women's Sports Foundation declined to buy a bloc of tickets for the
tournament, organizers said. Corporate giants such as Coca-Cola and
McDonald's, which spent hundreds of millions of dollars promoting
the Olympics and the men's World Cup, did not muster advertising
campaigns for the Women's World Cup. Organizers were guaranteed
only $6 million in revenue from the marketing arm of FIFA, soccer's
world governing body, compared with $40-plus million that the 1994
men's World Cup organizers generated. A $2 million sponsorship
offer from Sears had to be declined because FIFA perceived a conflict
with Adidas, one of its corporate backers.

"I was disappointed that Coke and McDonald's never got behind
the tournament in a meaningful way," said Marla Messing, the chief
organizer of the Women's World Cup. "They missed a huge opportunity. Our demographics were right in their sweet spot."

Even FIFA never possessed any grand vision for the Women's World
Cup. It proposed that the tournament be held on the East Coast in
small stadiums of 6,000 to 15,000 spectators as a way to save money on
travel costs and to avoid the potential embarrassment of tens of thousands of empty seats. As planned, the final would have been held at RFK
Stadium in Washington, D.C. As it turned out, RFK's capacity of
56,500 would have been one of the smallest crowds to see the American
women. The final match against China drew nearly as many spectators
as the 112,000 who saw the entire 1995 Women's World Cup in Sweden.

The idea to move the tournament into huge football stadiums
gained legitimacy during the 1996 Olympic tournament. The Ameri-

can women played the semifinals against Norway before a crowd of 64,196 at the University of Georgia, and the gold-medal game against China before 76,489 spectators. Messing, who was eight months pregnant at the time, attended those matches with Alan I. Rothenberg, then the president of the United States Soccer Federation who had organized the most successful men's World Cup ever in 1994 by selling 3.5 million tickets and turning a $60 million surplus. Also sitting with them was Hank Steinbrecher, then the federation's executive director. Three months earlier, the 1999 Women's World Cup had been awarded to the United States, and already Rothenberg had an idea for something on a grand scale. This convinced everyone. "The sentiment was, here we are in a giant stadium, and it is full and we need to make it big time," Messing said.

"In everything we did, we treated it as a major event," Messing said. "Our choices in this country are stadiums with 5,000 or 10,000 seats, or stadiums with 50,000, 60,000, or 80,000 seats. Once you decide on 5,000 or 10,000 seats, the image of what you are selling is second class. Putting it in small stadiums would have sealed the fate of the tournament. You had to sell the image of a major event. Right away it was major because it's at Giants Stadium and the Rose Bowl."

At the conclusion of the Olympics, Messing, then 32 and a graduate of the University of Chicago law school who had been executive vice president of the 1994 men's World Cup, agreed to write a business plan for the Women's World Cup. Her initial projections were for 312,000 tickets to be issued, three times what had been sold in Sweden in 1995, but only half of the eventual gate for 1999. FIFA, having seen the previous American success at organizing an international soccer tournament, agreed to move to larger stadiums. But how to fill them? Facing a limited budget and limited interest in the mainstream media, Messing went underground to the American grassroots soccer community. Eventually, her business acumen nearly doubled an original revenue projection of $21 million to a total of $38 million and left organizers with a surplus between $2 million and $3.5 million.

On Columbus Day weekend of 1997, organizers put up 10 tents at youth soccer events around the country, handing out bumper stickers, getting the word out about the Women's World Cup. In May of

1998, a million pieces of direct mail were sent to sophisticated fans, to coaches, parents and referees. "That was the big question," said Donna de Varona, chairwoman of the World Cup organizing committee. "Would they buy tickets? Would they put their money where their mouth was?" They would. By December of 1998, without spending any advertising dollars, without sponsorship promotions having kicked in, organizers had already sold 200,000 tickets.

In early 1999, with the Women's World Cup only several months away, Messing and her staff made a key decision that went against conventional wisdom but would pay off with a boost in ticket sales. Soccer moms had become a popular political demographic during the 1996 election season, but Messing went after soccer dads for the World Cup.

"Everyone told us we should target soccer moms," Messing said. "But we found that dads were looking for experiences to have with their daughters. There are not a lot of sporting events where they can do that. Soccer was something their daughters played and could even hope to get a scholarship from. Dads would enjoy taking their daughters. And men are the ones who are accustomed to buying tickets to sporting events."

Teenage girls, who found in the American players trading-card idols, validation of their own interest in sports and the possibility of future achievement, were also targeted, as were visible women in government such as Tipper Gore, the wife of Vice President Al Gore, and Donna Shalala, the Secretary of Health and Human Services. The solicitation of Capitol Hill support almost embarrassingly backfired, however. President Clinton and the First Lady had agreed in August of 1998 to be honorary chairpersons of the Women's World Cup, but a few days later, the President appeared on national television to announce that he had had an inappropriate relationship with Monica Lewinsky. He would later be impeached, and the announcement of his affiliation with the Women's World Cup had to be postponed until late February 1999.

"Here's a women's team and he's the honorary chairman," Julie Foudy said. "They couldn't announce it. It would have been a media nightmare."

It was not lost on the players that Clinton was attempting, in part, to rehabilitate his image with women by supporting the American soccer team. When the team visited the White House after the World

Cup, Foudy, the co-captain with cobalt blue eyes and a mordantly blue sense of humor, handed a cigar to a teammate and said, "The President wanted me to give you this."

Still, the players did appreciate that he had attended two matches. "At least he didn't jump on board at the end," Kate Sobrero said. And Clinton would later tell the team that he had tried to think of a more exciting sporting event but could not.

It hardly mattered that the players could not count on a ton of visible presidential support. For more than two years they promoted the tournament themselves through personal-services contracts with the World Cup organizers. A core group of the women had begun their sport with a lemonade-stand earnestness in the 1980s, and they sold the World Cup door to door as if the games were encyclopedias. The players appeared at sporting goods stores, schools, soccer camps, signing autographs after games with a missionary appetite for conversion, convinced there was a wide audience appeal for their exuberant teamwork. They came to possess a pioneering hardness, a horse-tail flick against the doubters who dismissed them or believed they should be sequestered in small stadiums. One of the least-remarked but most significant moments of the 1999 Women's World Cup occurred during the United States' semifinal match against Brazil, played before 73,123 fans at Stanford University on the Fourth of July. Rather than wait around for the men's portion of a doubleheader, one that featured D.C. United, on its way to a third championship in Major League Soccer, 60,000 fans got up and left.

"We want girls to know that they can play at the highest level," Kristine Lilly said about the years of patient autograph sessions. "We didn't look up to anyone on the national team, because there wasn't one. We didn't wait for autographs, because there was no one to wait for."

Although the American women were largely missing from the sports pages as the World Cup approached, they circumvented this disinterest and reached their audience anyway by appearing in such disparate publications as *Seventeen* and *Cosmopolitan*, *Teen People*, *Sports Illustrated for Kids*, a men's magazine called *Gear*, by appearing on the *Late Show with David Letterman* and in clever, powerful commercials sponsored by Adidas, Bud Lite, Gatorade and Nike, which has a $120 million affiliation with the U.S. Soccer Federation and which launched a $5 million television ad campaign in May and June of 1999.

"Historically, the federation looked upon the women's team as a financial drain," Messing said. "But Nike saw some magic in the team, which dovetailed with its interest in female athletes and the female sports market. I believe Nike persuaded the federation to give women more attention and to treat them more favorably. Nike said, 'This is important to us, it should be important to you.' To the federation's credit, it realized the value of this investment and spent a lot of money preparing for the 1996 Olympics and both the 1995 and 1999 World Cups."

Three days before the opening match, Brandi Chastain appeared with Letterman, who happened to have a copy of a *Gear* magazine photo in which she was crouched and wearing nothing but her cleats, her rippling muscles and a strategically placed soccer ball. "Soccer moms?" Letterman said. "Soccer mamas!"

After Chastain's segment, Letterman could not hold back any longer. "The U.S. team—and this may come out wrong; I'll just say it now and forget about it—is Babe City, ladies and gentleman. Babe City!"

Nightly, Letterman began showing a picture of the team in which the players stood shoulder to shoulder like beauty contestants and appeared only to be wearing *Late Show* T-shirts. After the final, the players would return to visit Letterman. Talking with Mia Hamm and Chastain, he would go on for as long as he could about how superbly athletic and graceful the players were, about what terrific role models they were, how nice and smart and intelligent they were, but finally he would not be able to resist their sensual attraction.

"They're just hot," he would say. "Certifiably babes."

The American team played along with Letterman's comedy of lechery. He had declared himself the team's spiritual leader and had put the players nightly into three or four million homes "in a way that's positive for us," Hamm said. "He was talking tongue in cheek," she said. "He's a comedian. He's supposed to make fun of things."

The nightly laughter gel-coated a pill that has never been easily swallowed in this country about the legitimacy of referring to the physical appearance of female athletes and the residual panic about lesbianism. A debate ensued among players, officials, expert observers, feminists and the media about the roles that gender, sex and beauty played in the popularity of the team and about the manner in which it was portrayed to the public.

In classical antiquity, the Greeks were endlessly outspoken about the erotic appeal of athletic bodies, both male and female, and only with the coming of Christianity did a powerful ascetic streak emerge that denigrated the body, contrasting it as sinful with a superior soul, noted Allen Guttmann, a sports historian and professor of English and American studies at Amherst College. Guttmann is the author of a book called *The Erotic in Sports*, in which he argues that we ought to accept and celebrate that male and female athletes are physically attractive instead of complaining about it and pretending it is not true.

"To acknowledge the erotic aspect of the body in sport is not to deny that we're interested in performance," he said. "They are not mutually exclusive. Some radical feminists talk as if they were. As if either I'm impressed by the skill or I'm simply ogling. The point is, the body as it is used in sports performance is impressive and attractive. It's not an either-or; at least it doesn't have to be."

Rick Burton, director of the Warsaw Sports Marketing Center at the University of Oregon's college of business, said his graduate students—both male and female—were in widespread agreement that the attractiveness of the American players was relevant to their popularity. "This is the first time I had seen that," Burton said. "The women in the class did not find it threatening, sexist or offensive. The line that was used was 'Soccer babes rule. Soccer babes rock.'"

Only in recent years have women in pursuit of beauty had the option to pursue a body custom-built for athletics, instead of one custom built either for clothes or sex, Holly Brubach, then the style editor of *The New York Times Magazine*, wrote before the 1996 Atlanta Olympics. "Though their bodies have been meticulously cultivated, their bodies aren't the point: the point is their ability to perform," Brubach wrote of athletes. "What is most striking, given that it's the other two ideals that are calculated to please—to win the admiration of women or the affection of men—is the fact that these athletes seem content in a way that other women do not."

Sports Illustrated and Condé Nast now have sports magazines aimed specifically at women, and athletes like Hamm and the basketball star Sheryl Swoopes have shoes named after them. A widely disseminated photograph of the women's soccer team appeared during the week of the final, showing a group of players jogging on a track, the muscles in their arms and legs exquisitely sculpted from years of pumping iron.

"It is a kind of fetishism—albeit a healthy one—that has taught us to appreciate women's bodies in detail," Brubach wrote. "Our education has been gradual, requiring the better part of the last hundred years. Fashion designers, models and movie stars have been our tutors. We have learned to love a woman's pelvis, her hipbones jutting out through a bias-cut satin gown. We have come to admire the clavicle in its role as a coat hanger from which clothes are suspended. And, more recently, we have discovered elegance in the swell of a woman's quads, in the tapering form of her lats, in the way her delts square the line of her shoulders. Women, as they have gradually come into their own, have at last begun to feel at home in their bodies, which previously they were only renting. In athletes, we recognize women who own their bodies, inhabiting every inch of them, and the sight of their vitality is exhilarating. Our own potential has become apparent, thanks to their example. We want to be like them—alive all over."

Mostly ignored by the media and corporate world during their careers, the players on the U.S. soccer team seemed free to act themselves, unguarded, unrehearsed, unself-conscious. It was the most human and engaging of sports teams, a complex group of players, among whom could be found stories of privilege, and also stories of prom dresses sewn at home and canned preserves put up to stretch paychecks, stories of strong family support and ruptured parental ties, of sustained health and chronic illness, of blithe athletic success and eventual achievement after protracted struggle. They appeared largely unencumbered by sexist myth that female athletes were weak, unwomanly, lesser than men. Within the team environment, the players, whatever their sexual preference, could live openly and their private lives were respected as just that—private.

The American women had arrived at a cultural intersection where feminism and postfeminism converged and sometimes collided. On one hand, they were groundbreaking athletes in the pioneering spirit of Babe Didrikson. On the other hand, they were viewed as soccer babes and were willing participants in the sexualization of the team.

Hamm was named one of *People's* 50 most beautiful people. Foudy appeared with her husband in the *Sports Illustrated* swimsuit issue. Like the figure skater Katarina Witt, who appeared in *Playboy*, and the American track and field stars, who posed nude in a calendar, Chastain belonged to a generation of female athletes who believed that their exposed bodies would be as appreciated for strength and power as for sex appeal, certain that nothing would be denied them or taken away, neither their reputations, their careers nor their financial opportunities.

"I ran my ass off for this body," Chastain said. She explained, "I have biceps and shoulders as big as my dad's. I'm not going to hide it."

Before a United States match against North Korea in Foxboro, Massachusetts, several men showed up at practice in construction-worker chic, with "Brandi Chastain Fan Club" scrawled on their T-shirts. If the attractiveness of the players brought some fans to the stadium, reasoned goalkeeper Briana Scurry, it was the attractiveness of the soccer that kept them interested.

"I don't think you have to run around naked to sell the game, but it's good to at least be on the minds of people," Scurry said. "I don't think it's degrading. People who see us on Letterman and come to the game realize we don't just strut around in our little skirts. Women play just as hard as anybody."

Still, a certain wariness developed among the players as they were peppered with questions about their looks. "What's it like to have 13-year-old boys think you're hot?" a female reporter asked Foudy before the semifinal match against Brazil. She smiled, but firmly said, "Stop."

"I think if you ask 99 percent of the fans, are they there to see someone who posed naked or to see soccer, they're going to say they come for the team," Foudy said. "You're never going to escape sexual references with women. If we can make sure we're successful on the field, I think people will come for the product, rather than what the product looks like."

Several days before the championship game against China, Chastain was asked this question by Christine Brennan of *USA Today*: "If you were all ugly, if you were not wholesome, attractive—words that have been attached to you—would this team be as popular?"

Somewhat surprisingly, wrote Mike Penner of the *Los Angeles Times,* "the questioner wasn't cursed or insulted, Chastain didn't stomp away amid a stream of expletives and the player actually hung in there to make a sober, rational response."

Chastain's response was this: "There are those people who come purely for the soccer. There are those people who come purely for the event. And there are those people who come because they like us, to look at us. Those are three great reasons to come."

Some in the media and on the team, however, believed the focus on the physical attractiveness of the players devalued and trivialized their accomplishments as athletes. As the millennium approached, had women finally reached the point where they could show a sensual side and could still be taken seriously as athletes? Or was it still necessary to use sex to sell women's sports, the way it had been used to sell everything from jeans to cars in advertising?

To Gwen Knapp, a columnist for the *San Francisco Examiner,* it seemed as if the Women's World Cup was being played "like the talent competition in the Miss America pageant, rather than as a sporting event." Michelle Akers, the American midfielder, said she was a "bit uncomfortable" with Chastain posing in *Gear* magazine. "Everybody has to make their own decisions on how they wanted to be portrayed," Akers said. "Regardless of that, it has a reflection on us as a team and women's sports as a whole. You don't want something like that to detract from the excellence of this team and the message that we're striving to put out."

When describing the attributes of the American team, Messing, the World Cup's chief organizer, said she intentionally would name attractiveness near the end of the list. It remained a delicate issue, even in verbal positioning in a sentence. "It's a fact, in our culture, it helps to be attractive, whether you are a man or a woman," Messing said. "If you are talented, intelligent and attractive, you shouldn't have to apologize. But if they weren't great athletes, there would be no interest. If they were a miserable team, no one would care." Still, she disapproved of the team playing along with Letterman's licentious comedy, saying that "it became too much about titillation."

"If someone else says that about you, that's one thing, but to take time to overtly play along, that didn't sit well with me," Messing said.

Donna de Varona, a 1964 Olympic swimming champion, said that posing for a magazine should be an individual decision. The U.S. women's team seemed "totally free in its choices," she said. "I come from a different era where we were punished for our sexuality or accused of not having it. Maybe this is progress, freedom to show pride in our bodies."

However, de Varona said she had conflicting feelings about Chastain posing for *Gear* magazine. Had Chastain posed for a more upscale publication, her attempt to portray strength instead of sex may have gained more validity, she said. De Varona also felt uncomfortable with the fact that women still have to defend their athleticism by also projecting a feminine side. "We always have to prove that we're feminine and sexy," de Varona said. "We can be tough and sweaty and a sex symbol; if we do that, we're acceptable. Michael Jordan didn't have to take off his clothes."

During her own swimming career, de Varona said, she was careful to paint her nails and to wear long-sleeve shirts to hide her muscles. Babe Didrikson, voted by the *Associated Press* as the top female athlete of the first half of the 20th century, remade her image after setting three world records in track and field at the 1932 Summer Olympics and joining the golf circuit, letting her hair grow, wearing makeup and marrying a 278-pound wrestler named George Zaharias. "Babe is a Woman Now" said one headline of the day. After the World Cup, members of the Ohio State women's rugby team, which did not have varsity status, would find it necessary to remove their shirts at the Washington Monument to gain attention and revenue from photographs of their bare-breasted escapade. This attempt at public endearment was known by feminists as the "female apologetic."

"To be successful in sports is to buck the traditional female role," the author Mariah Burton Nelson said. "The deal is, 'If you let me play sports, I will go along with how you want me to behave, as a lady, as a tramp, or whatever female role you want to put me into.' Billie

Jean King and Martina Navratilova come to mind as two striking exceptions to that role. Women who wear pants, women who don't wear a lot of makeup, who say no to offers and suggestions they should degrade themselves through sexual positions."

Posing nude in *Gear* magazine was a mistake for Chastain, who allowed herself to be exploited, Burton Nelson said. "I don't think women can retain their dignity—or it would be in rare circumstances if they did—if they take off their clothes," she said. "We make up lots of excuses. We try to show off power, to redefine beauty. But we can't control what people do with those images. There is still a struggle about who's going to define female beauty, who's going to define what women should wear and how they should behave. Women's sports will not have arrived until we are writing those rules for ourselves."

Indeed, Chastain would come to regret how her pictures were used in *Gear.* She had not been sophisticated enough to secure the rights to the photographs. A second *Gear* layout, after the World Cup, would picture Chastain in poses of laughing naughtiness and would cause her corporate sponsors to caution that it might hurt her marketability. Donna Lopiano, the executive director of the Women's Sports Foundation, dismissed the *Gear* photographs as "soft porn." Kane, the sports sociologist, said, "It set us back a million years."

"The people I work with were nervous and upset," Chastain said. "You get involved with corporations and become a spokesperson for them, you have to be sensitive to their values, their morals. It was a little bit of a shock to my business associates, who were saying, 'This could be bad for you.' I did it one time, for the right reason. If I had known what kind of magazine it was, I wouldn't have done it. That's my fault. I'm always naïve. I have this belief that people are only going to do right by you. I'm open and honest, but I've learned a couple of things. You have to protect yourself."

Even locker-room jokes could take on unintended meanings. Foudy had jokingly referred to a group of 1996 Olympic housemates as "booters with hooters." It was meant, she said, to be an ironic referral to the fact that the players were flat-chested, as well as a skewering of the Hooters restaurant chain, which requires its waitresses to dress in tight T-shirts and brief shorts. "People need to lighten up," she said. "It was obviously a sarcastic joke." But she lost control of the line's intent when "booters with hooters" became public currency and seemed to give sportswriters license to write about the players looks instead of their soccer skills.

In a column headlined "Goal Goal Girls," a takeoff on go-go girls, Rick Reilly of *Sports Illustrated* wrote that he had been expecting "Joe Torre in heels" from the American women but found instead that "They've got ponytails! They've got kids! They've got (gulp) curves!"

To their fans, and their corporate sponsors, and to many members of the media, the ponytailed Americans presented a safe-sexy picture of bouncy femininity. The ponytail was even incorporated into the official Women's World Cup logo. It was an unthreatening symbol that may have felt restrictive to players on the team not eager to conform to such an portrayal, a sign that organizers still felt it necessary to sheath women's sports in the image condom of heterosexuality.

"They belied the belief that you couldn't be all-American and feminine," said Marty Mankamyer, executive assistant to the president of the United States Soccer Federation and a long-time activist for women's soccer. "A dad could have his daughter go into the sport of soccer and know that she can still be feminine."

Feminine has come to be a code word for heterosexual, and, while the public acceptance of female athletes has never been greater, gusts of homophobia persist like tropical flurries from vestigial hurricanes. After Australia's team performed disastrously with two defeats and a draw in the World Cup, the Australian women's soccer federation underwent a power struggle as it began preparing for 2000 Summer Olympics. Two months after the World Cup, the *Sydney Morning Herald* would carry a story that said, "The gay lobby is aiming to regain control of the sport," which, the paper said, was leading to much angst as the Olympics approached. Then in December of 1999, 12 members of the Matildas, as the soccer team is known, would pose naked for a calendar. "We are not big, butch, masculine, lesbian football players," the defender Amy Taylor told *Sports Illustrated*.

If she is talking to a group of guys, and mentions that she is a member of the American women's soccer team, said the defender

Kate Sobrero, the question unfailingly comes up: "How many lesbians are there on the team?"

"It makes me so mad," Sobrero said. "Who cares? Why does that matter? I'm sure there's gay male athletes. No one asks. No one assumes. They assume we're butch, they assume we're lesbian. I wish I knew why this was such a big deal. Maybe it's a way to dismiss the achievement of women. To think that somehow we're not normal. How could we not be normal? I have a huge issue with that. It's none of their business."

For decades, athletes, coaches and promoters have confronted these suspicions by denying the existence of lesbianism or by deflecting masculine and lesbian stereotypes through the highlighting of motherhood, boyfriends, husbands, babies. Women like Billie Jean King and Martina Navratilova who admitted homosexuality were faced with the abandonment of corporate sponsors. Players in the All-American Girls Baseball League, which existed during World War II while many male ballplayers were in the service, compensated by wearing dresses. Members of the 1996 women's Olympic basketball team did a television commercial in which they were shown applying lipstick and wearing tight-fitting dresses. Stars in the Women's National Basketball Association such as Lisa Leslie and Chamique Holdsclaw frequently speak of being feminine, as if to say they are not homosexual in a league with a wide lesbian fan base, according to reporters who cover the league. Women on the U.S. soccer team had a pre-game ritual of painting their fingernails and features on the team's soccer moms appeared everywhere from *People* to *The New York Times*.

If the American team represented an ideal, it was primarily a white suburban ideal. The United States faced China with no Hispanic players and with two black players on its 20-player roster, the goalkeepers Briana Scurry and Saskia Webber. In most places around the world, soccer was a game of the urban poor. But, in the United States it was suburban sport, played mostly by middle class and upper middle class whites. The racial makeup of the team—and the audience at the Rose Bowl—mirrored the racial demographic of the sport in the United States. Soccer was one of the few team sports in which white suburban Americans held the large majority of roster spots. To

Tony DiCicco, the American coach, the U.S. women reflected, like no other team, the values of mainstream, middle class, middle of the road America. "That definitely struck a chord," he said.

To others, the racial makeup of the team carried a whiff of exclusion, of a lack of playing fields and opportunities for inner city kids, a lack of role models, a lack of urgency by the United States Soccer Federation to cast a wide talent net for black and Hispanic players. This at a time when the country-club sports of golf and tennis were rescued from their plaid indifference by black superstars such as Tiger Woods and the Williams sisters, Serena and Venus, who were not only more entertaining than most men, but served harder, too.

"It was a socially acceptable team," said Lopiano, executive director of the Women's Sports Foundation. "Soccer is where football was 25 years ago, no black quarterbacks. It needs to address the diversity issue; so do most sports. I think the team had great appeal to middle America, to corporate America, because this was pretty much an all-white, little-girl-down-the-street, not-too-tough group. That's advantageous from a p.r. standpoint. But it always concerns you when you don't take all women, color, body type or being. Stereotypes are destructive."

The 1996 women's Olympic basketball team was just as accomplished and just as well-educated as the women's soccer team, but most of the players were black, and they did not receive the same portrayal as the girls next door by the predominantly white media.

"I was grateful the press paid attention to the women's soccer team, but I think it was easier because most of the journalists could consider the athletes their sister or daughter," said Anita DeFrantz, a member of the International Olympic Committee from the United States. "That would not be the case with the women's basketball team of 1996."

At the same time, in places like Latin America, the Middle East and Africa, the American soccer team presented a provocative, even radical, notion that women could succeed at the ultimate macho sport, that female athletes could viewed as forceful and womanly, that they were not automatically assumed to be lesbians, that they could bear children and not be concerned that rigorous play would cause their uterus to fall out.

In Ghana, which was participating in its first Women's World Cup, girls of the West African nation are still subject to genital cutting, which involves the amputation of their clitoris and some or all of the genital lips by broken glass, a razor blade, scissors or a pen knife—generally without anesthesia—in a ritual born of custom and tradition in 28 African nations. There is often a belief that genital cutting will reduce a young woman's sexual pleasure and thus insure fidelity to her future husband and docility in a society where women's lives are controlled by men. This practice of genital cutting, banned in the United States, can lead to infection, hemorrhaging, even death. Two soccer players and a referee from Ghana remained in America after the African team was eliminated from the World Cup. Although organizers believed there was no connection between the players' defection and the mutilation ritual, a month after the championship game another woman from Ghana became the second person ever to be granted political asylum in the United States because of genital cutting.

Mexico, where soccer has generally been perceived as too rough for women in a macho society and where the women who play are considered butch, relied on Hispanic Americans to fill out half of its World Cup roster. While they trained in Mexico City, players said, guards patroled the training camp and the women were not allowed to leave without permission, for fear of their safety. Once the team essentially had to hijack a city bus to a local stadium for a World Cup tune-up match when its scheduled transportation did not arrive. A top official in the Mexican soccer federation said the women were less important than even the teenage men's national team. While the American women trained for six months outside of Orlando, Florida, and lived on a golf course, the Mexican women sometimes bivouacked at a mountain training site that had no heat and little running water, requiring the players to build their own fire and to sleep in several layers of clothing to keep warm.

"We're fighting the myths and prejudices that women's soccer felt in the U.S. in the '70s," said Andrea Rodebaugh, the captain of the Mexican team who played collegiately at the University of California at Berkeley. "That there are sports for boys and sports for girls and that soccer is not for girls, not feminine."

The women of Nigeria, the perennial African champion, were household names, with two weekly half-hour television programs devoted to the team, yet they played soccer despite immense pressure to give up the sport at age 18 so they could marry and have children. The flamboyant goalkeeper, Anne Chiejine, who dyed her hair white and wore colorful bandanas for the 1999 Women's World Cup, was the only wife and mother on the Nigerian team. She had two daughters, ages 5 and 3, and served as a powerful rebuttal to those who believed that sports would sabotage motherhood. Still, she said she felt it necessary to orchestrate routine saves with ostentatious leaps and dives in order to show her husband that she was working hard and had a legitimate reason to be away from her family.

"Some feel that when you get married, that is the end of your career, and that if you play football, you won't be able to have children," Chiejine said. "I am showing that you can still play and it will not disturb you."

Five months after the World Cup, women's soccer was outlawed in one northern state in Nigeria because it was considered un-Islamic. During the African qualifying tournament for the World Cup, Mankamyer of the U.S. Soccer Federation said she received a newspaper article from Nigeria saying that the team would be playing its next match without its talented, transsexual midfielder.

"It was such a joke; they apparently put this player on the team so they could win," as if this were just women's soccer and no rules applied, Mankamyer said. "The African confederation regarded it so lightly, they didn't care either. I was concerned that a heavily muscled transsexual could cause havoc, rip up someone's knee."

Brazil is the most improved women's team in the world. In a breakfast match prior to the United States–China final, the Brazilian women defeated Norway in penalty kicks to finish third in the World Cup. They play the same beautiful game as the Brazilian men, and, like the men, they are sponsored by Nike, which supported the team on a month-long stay in the United States in preparation for the World Cup. But the games were not telecast live back to Rio de Janeiro and São Paulo, and none of Brazil's top newspapers sent a soccer correspondent to cover the tournament. Female players in Brazil still faced the stigma that they

become masculinized and that they were incapable of legitimately playing a sport as physically demanding as soccer. One of the team's top
players went by the nickname of Pretinha, which translates from the
Portuguese as "little black girl." When a national club championship for
Brazilian women was organized for the first time in the early 1990s, a
priest in the city of Arceburgo went on strike, closed his church and said
he would not say mass as long as the women's tournament was in
progress in his town.

"He said that soccer was a men's sport and that if women played,
they were trying to be like men," recalled Luis Miguel Estevao, the
general manager of the women's national team.

As hurricanes once were, soccer balls are always female in Brazil,
to be caressed and kissed, to be called "pudgy" and "baby." In neigh-
boring Argentina, one of the game's greatest players, Alfredo di Ste-
fano, built a home monument to the object of his affection, consist-
ing of a bronzed ball and a plaque that said, "Thanks, old girl."

"She is loyal," the Uruguyan author Eduardo Galeano wrote in his
book, *Soccer in Sun and Shadow*, depicting the ball in South America as a calculating seductress. "The ball can also be fickle sometimes, refusing to enter the goal because she changes her mind in
mid-flight and curves away. You see, she is easily offended. She can't
stand getting kicked around or hit out of spite. She insists on being
caressed, kissed, lulled to sleep on the chest or foot. She is proud,
vain perhaps, and she's not lacking a motive: she knows all too well
that when she rises gracefully she brings joy to many hearts, and
many a heart is crushed when she lands without style."

Some of the verbs used in popular speech to describe possession of
the ball in Brazil are also the words used to describe sexual inter-
course, Larry Rohter of *The New York Times* wrote from Rio during
the World Cup. The most common word for ball, "bola," also sug-
gests the voluptuous shape of a woman's breasts and buttocks. Soccer
in Brazil carries an erotic component associated with the idea that a
man subdues the ball as he would a woman.

"In Brazil, soccer has a strong gender demarcation that makes it a
masculine domain par excellence," Roberto da Matta, a prominent
Brazilian anthropologist and sociologist, told Rohter. "It is a sport that

contains all of the various elements that are traditionally used to define masculinity: conflict, physical confrontation, guts, dominance, control and endurance."

Several of the American women played professionally in Japan in the early 1990s, and they faced questions about their assertive play in a society where women have traditionally been subservient. Men brought six-packs of beer to watch women play, Shannon MacMillan said, adding, "I don't think they cared about soccer at all. I think they just wanted to see women run around and sweat." In an exhibition prior to the 1999 World Cup, the Japanese women played so deferentially against the Americans that they took not a single shot, compared to 35 for the Americans, in a 9–0 defeat.

"We're not second-class citizens like women in some other countries," Scurry said. "Our personality is, we go after it. We want to beat the crap out of whoever we play. Other teams are aggressive, but there is a difference."

The seriousness of the American game is precisely what drew Claire Scanlon, a diminutive forward from Ireland, to the television for the conclusion of the United States–China match. After playing in the semi-professional Irish league, she went home to see the final few penalty kicks. The Irish national team could not even afford to fly all of its players in from their European club teams for home games. One of its top players, an American named Holly Pierce, was recruited by e-mail. The Irish women had never played before an audience larger than 4,000. But, across an ocean that might as well have been a galaxy, the United States and China were playing before a crowd more than 20 times that size. Scanlon sat, drawn by the tension, by the distant confirmation that her sport could be taken seriously.

"The problem in Ireland is that most men and women see women playing soccer as recreational," Scanlon said. "They don't see a lot of highly competitive teams. They see female soccer players as too masculine, not feminine at all. I hope this did away with some of those myths. The Irish media could see that these were athletes before they were women. They weren't middle age women out there just kicking around."

4

"I'm Expecting Great Things from You"

E ARLY ON THE MORNING of the final, Dainis Kalnins set out the American uniforms in the equipment room of the team hotel and placed a red, white and blue rose on the jersey of each player. This being Pasadena, California, home of the Rose Bowl parade, Kalnins had no trouble finding a florist who could dye a rose blue. Among the 2,000 pounds of uniforms, shoes, T-shirts, balls and digital computer equipment that he carried as the team's equipment manager was a coffee thermos that bore the label: "Michelle's Secret Recipe." The reference was to Michelle Akers, and the label carried a comic warning: "This stuff may turn you into superwoman."

Often on the road, as the team barnstormed the country on a pre-World Cup tour, Kalnins and Akers had coffee together at 6 or 6:30 in the morning. Sometimes they were joined by Brandi Chastain, an insomniac who could not sleep more than five or five and a half hours. It was Kalnins, a former collegiate volleyball player, who worked with Akers and Chastain daily after practice, standing in goal while they rehearsed penalty kicks. After scoring the decisive penalty-kick goal against Brazil in the semifinals, Akers ran to the sideline and kissed him on the forehead. At these early morning coffee klatches, Akers answered her voluminous e-mail, made small talk with Kalnins and gave updates, like personal weather forecasts, on the state of her physical well-being. She had struggled for seven years with chronic fatigue syndrome, which, at its worst, left her with debilitating migraines, low blood pressure, memory loss, dizziness, bouts of vomiting and an overwhelming feeling of lassitude.

"I feel pretty good today," Akers would inevitably say, as if her words might convince her body. "I'll be ready. I'll get it done."

"It was never, 'I can't do it, I don't have it,'" Kalnins said. "Her answer was always with hope."

Yet, as the World Cup approached, the American coaches, trainers and doctors had become concerned about a curious phenomenon. Akers repeatedly grew fatigued after the first half of exhibition matches played at night. There was a verbal shorthand between player and coach. "I have to come out," Akers would tell Tony DiCicco and he would immediately find a replacement in midfield. Akers's face would have the familiar flushed, hollow look of exhaustion and nothing more would need to be said. After so many years together on the soccer field, DiCicco could read her face as if it were an X-ray. But two night games were scheduled during the World Cup and the coach could not afford to be without the game's seminal star, the person who had legitimized women's soccer with her raw assertiveness, who signed the first shoe endorsement, who had scored 10 goals in the inaugural Women's World Cup in 1991 and who would anchor the midfield in 1999. Finally, it dawned on the staff. Halftime came about 8:30 P.M., the same time that Akers usually went to bed.

"Michelle, you've got to stay up later," trainer Sue Hammond told Akers in March or April, with the World Cup less than three months away. "Your body is shutting down."

A plan was devised. When sleep came on, Akers tried to find a friend or a teammate to talk with, and she took walks at night and naps in the afternoon, pushing herself to stay awake until 10 or 11 P.M. The Americans also asked organizers not to play the second match of a quarterfinal doubleheader in suburban Washington that started at 9:30 P.M. And Akers began drinking coffee from her secret recipe thermos before each game and during halftime of each match, day or night. In large doses, the caffeine stimulation of coffee was banned by soccer's world governing body as a performance-enhancing drug. But that would require eight or more cups, two or three hours before game time. In smaller amounts, it was an acceptable way to rev up her body's engine and to boost her low blood pressure, which she found difficult to regulate during times of stress.

During the Women's World Cup, the team gave Akers a room of her own on the road, so she could get sufficient and uninterrupted rest. On the morning of the final, she awakened early as usual, had her first cup of coffee, answered e-mail, read from the Bible. She was 33, and she would be playing for the final time in a World Cup match. As she did every game day, Akers climbed out of bed and did the equivalent of kicking her body's tires. She felt tired, diminished, and her right shoulder ached. It was her luck to have dislocated the shoulder while high-fiving a fan after an opening-round match against North Korea in which she hadn't even played. In relative terms, though, she felt okay. "I didn't feel like I was going to puke," she said. "I didn't feel like I was going to die on the spot."

As she was leaving the room, she said she looked at herself in the bathroom mirror. The bridge of her nose bore a scab that resulted from a cleat that raked her face six days earlier in the semifinals against Brazil. On her left cheek she could still see discoloration from 25 stitches, three fractures and a black eye she had suffered in a game five months earlier. She was a devout Christian, and soccer to her was part of a spiritual journey. This was be her final match of her third World Cup. She would be retiring from the national team after the 2000 Summer Olympics and, as she stood before the mirror now, knowing that this game, like all games, would end in pain and impairment, that her muscles would revolt and her mind would grow foggy, she wondered how far she would be able to push herself. She had been asking this question throughout the World Cup and today she would finally get an answer.

This is a defining moment. This is my third World Cup, and I played through the Olympics, and this is going to be a huge challenge. Who will I be when I come back? Who will I see? What will have been revealed? Will I be proud of myself? Will I be disappointed? Will I have the courage to extend myself until the end? Will I not be able to play to the level I know I can if I'm healthy? Will I quit? Will I be gutsy enough? Will I be strong and courageous? It's not an option.

As she did the day of every game, Kristine Lilly listened to an audio-tape of motivational phrases. The Americans were pioneering in the explicit use of sports psychology as a team. They believed that the development of mental skills was as vital as the development of dribbling and passing and shooting skills. That the same scientific approach used to develop fitness and endurance could also be used to refine confidence and focus and control and the reliance on team-work. That, in a sense, the mind was a muscle to be pumped-up like a calf or a biceps. The morning of the final, individually and in groups, players watched fast-cut videotapes that showed them mastering particular individual skills: Briana Scurry making acrobatic saves. Akers heading the ball. Kate Sobrero making assertive tackles. Lilly running at full speed, showing strong emotion on her face, playing insurgent defense. Success imagined and visualized alone in quiet darkness, the theory went, was more easily replicated in the heat and chaos and live-wire jolt of a filled stadium. Soccer, more than most, was a game of patience and attrition, long periods of equilibrium shattered by a moment's distraction, a routine disturbed, a head turned, a step taken too early or too late. Concentration maintained, confidence preserved, could make the difference in a game, a tournament, a world championship.

Lilly listened to the phrases she had chosen for her audiotape. She listened once, then listened again.

"I make an impact."

"I want the ball.

"I make a difference."

"It does matter that I'm on the field."

"Little things do matter."

While still at the team hotel, the Americans also watched a videotape of Chinese matches that had been compiled by Lauren Gregg, the assistant coach. The coaching staff traveled with a library of 60 to 80 videotapes, at least 10 of which were matches involving the Chinese. Using a digital editing system, the coaches had logged every corner kick, every free kick, taken by China in the World Cup. Another sophisticated bit of technology recorded every touch, every pass of the ball, by made by every Chinese player in the tournament. The resulting set of overlapping lines, known as a computer spine, looked like an airline route map. Gregg had edited videotape of each Chinese match after it was played, preparing for a likely meeting in the final. In the six days leading up to the championship match, she estimated that she watched 30 hours of videotape on the American opponent. She knew which foot each of the Chinese players preferred, which teammate they most often passed to, whether the corner kicks and free kicks of a particular player swung inward or outward. Soccer was a free-form game, not regimented like American football, and coaches were sometimes criticized for overly managing the matches. But Gregg believed that, if videotape accounted for five percent of the American preparation, it provided valuable readiness.

The point of comprehensive preparation was driven home by Colleen Hacker, the team's sports psychologist and a former champion soccer coach on the collegiate level. Hacker liked to tell the story of the blue car and the red car, showing players a picture of the blue car edging the red car by six feet after 500 miles of racing at Indianapolis. The American soccer players, like the driver of the blue race car, she told them, must be prepared to take advantage of the slight edge.

"How do you know which moment amounted to those six feet?" Gregg said. "Was it a tire change? This turn or that turn? You have to seek the moment's influence. Ninety-nine percent of the things you prepare for don't happen. But you don't want to have the one percent you didn't prepare for happen."

*   *   *

Once the Americans arrived by bus at the Rose Bowl, the players went about their familiar pregame rituals. Saskia Webber, the reserve goalkeeper, found a locker in a corner, so she would not feel the phone-booth pinch of teammates dressing on both sides. Mia Hamm made sure she sat next to Lilly and Carla Overbeck. Before the semifinals at Stanford University, Tisha Venturini, a reserve midfielder, had interrupted this harmonic seating arrangement. Hamm had, in her words, "freaked" and given Venturini "the look."

"Get up, you're in my seat," she told Venturini.

"They had never done this before," Venturini said. "I got a big laugh, but she didn't think it was funny. After the game, I'm like, 'You jerk,' and she started laughing. I laughed about it beforehand, but she didn't. She's pretty intense."

As she did before each game, Webber had her hair spray-painted red, white and blue by teammate Christie Pearce. For the final, Pearce had painted three flags, one on the top and one on each side of Webber's head. The goalkeeper had considered abandoning the ritual, believing it might be detracting from the team's focus, but Pearce said, "What are you talking about?" and Webber relented.

"I realized it had become part of everything, a bit of superstition," Webber said.

Tony DiCicco, the head coach, had become concerned about the hair coloring during an earlier match against Nigeria. Hamm almost had to retreat to the locker room to change jerseys, he said, when a sideline official saw red on her shirt and thought it was blood. "No, it's hair color," DiCicco told the official and Hamm remained on the field. Could anyone imagine that? A World Cup decided by runny hair coloring? Despite his wariness, though, the coach could not bring himself to ban the Old Glory hairdos.

"Not that I'm superstitious, but I said, 'Let's not change anything,'" he said.

As had become custom, players painted their fingernails and toenails red, blue and flag-patterned before the championship match. They held a dance party in the hallway of the team hotel before the opener against Denmark, but the mood was slightly more subdued for the game against China. A world championship was at stake.

Still, music played in the locker room and several players, including the goalkeeper Scurry, danced to the party beat from emanating from a CD player.

A day earlier, the players had seemed curiously relaxed while doing interviews in the same locker room. The enormous pressure, they said, had lessened after the semifinals. They had done their part, marketing the tournament, reaching the final, guaranteeing a filled stadium and a huge television audience. All they had to do now was play. Julie Foudy, the co-captain, had spent the morning in her hotel room ironing her clothes for the postgame party, nervous but confident of victory. Later, Hamm looked closely a team picture that had been taken in the locker room and noticed that there seemed to be no anxious creases on the American faces.

"It was pure joy," Hamm said. "We were just so happy that our game had come this far. In our minds, the sport had won. That was most important. We still had a job to do, but we had accomplished a lot."

Venturini, though, felt a twinge of melancholy.

"We couldn't believe all these people were coming to watch us play," she said. "Everywhere we went, everyone was talking about us. Every newspaper, every news channel. It was kind of sad that this was the last game. It had been such a great tournament. Everything was so awesome. And this was it. The game would be done and that would be it. You wanted to play, but then it was going to be over."

On charts in the locker room, DiCicco wrote a detailed list of offensive and defensive sets and added this reminder: "You must be prepared to take and make a penalty kick."

"You've written the script, you've created an incredible aura about this event," he said in his pregame speech to the players. "There's such excitement out there. It's all there for you to go out and finish the final chapter, the final sentence. We've come too far to have anything else written in that script but victory and fulfillment."

A group of employees from his soccer-camp business had sent DiCicco and the American players a card wishing them good luck. Each had written a personal note, but it was not until a month later, while vacationing in Hawaii and using the card as a bookmark, that DiCicco would notice something startlingly prescient in one of the missives. One of his employees, Sean Kelly, who had a crush on Brandi Chastain, had written, "Brandi will score the winning goal."

The first sign that this would be a hard afternoon occurred during warm-ups. The consolation match between Brazil and Norway had also extended through two overtimes and penalty kicks. And now the singer Jennifer Lopez was performing during the closing ceremonies, wearing a miniskirt and calf-high boots as if she had walked out of a Nancy Sinatra museum. This meant that neither the Americans nor Chinese would be able to warm up properly on the field. Muscles would not be thoroughly stretched, pent-up tension would not be adequately released. Akers was upset. "This stinks," she said. "The biggest game of our careers and we can't even warm up." But DiCicco calmed his players, who broke a sweat by running in a narrow, Astroturfed corridor under the stadium, the reserves slapping high-fives as the starters jogged past. The Chinese players also ran in the corridor, separated from the Americans by a set of bicycle racks. "It was kind of like a stare-down match," forward Tiffeny Milbrett said. DiCicco warmed up his goalkeepers on a bus ramp, careful to avoid a puddle of water, the ball thwocking against the cement wall with the sound of hollow collision. Dozens of fans pressed their faces to openings in the covered fences that rose above the ramp, like painted-face commuters gawking at a construction site.

Hammond, the team trainer, and Kalnins, the equipment manager, set bottles of water against advertising placards that ringed the field, removing the label from each bottle to avoid conflict with sponsorship rules. Any time there was a lull in play, players could run to the sideline and grab a drink. Each American player on the bench had also been assigned to a teammate on the field and was to remind her to drink at every available opportunity. Special attention would have to be paid to Akers. At the Olympics, energy bars had been tossed onto the field so she could refuel as her tank began to empty. Sometimes, she cut the bars into pieces and stuffed them into her socks. But she had recently learned that the bars contained dairy products, to which she was allergic. Before the team left the locker room for the World Cup final, Akers drank a half cup of coffee and ate a peanut-butter granola bar that would have to sustain her until halftime.

As the Americans took the field, emerging from a stadium tunnel in numerical order to a throbbing roar, Lilly reached behind her and did a chicken-pecking handshake with the next player in line, Joy Fawcett. It was part of her game-day rituals that included another a fist-bumping handshake with Venturini, three jumps to simulate headers at midfield and a calling out of "Bri" to Scurry, who acknowledged her. Earlier, Lilly had shaved her legs and had checked to make sure that Kalnins had also shaved his beard.

"I'm expecting great things from you," he told her as part of their routine.

The Rose Bowl seemed to be buzzing like a giant hive, and as she always did, Lilly felt a tightness in her throat as she stood with her teammates for the national anthem. At 27, she had already spent 12 years, nearly half her life, as a member of the American soccer team. When she joined, she carried a stuffed tiger as a sort of security blanket—her teammates immediately strung it up by its neck on a doorknob—and her grandmother still gave her a dollar for every goal she scored. She took in the expanse of the crowd in the low, wide-scooped bowl and flashed back to the late 1980s and early 1990s, when the team had to schedule its training around the one hour a day of hot water at a hotel in Haiti, when travel in China was on a coal train that left the players' faces blackened with soot, when all she could force down in Bulgaria were cucumbers on an "if you can't peel it, don't eat it" diet.

"All I could see was people, a sea of people," Lilly said. "I could have bawled. We had been waiting so long for people to come and watch us. We knew they would enjoy it. I'm just glad it kicked in before the new millennium. There was a time when we didn't need a police escort to the stadium. We could have walked. Our parents were our fans. Now we were driving on the shoulder, everyone was honking at us. And there were so many people in the stands, not just our families. We were the queens for a while."

5

Savages and
Blunt Instruments

JULIE FOUDY, the American co-captain, could not suppress a
smile of vindication as she stood on the field. How many times had
she heard it? How many times had someone said, "You can't do this
in big stadiums. You won't draw." Even FIFA did not really believe it
was possible. Joseph "Sepp" Blatter, the Swiss president of soccer's
world governing body, was fond of saying "the future is feminine," but
he apparently did not mean the future is equal. At the inaugural
Women's World Cup in 1991, FIFA staged matches 80 minutes in
duration, concerned that women did not possess the stamina to play
the 90 minutes that men play. For the 1999 World Cup, FIFA also
briefly considered deflating the ball slightly so that it would not hurt
the women when it hit them and would be easier to control. But the
Americans objected, sensing a European scheme to slow the game

down by taking air out of the ball. Foudy sometimes joked with her British inlaws that female teams were made to use 20 players on the field instead of 11 and that the women's goal was three times as large as the men's goal.

"You mean you head the ball?" her astonished mother-in-law said upon meeting her.

"Yes, Ruthie, and we even wear cleats!" Foudy responded.

She and her teammates had spent years like this, trying to convince the unconvinceable. Now she stood before 90,000 people who validated her convictions.

"Coming out on the field, I kept thinking that for so long we had talked about how successful this team is and what a draw it could be," Foudy said. "Every time someone comes to watch, they fall in love with this team. And then I thought of all the negatives we heard. Five months before the World Cup, we had a press conference to announce the draw. The first two questions, we get hammered by Americans. 'You're lying about tickets sales. You haven't sold as many as you say you have. You're downsizing the stadiums and you won't admit it. You're crazy to do this.' That was the theme of it. I was like, man, that's always the attitude. 'You shouldn't, you can't, it's not going to happen.' And then I walked into this huge stadium and I kind of looked around and smiled and said, 'Yes.' I knew some attitudes had changed."

This would be the last uncluttered moment for the American team, the bright, clear, suspended time before cell phones and conference calls became a corporate necessity, before talk would turn to taxes and agents' fees at rounds of afternoon golf, before "people either would be kissing your butt or trying to bring you down," Kate Sobrero said. When Sobrero would return from the tournament to her parents' home in suburban Detroit, a guy she didn't know would tape a message to the front door, leaving a picture of himself and asking her on a date. Another man would approach her at a party, someone she had never met, and he would sniff, "You must think you're big stuff."

The flicker of recognition would soon burst into the flame of celebrity, which meant a parade at Disneyland, free tickets to Bruce Springsteen, book deals and movie cameos, fans pressing for autographs just as fork reached mouth in popular restaurants. Private accomplishment would become public property and fame would bring the joust of reward and burden. A shirt would be removed, a sports bra would be exposed. Would it be improper to remove the shirt? Was it a spontaneous celebration or a cynical marketing ploy? A goalkeeper would come off of the goal line prematurely to make a save. Was it cheating or acceptable gamesmanship?

The players had longed for opportunity and professionalism, a chance to make a secure living at their sport. They would now earn six-figure incomes, $150,000 to $200,000 apiece in World Cup salary and bonuses and income from a victory tour. They would be taken with a new seriousness as athletes. "You can say you're a soccer player and people think it's cool," Brandi Chastain said. "You're no longer a second-class citizen." They would endorse sports drinks and insurance companies and fitness centers. They would judge beauty pageants, and they would become questions on game shows and answers to crossword puzzles and they would air-kiss celebrities who told them call anytime they were in town. They would be invited to the White House for equal-pay initiatives and to Capitol Hill for State of the Union addresses and they would fly with Hillary Rodham Clinton to see a space shuttle launch. They would find the fame fun and ordinary and complicated, and like Bill Bradley before them, in his basketball days at Princeton and with the New York Knicks, they would also come to feel as if they were on display.

"Welcome to the zoo," Kristine Lilly would say as the team arrived at practice in Kansas City for a match after the World Cup, fans on one side of the fence, the players on the other.

Four months after the World Cup, coach Tony DiCicco would resign, and his top assistant, Lauren Gregg would be overlooked as his successor. DiCicco would be replaced instead by April Heinrichs, one of the first stars of the women's national team. The entanglements of business and politics would inevitably collide with the simplicity of sport. In three weeks, the women's team had done more for soccer in the United States than any team had ever done. Yet, the United States Soccer Federation was unprepared and unwelcoming in its acerbic response to the women's success. With petty, resentful, chauvinistic behavior, the federation would bungle what should have been its greatest moment as a national governing body. Its leaders would criticize DiCicco instead of congratulating him, they would threaten to sue the women over an indoor victory tour and they would wait an unacceptably long period before entering into contract negotiations with the team. Then, at the end of the year, the federation would offer a deal that the women found insulting. Unwilling to trust that the federation was bargaining in good faith, the women would boycott a trip to a tournament in Australia. They would become champions of the world, embraced by the president, by the largest crowd ever to watch women play and by the largest television audience for soccer in this country, embraced by everyone, it seemed, but the officials who ran the sport with the vision of a student council. Increasingly, it appeared, the only amateurs left in sports were the people running the federations that governed them.

"The women are restrained now not by their own ability or the advertising industry, but by the soccer federation itself," said Donna Shalala, the Secretary of Health and Human Services who has been a vociferous supporter of the women's national team. "It is not modern. It is all males, narrow. I'm just appalled. It doesn't have anything to do with equal pay. It has to do with being prepared to let the women's team lead them into the next century. It will take years before the American soccer men are able to sustain a high level of play. I think they're jealous. They've never invested as much in the women. They were surprised and didn't know how to handle success."

Women's soccer had always been a hard fight. At one point, just getting onto youth club teams required that a federal case be made. In 1975, a nine-year-old goalkeeper named Amy Love of Danville, California, sued the state's youth soccer association, which prevented her from playing on an all-star team called the Rustlers. Three years after its passage, Title IX languished, ignored, unenforced. The daughter of a Coca-Cola executive, Love had come to play goalkeeper as a way to get into games with her older brother and his friends on the beaches of Rio de Janeiro. When the family returned to northern California, she was the only girl chosen among 13 who tried out for a traveling all-star team. The state youth soccer association objected because she was a girl, and she filed suit.

"I wanted to become the next Pelé and the next Hank Aaron," said Love, who was born in Atlanta and is the founder and publisher of *Real Sports* magazine. "My parents were very supportive. They never said there was not a single women's baseball player or soccer player. Soccer season came around, and I made the team, got my uniform, and my parents sat me down and said there was a problem. 'You can't play because you're a girl.' I said, 'What does the fact that I'm a girl have anything to do with my ability to play soccer?' We met with some attorneys in San Francisco, equal rights advocates, and they said, 'It can no longer be about Amy Love. It has to be about providing equal rights for all girls. The reality is that you can't be average. You have to be the best.'"

The case became widely publicized. Love appeared with Pelé, the Brazilian legend, on the cover of *SoccerAmerica* magazine, a weekly publication that is a leading voice for the sport. The magazine was new at the time, and so was the idea that women should be welcomed to play. The publication's founder, Clay Berling, reminisced in a column that it was so difficult to find soccer shoes, players often improvised with baseball spikes. Eventually, Love prevailed in federal district court, but the victory was not without its costs. Even with supportive parents and some sympathetic media coverage, Love faced prank phone calls, the egging of her house, columnists who said she was destroying youth sport, parents of other kids who questioned whether her sexual organs would become "endangered." Her parents were even tossed out of their bridge club, she said.

For 6 years in the 1970s, Hank Steinbrecher, the former executive director of the United States Soccer Federation, coached soccer at tiny Warren Wilson College in North Carolina, where the budget was so minuscule that players slept eight to a room on road trips. There was no team for women, so Steinbrecher said a player named Glenda Wells played on the men's team. "We'd go to Sizzler, buy the salad bar and pass the plate around," he said.

In 1978, Lauren Gregg graduated from high school in Wellesley, Massachusetts, attended Lehigh University in Bethlehem, Pennsylvania, and tried out for the men's junior varsity soccer team. There was a club team for women, but Gregg wanted the highest caliber of soccer she could find. She changed clothes in restrooms because there was no women's locker room and she ignored the convention that said women should not be competitive. "Women on the club team were saying, 'You think you're too good for us,' and the guys thought I was trying to prove something," Gregg said. "I wasn't. I just wanted to play soccer." She transferred to Harvard for a year as a visiting student, and her team reached the championship match sponsored by the now defunct Association of Intercollegiate Athletics for Women. Still, when she made sliding tackles and flicked the ball over someone's head, the response she got was often not one of acceptance but of resentment. *What's up with you? Why are you trying so hard?* Finally, Gregg transferred again, to North Carolina. In 1982—a full decade after the passage of Title IX—the NCAA sponsored a national championship for women's soccer and Gregg played on the team that won the first title. No longer were female collegiate teams left to compete in a mire of informality and, by extension, inauthenticity.

"I couldn't stop the desire," she said. "I couldn't keep quiet the voice inside. I love the game, the expression of yourself through the game. No matter what your day is like, when you walked on the field you were free, expressive, open."

The United States Soccer Federation, however, remained a closed shop to women who wanted positions of authority. Marty Mankamyer was a youth-soccer official from Colorado Springs, Colorado, when she attended the United States Soccer Federation's annual convention in Dallas in 1980. In the back of the room, there was a contest for stacking beer cans, she said, and the wife of one of the federation officials took off her clothes and jumped into a hotel pool.

"I was seeing it as a marketer's dream and all they were interested in were getting a free trip and drinking beer," Mankamyer said. In those years, she said, "It was a nightmare. There were no leagues, no national team for women, no plans for one."

In 1984, as chairwoman of the United States Youth Soccer Association, Mankamyer became the first woman to join the soccer federation's executive committee. She had decided to change the sport by working from the inside, she said, but was still resented by many officials, who sometimes made decisions by convening in the men's bathroom, where she could not follow. She said she threatened a lawsuit unless the federation began a national program for women, and turned her attention to getting women's soccer into the Olympics.

The women's national team was hastily born in the summer of 1985, when the U.S. Soccer received an invitation to participate in an international tournament against Italy, Denmark and England. A metallurgist from Seattle named Mike Ryan, who had won three national amateur club championships, was chosen as the American coach. By that time, Mankamyer and others had persuaded the United States Olympic Committee to accept women's soccer at its Sports Festival, held in the summer for developing athletes. Ryan was approached at the festival in Baton Rouge, Louisiana, and was told that he would be taking a national team to Italy. In a week.

Michelle Akers, who was 19 at the time, said that the players chosen had no idea what a national team was. Ryan made them sing the national anthem so they would understand the importance of the moment, she said, "and when we didn't do it right, he made us start over." Training for the tournament lasted all of three days at C.W. Post University on Long Island, where the players were housed in a dorm with participants in a high school cheerleading camp.

"We woke up to cheerleaders yelling their heads off," Akers said.

Funding for the team seemed to come from the proceeds of a parking meter. There were no salaries for the players, only $10 a day meal money. Even if there had been money, the college-based players would not have been able to accept it. Ryan said the federation did not reimburse his $1,000 in expenses for six months. Not only did the team lack any history, it also lacked any uniforms. When suitable shorts and jerseys were rounded up, they turned out to be men's uniforms. Contrary to popular myth, the team did not have to sew U-S-A across its white jerseys, Ryan said. The letters and numbers were ironed on at a sporting goods store. But, the night before the team left for Italy, players and staff were pressed into action as tailors, trimming the legs on warm-up suits, hemming shorts, sewing the front of v-neck jerseys.

"It was like Christmas," said Ryan, a native of Dublin. "The girls were opening boxes, putting on these suits, and everything came around their ankles. They looked like little gorillas walking around. We were up 'til 12 or 1 sewing, fitting everything to size."

The Americans flew to Milan, then traveled five hours by bus to Jesolo, Italy, where they stayed up late for a welcoming reception. The next day, exhausted, they trailed Italy 1–0 at halftime, then had a chance to tie in the last minute on a penalty kick. "We missed," Ryan said.

The United States managed a tie in three matches, never losing by more than one goal, a promising start. Yet when the American women gathered the next year, in 1986, the coach was now Anson Dorrance, who was on his way to winning 16 national collegiate championships at the University of North Carolina. Ryan is still not certain exactly how or why he was relieved of duty. "No one ever called to say thank you or kiss my ass," he said. "You'd think they'd acknowledge you."

Very quickly, Dorrance began assembling what would become the world's dominant team. He jettisoned older players and brought in teenagers such as Mia Hamm, Kristine Lilly and Julie Foudy, along with Joy Fawcett, Carla Overbeck and Brandi Chastain, forming the backbone to support a decade of American success. He also stressed that the players must "sell the game," in the assertive way they played, in marketing it to a public that did not yet know or care that they existed. And he became a sort of cultural scofflaw, encouraging players to run through the red lights of social restraint that prevented some women from competing aggressively against friends and teammates.

Shortly after he took over the national team, Dorrance got a call from a coaching friend in Texas. There was a kid named Mia Hamm whom he had to see. Skeptical, Dorrance went to watch her play in a tournament in Louisiana.

"The team kicks off, a girl passes the ball to the right about 30 yards and I see this skinny brunette take off like she had been shot out of a cannon," Dorrance recalled.

He walked around the field and approached his coaching friend.

"Is that Mia Hamm?"

"Yes."

"We've got something here."

But Hamm was only 14. At 15, she would become the youngest player, male or female, to join the national team

"When you have a potential genius, you don't want to crush their spirit and shatter their confidence if they don't succeed," Dorrance said. "I decided we couldn't wait. The rest is history."

Women's soccer was played largely as a chess match as it expanded on the international level in the mid-1980s, but Dorrance introduced a cowboy element. Or at least he introduced the cowboy myth as expressed by Tom Cruise the fighter pilot. The year that Dorrance took over the national team, the movie *Top Gun* was released. Dorrance was smitten with Maverick, Cruise's character. He wanted the same thing in his soccer players, athletes who were creative, reliant on instinct, irreverent toward conventional wisdom, possessive of a "wonderful arrogance" about their abilities.

Taking a cue from Dean Smith, the fastidious North Carolina basketball coach who logged every shot, every rebound, every turnover in practice, Dorrance began keeping meticulous results of every soccer training session. He even had a *Top Gun* drill, where players squared off in one-on-one contests. Every player was ranked in every drill. The results were posted for everyone to see. After each practice, players knew exactly where they stood in relation to their teammates. Dorrance was creating a powerful psychological dimension, which would come to be known as the "USA mentality." In his hyperbolic manner, he referred to his players as "savages" and "blunt instruments."

"Practice became a legitimate war," Dorrance said. "It was a war you were permitted to fight in, to go after each other. It was honorable to carve up your teammates. It was the only way to practice. We ended up with a wonderful dichotomy, which was, 'When you cross the line of the field, I'm going to cut you in half to get that ball. Off the field, we take care of each other as family. If you are carrying three bags from the bus to the terminal at the airport, I'm going to grab two bags off your shoulders and carry them myself, even though that welt in back of your thigh is my cleat mark.' "

The personification of the emerging American style was a forward named April Heinrichs, whom Dorrance had recruited to North Carolina out of Littleton, Colorado, in 1983. In 1986, he would make Heinrichs the first captain of his national team. "She intimidated everyone," Dorrance said. "She even intimidated Michelle Akers."

When she joined the team in 1988, Brandi Chastain remembered, she went to take the ball from Heinrichs during a drill, "and I've never been chewed out or yelled at like she yelled at me. Her face turned bright red. I didn't know what to do. It scared the hell out of me."

It was during Heinrichs' college career, Dorrance said, that he came to believe that men and women were motivated differently. That for women, relationships meant as much as competition. And that many women found it difficult to compete against their friends, for fear of destroying their personal relationships.

"How does your team get along?" Heinrichs kept asking while he recruited her.

"Who cares?" he kept thinking to himself.

Then it dawned on him why she asked the question.

"She came in and crushed everyone," Dorrance said. "She had no respect for the seniors, juniors, sophomores, freshmen. She buried everyone equally. Instantaneously, she incurred everyone's wrath. One player after another would come into my office. 'What are you going to do about April?' 'Clone her?' I was thinking. Most women, when they come into this environment, spend the first three or four months genuflecting to everyone. April didn't genuflect to a soul. When you go after people, you are considered a bitch. You're taking it too seriously. The way people get back at intimidators is in backstabbing ways, going after them them socially, or how she dresses. The parents don't like her until there's two minutes left, and then it's 'Give the ball to April.' Those kind of athletes spend their lives suffering from criticism. Then of course everyone relies on them. They are brought up in this incredible hypocrisy. The thing I admired about April is, she wanted to be liked, wanted to be on a team that got along, but she wouldn't sacrifice her level of excellence to be like everyone else, wonderfully mediocre. We took her mentality and framed the culture of the national team around her."

The idea that she was a social outcast and had to be protected was a good banquet story but not the truth, Heinrichs said. However, she added, "Did I compete without fear of social ramifications? Absolutely. Did I put a premium on my friendships on the field? No. My premium was on winning."

The culture that trains women to be acquiescent is fundamentally at odds with the culture of athletics, Dorrance said. And even though soccer is a team game, stars who win games at the highest level are what he calls "personality players," those who possess an individual willingness, an essential haughtiness, to take control.

"I've spent my life trying to develop this kind of player," Dorrance said. "And to protect them from the sociology of their culture, protect them from their teammates who want them to pass the ball, from the parents of their teammates who are screaming that they're selfish, from everything in the world that tells them a pass is better than a shot, which is a crock. A shot is better than a pass. And it is only the really powerful personalities who are capable of taking the shot all the time, despite the criticism and some watered-down media image of what team success is all about. "

One of his favorite stories on the banquet circuit concerns a summer soccer camp, when, on parents' night, one aggressive girl came charging in on another and broke her leg on a fierce tackle. The next day, the aggressive girl, whom he respectfully called a "savage," charged another girl and "cut her in half" on a similar tackle.

According to Dorrance, "The second girl stood up and said, 'Listen, if you want it that badly, just tell me. This doesn't mean that much to me.'"

"You want a collection of these savages who are uncompromising," Dorrance said. "It has to mean something to them. The problem with the socialization of women is, they are trained for this not to mean that much to them. We wouldn't be in the World Cup final if we had that attitude. It has to mean something. It is part of my job to reconstruct that sociology, to get them to accept that competition. I have to protect the savages from their teammates and make it acceptable. Not acceptable, make it admirable."

Not everyone welcomed or thrived in this system. Tiffeny Milbrett declined to attend North Carolina out of high school and did not respond to Dorrance's coaching methods on the national team.

"I honestly felt there were times when he was really mean to me," she said. "He ridiculed, he was harsh. That's his coaching style. I don't fit well in that kind of style."

Other players on the national team, especially those who also played for Dorrance at North Carolina, found confirmation in an atmosphere where they did not have to offer excuses or atonement for being aggressive.

"Anson gave us the feeling it was okay to feel good about your success," Hamm said. "You should want to win. I still remember when I was little. Girls would score a goal, and we would walk together, high-five, and walk back to our positions. Boys are running around, going 'I'm Number One.' It wasn't like that for young girls. With girls, if you miss the ball on a tackle and hit the other player, it's like, 'Oh my God, I'm so sorry.' With Anson you didn't have to apologize for being good and wanting to be better."

If the women's national soccer team was forged by demanding aggressiveness, it was also stamped in anonymity and by the humor and adversity of shoestring travel. The team flew to Italy in 1988 on a cargo plane. Trips to China in the late 1980s meant living on Snickers bars and Pop-Tarts, weight losses of up to ten pounds a player, barren hotel rooms that flooded or were so grungy that players slept in their clothes. Akers said it was the first time that she had ever taken photographs of her food before she ate it.

"We never knew what we eating," said Sue Hammond, the team trainer. "We probably ate a little dog, cat, rat and survived. We stayed at some of the worst hotels. One of them had running water, or hot water, only an hour or two a day. We had to do our training around that. One of the places was so filthy, no one would take their shoes off. They laid on the covers fully clothed. The bathroom was a hole in the floor. It smelled so bad, we would get gauze sponges and put alcohol on them, put them under our noses, and run in and go to the bathroom and run out."

In parts of China where few Americans traveled, people would approach the players and touch their hair, Foudy said. These feelings of serious dislocation, though, were tempered by serious fun. Foudy said that the team was trailed constantly by Chinese security officials on scooters, and "we'd hide behind cars, in alleys, and jump out and scare them." "They didn't think it was funny," Foudy said. "We thought it was the funniest thing ever."

In these early years, the team seldom played in the United States. In fact, it seldom played. In 1989, with the inaugural Women's World Cup two years away, one match was scheduled. In 1990, six matches were played. However, it was on the road that the American team began to see the flash of possibility, the hint of national absorption, for the women's game.

The 1991 World Cup qualifying tournament for the North American, Central American and Caribbean region was played in Haiti. The hotel electricity was unreliable, hot water was scarce and, according to Heinrichs, "You'd see the power go off and hope there was one more flush in the toilet." She took to bathing in the hotel pool with a dab of shampoo in the palm of her hand. At night, she said, the players would sit around in their underwear, playing cards by candlelight. "This was the era prior to bodies that were cut like Brandi Chastain's," Heinrichs laughed. "Some of us shouldn't have been hanging out in our bras and underwear."

When it came time to play, fans clung to the back of the American team bus and packed Haiti's national stadium, even climbing light poles when they could not find a seat. At the World Cup final in Guangzhou, China, formerly Canton, the Americans defeated Norway, 2–1, before a crowd of 65,000. It appeared to be a rigged crowd, with Chinese workers given free tickets or instructed to attend, but, at the time, it was the largest audience to have ever watched women play soccer.

Where the American women once slept under mosquito nets in China, they were now housed in a four-star hotel at the inaugural World Cup. Where they once lived on candy bars, they now had meals of pasta and marinara sauce overseen by Dorrance's brother, Pete, and Carla Overbeck's future husband, Greg, both restaurateurs from Chapel Hill, North Carolina. McDonald's hamburgers were flown in from Hong Kong by the American consulate. The tournament took place during Thanksgiving, and fearing that a traditional dinner would not be available, a tour promoter secured several live turkeys and stashed them in a hotel room, Pete Dorrance said. It was unnecessary, though, and the turkeys were released, many feathers but no gobbler lives having been shed.

"Our friends would say, 'Aren't you guys bummed that you're not in the U.S?'" said Amy Allmann, a reserve goalkeeper on the first World Cup team. "We said, no. We loved the mosquito nets over the beds, the bad food. That was half the fun. At least people came to watch us. We played for ourselves. No one else cared. We rarely played in the U.S. Parents hardly ever came. We would tell them stories, but they didn't realize at all what was happening. I think that's why we won. We kept telling ourselves, 'We didn't go through all this to lose.' It wasn't until the parents got to China for the World Cup, and saw all the signs, the nice hotel, people climbing on our bus, that they realized it was a big deal. It was a whole new ballgame."

The cowboy soccer was not particularly sophisticated but it had the overwhelming, dust-raising momentum of a cattle drive. At the regional qualifying tournament in Haiti, the Americans scored 49 goals in five matches and surrendered none. Chastain scored five goals by herself in a match against a Mexican team that had been assembled all of three weeks earlier. During the World Cup in China, Akers scored five goals in a 7–0 rout of Taiwan, and collected both American goals in the 2–1 victory over Norway in the championship game. The American forwards—Akers, Heinrichs and Carin Gabarra—were nicknamed the "triple-edged sword" by the Chinese media, and they attacked with ferocious, inexorable slashing as if carving their way through Thanksgiving dinner.

The Americans won with speed, fitness, a bludgeoning defense and a mentality that, according to Allmann, seemed to scare some of their opponents, who shrank in defeat that was both athletic and cultural.

"I think you're born with a competitive side, or you're not, and it is shaped by society," Foudy said. "I was born with a competitive nature, sports, academics, whatever, I wanted to be good, I wanted to stand out. That's the common thread on this team. Anson set that tone; you keep score, you compete, you make each other better. The worst thing would have been to have all this competitive energy and to have a coach who never really pushed it. It became the way of our team. That's why so many of us stayed on the team. That drive, that refusal to lose."

This drive, this fierce commitment, however, was lost on the world outside of the team. Foudy returned to classes at Stanford, and her professor said, "You won the World Cup? Great. Here's your exam in human biology." Overbeck told friends that the Americans were world champions and the friends replied, "Oh, we didn't know you had a team." There was little media interest in the 1991 Women's World Cup, so some American players had resorted to sending faxes to their friends from China, and the friends distributed the faxes like chain letters. One of the team's corporate sponsors took out full-page newspaper ads to tell the story that sports sections had largely ignored. When the team returned to the United States, the welcoming party consisted of four people plus baggage handlers.

"I think there was one reporter there, but he was catching a flight to somewhere else," Chastain said.

The team began to drift, playing only two games in 1992. Players continued their college studies or worked part-time jobs. Overbeck worked as a teacher's assistant in Chapel Hill, North Carolina; her husband hired players who came through town to work at his restaurant for short periods. By 1994, Dorrance was gone from the national team, saying he wanted to devote all of his time to coaching North Carolina. Tony DiCicco, who had been the goalkeeper coach, became head coach. But he was hesitant to make changes in either style or personnel, and the team entered the 1995 World Cup in Sweden complaining of being tired and overtrained and distracted by a dispute over which brand of shoe to wear. Seven minutes into the tournament, Akers jumped to head a ball, collided with a Chinese player and was knocked unconscious. She did not return until the semifinals against Norway, when the six-foot-tall forward, Ann Kristin Aarones, flicked a header past Briana Scurry's outstretched arm on a corner kick. The Americans had been favored to repeat as champions, but now they had lost 1–0 and would not even reach the final. Disconsolate, the players gathered at midfield.

"For some of us, it was the worst day of our lives," Overbeck said. "We were determined never to let this happen again."

Scurry had tried vainly to muscle through a wall players on the corner kick, and the ball whistled past her, inside the near post, seemingly no more than an inch beyond her fingertips. When the game was over, the Norwegian players crawled on the ground, linked hand-to-ankle like human boxcars in a victory ritual called the Train. Hege

Riise, the team's star midfielder, had seen a men's team celebrating this way on television, "and I thought it would be fun."

It was a harmless celebration, but it was humiliating to the Americans. The sight of the Norwegians choo-chooing around the field became as indelible for Scurry as the tattoo of a panther on her shoulder.

"I burned it into my head," she said. "I felt I wasn't strong enough to get to the ball, so I hit the weight room hard. I was determined to knock a few Norwegians around."

A year later, the United States and Norway met in the semifinals of the 1996 Summer Olympics. Women's soccer had been added to the Atlanta Games, in part as a political bargaining chip, American officials said. Juan Antonio Samaranch, president of the International Olympic Committee, wanted the world's best athletes from each sport participating in the Winter and Summer Games. Joao Havelange, then the autocratic president of FIFA from Brazil, had placed an age limit of 23 years for Olympic soccer players, concerned that the Olympics might eventually overshadow the men's World Cup. If Havelange would allow three players above 23 on each Olympic team, Samaranch would agree to add women's soccer to the Atlanta Games. A deal was struck.

By then, Scurry had added 15 pounds of muscle for the rematch, weighing about 150, and she stood her ground as the Americans prevailed, 2–1, in overtime. Three days later, the Americans won the Olympic tournament over China, and keeping a promise she had made to a reporter, Scurry streaked down a secluded street in Athens, Georgia, wearing nothing but her gold medal.

"There was such a release of anxiety from the year before," she said. "I did not cry a tear until we beat them in the Olympics. That's when I cried."

Still, there was a score to settle in the 1999 Women's World Cup. The Americans felt a redemptive need to defeat Norway, the defending champions, to derail the Train once and for all. Even after the Olympics, Scurry had made a nightly ritual of thinking of the Norway game from 1995, of reliving the lone goal, the humbling celebration of players crawling on the field. "Every time I went into the weight room and felt tired, I would see that game," she said. "It was like a light went on and opened up in my head."

The World Cup rematch would never come. Norway was dismantled 5–0 by China in the semifinals. As the Americans warmed up for the championship match, Norway lost again in the consolation game, on penalty kicks to Brazil. It felt vengeful, but Scurry could not restrain the surge of happiness that welled in her at the news of another Norwegian defeat. *That's what happened to you because you were gloating. What goes around comes around.*

6

The Great Wall
of China

S UN WEN, the Chinese captain, stood over the ball at midfield,
hands on her hips, tapping the ground with her foot in nervous
anticipation, then nudged a pass to a teammate and began a slow jog
upfield. The game was on. Both teams settled into their tactical align-
ments, which, in soccer, read like the combinations to briefcase locks.
China used a conventional formation, the 4–4–2, with four defenders,
four midfielders and two forwards. The Americans employed a 4–3–3,
with four defenders, three midfielders and three forwards. This gave
the United States an extra forward on attack, but it also left the team
without midfielders on the flanks. This could prove dangerously vulnerable on a field 72 yards wide and 116 yards long, especially against
the Chinese who surged down the wings, scoring 19 goals in their first
five matches while surrendering only two. China played a triangular

offense, advancing the ball from the outside backs to the central midfielders to the flank midfielders. China's two outside backs, Bai Jie and Wang Liping, often came forward to support an attack that operated on swift deception. Through the tournament, the Chinese frequently advanced on a feint down the left wing, only to score from the right side, slipping behind unwary defenses the way receivers slipped behind distracted cornerbacks in football. The most elusive of the Chinese was Sun Wen, who seemed to move as quickly with the ball as without, and who was tied for the lead with seven goals scored in the World Cup. Just when defenses ignored her for a moment, she seemed to materialize with the ball at her feet, threatening to score.

"Keep your eye on her, don't just watch the ball," Lauren Gregg, the American assistant coach, had warned Kate Sobrero, the young defender.

The Americans considered marking Sun man-to-man but opted to remain in a zone. The United States opened in soccer's version of the full-court press to burn off nervous energy and to force the pace, insinuating its will upon the Chinese. It was too hot and too disruptive to the American attack to maintain the press the entire length of the field, so the defense would quickly reposition at the top of the penalty area, where it could maintain pressure for three-quarters of the field. The plan was to neutralize China's superior speed and flank play by placing two of the American forwards, usually Mia Hamm and Tiffeny Milbrett, wide and by funneling China's attack inside toward Michelle Akers, Kristine Lilly and Julie Foudy in midfield. Akers would track Sun Wen in midfield then hand her off to Carla Overbeck and Sobrero in the center of the American defense. The defense was designed to work as a sort of lobster trap, luring the Chinese in, but not allowing them out.

If victory came for the Americans, it would undoubtedly come by the slightest of margins. The Americans had defeated the Chinese 2–0 in the consolation match at the 1995 Women's World Cup held in Sweden, after the teams drew 3–3 in the opening match. They drew, 0–0, in the early rounds of the 1996 Olympic tournament, then the Americans prevailed 2–1 in the gold medal game. Already in 1999, the United States had played China three times. Each time the result again had been 2–1, with China winning twice. China entered the World Cup final every bit the tactical, technical and athletic equal of the Americans, having dismantled Norway, the defending champion, by 5–0 in the semifinals. Tony DiCicco, the American head coach, had used classic subterfuge in the days before the final, attempting to ratchet up the burden on the Chinese by declaring them to be the favorites.

"You're going to hear me say some things this week, and don't believe them," he told his players. "Let them carry the responsibility on their shoulders for a while. Let them bear the pressure."

They had entered the shadowless heat as links in a human chain, wearing red uniforms, the Chinese flag etched on their jerseys and socks, each player holding hands with the teammate in front and in back. In previous years, this had been a sign to the Americans of a timid sameness, as if China's players were a paper chain of dolls, identical, unchanging, as mass produced as Andy Warhol's soup cans, so reliant on the group that the individual became reluctant and smothered. It is often said in soccer that a country's particular style of play bears the fingerprints of its social and political nature. Thus the Germans are unfailingly characterized as resourceful and organized, while Brazilians are said to dance with the ball to the free-form, samba rhythms of Carnival. In the husk of cliché lies a kernel of truth. The Communist system of China had produced a collectivist style of women's soccer from the early 1980s to the mid-1990s. "As recently as 1996, 1997, they would just pass, pass, pass and they would never shoot," said the American forward Tiffeny Milbrett. The Chinese had faced the Americans in almost every international event—the World Cup, the Olympics, the Goodwill Games—but they had yet to win a single meeting in an important tournament. "I think we always had the edge mentally; we could break them down mentally," said the American midfielder Kristine Lilly. "They could take us all over the field, but when they get closer, rarely have they finished a lot of goals against us. Maybe they didn't work on it as much as we did. I think society plays a role. Our mentality here is, you get what you want. Their society is, lean over toward the men.

Let them go first. But they've gotten a lot better about it. This time you could see they wanted it."

An early form of soccer had appeared in China in the third and second centuries B.C., called tsu-chu, which involved the kicking of a ball filled with hair, fiber and feathers through an opening in a small net fixed to bamboo poles. Chinese officials said the game resembled volleyball, three to a side, and the ball had to be kicked from one side to the other without touching the ground. It was a game for the upper classes, not commoners. There is some evidence that women played a form of soccer in China in the Middle Ages. In the modern era, a team that once seemed to suppress creativity in favor of regimentation was now playing free-flowing, open soccer, moving forward in attack with no wasted motion, advancing with short, quick passes, and the fast-forwarding of long balls, finishing with individual assertiveness. No team was more impressively unstoppable during the tournament, or seemed so inevitably victorious.

"We're seeing an evolution," said Gregg, the assistant American coach. "In the past, they were much more predictable and hesitant to express themselves individually. For the first time they are expressing their personality. And they are riding a tremendous wave of confidence."

Several days before the final, Sun Wen had said boldly of the American goalkeeper, "We will bombard Scurry with all kinds of shots. She had better be prepared."

If such a remark seemed intemperate, and wildly uncharacteristic, it was also reflective in a larger sense of the metamorphosis of women's soccer 50 years after Mao Zedong stood at the Gate of Heavenly Peace, looked out over Tiananmen Square and announced, "The People's Republic of China is founded!"

Once, Chinese women performed in an such a robotic, aggregate manner on the soccer field that they sometimes seemed to be workers instead of players. But now they had become the sporting extension of Deng Xiaoping's economic belt-loosening of two decades earlier. Just as market forces brought relative wealth and dominion over personal lives, soccer now afforded the chance for instinct and elegant artistry. In the capital of Beijing, Mao uniforms were long gone, given way to somber fashion. Drab Stalinist apartment buildings stood shoulder-to-shoulder with the hulking steel and glass of new hotels and office buildings. Even the once ubiquitous bicycles shared the streets with the four-wheeled joint ventures of Jeep, Peugeot, Buick and red Japanese taxis known as Xiali's. The golden anniversary of Communism coexisted easily with the golden arches of McDonald's. A Kentucky Fried Chicken—featuring a Buddha-esque Colonel Sanders—now stood at the Great Wall. Even the Chairman Mao Mausoleum had accumulated a sort of Pope-on-a-rope kitschiness. Around Beijing, Mao's likeness could be found on any manner of trinkets, including a cigarette lighter that played "Happy Birthday" and "Twinkle, Twinkle Little Star." Outside the Forbidden City, policemen played daily pickup basketball games while wearing replica uniforms of the Chicago Bulls. Soccer, too, had accumulated many Western influences. The Chinese women's team was sponsored by Adidas sportswear, and its marketing division was based in Switzerland. The Chinese and American women were in many ways similar. The players grew up on the outskirts of cities. They played attractive, attacking soccer. They succeeded at the highest level in a country where the men's national team was viewed as underachieving; the Chinese men, in fact, had never qualified for the World Cup, and the national's men's league was beset by match-rigging scandals. When they looked in the mirror, the American and Chinese women had begun to see each other's reflection. To reach the World Cup final, the Americans had become tightly connected by the ligaments of teamwork, while the Chinese had realized the necessary freedom of individual expression.

"This bears a close relationship to the reform of our country," said Wang Junsheng, the general secretary of the Chinese soccer federation. "The social reforms of the recent years say that we should follow the modern way. We must combine with the soccer family worldwide. Our federation encourages players to express themselves. If you have the ability at that level, don't be afraid to do that."

When American warplanes inadvertently bombed the Chinese Embassy in Belgrade, Yugoslavia, on May 7, 1999, during the crisis in Kosovo, shock waves reached all the way to the Women's World Cup.

For a brief moment, organizers were faced with the nightmare possibility that China would refuse to participate. If China withdrew in retaliation, the tournament would have lost its legitimacy and become less a competition than a coronation of the American team.

Unlike the students who surrounded the American Embassy in Beijing and hurled rocks and chunks of sidewalk in protest, Chinese soccer officials made no threatening gestures. "I did not say definitely we will come, and I did not say we will not come," Zhao Ginfu, a foreign-affairs official in the Chinese soccer federation, said in an interview a month before the World Cup was to begin. "Up to this point, there is no such problem that we will not come."

Perhaps, given all the tools of protest, women's soccer was not regarded highly enough to use as a political hammer. Or, theorized Alan I. Rothenberg, the former president of the United States Soccer Federation, "Maybe they thought they had more to gain by coming here and winning."

In the end, Rothenberg was right. The Chinese kept pursuing their lodging arrangements and they arrived in the United States on schedule before the tournament began. More than 30 Chinese journalists reporters accompanied the team, and their reports, portraying a women's game that was purer and more fundamentally refined than the men's game, aroused considerable public interest as China kept winning. The final match, according to China's soccer federation, was watched on television by 100 to 200 million Chinese viewers. One time zone encompasses all of China, where the game began at 4 A.M., Saturday July 10 in the States, having become Sunday July 11 in the Far East. Some restaurants in Beijing remained open all night. At the Soccer Buff Café, 11 candles, one for each of the starting players, were stuck in 11 bottles of beer and were placed around a soccer ball for good luck, according to *The Washington Post. The China Women's News*, a state-run, mass-circulation newspaper that is an advocate for women's issues, brought the parents of some players to a hotel in Beijing to watch the match. Tens of millions apparently went to sleep then awakened before dawn and flipped on the television for a game that would be engaging as much for political and nationalistic reasons as athletic reasons.

"The majority of Chinese thought that, no matter what the United States explained, that the bombing was deliberate," said Cheng Gang, an editor at *China Women's News*. "The Chinese thought they had been bullied by the U.S. If China could now beat the U.S. in the World Cup, on U.S. soil, it would be a way to vent our anger. Rationally, of course, we couldn't get even by beating the U.S., but sentimentally, emotionally, we could."

Before the final match, Chinese President Jiang Zemin personally telephoned Wang Junsheng, the head of the team's soccer delegation in Los Angeles, saying, "I have watched you performances. You have displayed excellent skills. Your performances have won appreciation by the Chinese and American people. We will celebrate and honor you, no matter the outcome of the final."

In this 50th birthday year of the People's Republic of China, Jiang eagerly sought to demonstrate that he belonged on the Communist Party equivalent of Mt. Rushmore, alongside Mao, the founding father, and Deng Xiaoping, the economic liberator. Along with the goose-stepping missile parades, designed to show military and personal strength, Jiang also made fervent political use of China's sporting achievements, courting the women's soccer team as a way to jump-start the dead battery of a relationship with the United States. The state-run *New China News Agency* would report that President Clinton wrote a letter to Jiang, and that he responded, on the day of the final. Three months after the World Cup, Jiang would also make an appearance at the world gymnastics championships in the Chinese city of Tianjin, but this would not exactly earn his human-rights reputation a perfect score of 10 from international judges. A week later, while Jang was on an October state visit to Britain, Western hotels in Beijing would carry jarring coverage from British television in which Amnesty International accused China of keeping 200 dissidents in jail 10 years after democracy demonstrations were suppressed in Tiananmen Square, of routinely carrying out torture and of meting out the death penalty for crimes as minor as the stealing of a cow.

"In my opinion, Mao used sport to elevate the portrayal of China into a big and strong nation, while Jiang uses sport to elevate his status and the status of the party," said Harold Xu, a former translator for Mao and Premier Zhou Enlai who has taught Asian studies and seminars on revolutionary China at two California universities. "Deng Xiaoping started all the reform. Jiang has to concentrate on portraying himself as a head of state active in foreign affairs. The Belgrade embassy bombing was a blow to his efforts. If he didn't get the initiative back in his hands, how would Chinese history portray him? The final at the Rose Bowl gave Jiang a chance to re-establish non-political contacts with Clinton. Clinton attended the match to break the ice. Then he wrote Jiang a letter after the match and Jiang responded the same day. They could talk to each other about soccer, without involving politics."

Just as Ping-Pong diplomacy was used to reconnect severed diplomatic relations with China a generation earlier, a sort of soccer summitry occurred through the guise of the Women's World Cup. This allowed a safe, sporting way to begin mending of relations that had been frazzled by the American bombing of the Chinese embassy in Belgrade, by America's continued weapons sales to Taiwan, and by charges against China of nuclear espionage and manipulative campaign donations in the United States.

After the championship match, Clinton would make an explicit effort to visit the Chinese locker room, to be photographed with the Chinese players, to speak of their competitive spirit and graciousness in defeat. He would mention the Chinese players again nine days later when the American team would visit the White House. A political thaw had begun. Two months later, Jiang would refer to Clinton as "my good friend" and the two leaders would meet in New Zealand. And by mid-November of 1999, the United States and China would enter into a sweeping agreement designed to open the world's largest market to international trade. In exchange for American support of China's entry into the World Trade Organization, China would reduce taxes on imported cars, allow international corporations to gain controlling interests in banks and telephone companies, double its import of foreign films. If the final of the Women's World Cup had failed to produce any goals in an athletic sense, it had scored significantly on the political front.

"I think the soccer diplomacy certainly helped," said Henry A. Kissinger, who was national security adviser when he made a secret trip to Beijing in July of 1971 to begin President Nixon's opening to

China, and who is an inveterate soccer fan. "It came at a critical time. It was not quite the same function as Ping-Pong diplomacy because it was not unexpected and totally new. But within that framework, it was certainly extremely helpful."

Although Mao proclaimed that women "hold up half the sky," and while their status has improved significantly with legislated equality in the People's Republic of China, women are still subjected to centuries-old prejudices and they face widespread discrimination in the areas of education and employment. In 1979, China announced a one-child policy as a means of population control in a country that now has 1.2 billion people, although in rural areas families are usually allowed two children and in some areas, three. Pregnancies must be authorized by the state, and, according to the New York–based Human Rights in China, women face physical coercion, psychological pressure and the threat of economic penalties to undergo sex-selective abortion, sterilization and the implantation of birth-control devices. Especially in the countryside, female babies are often considered the "difficult" or "wrong" sex, and families remain anxious to have a son to carry on the family name. Official surveys, human-rights groups and newspaper reports indicate that, each year, from half a million to nearly two million girls go missing due to abortion, abandonment, infanticide and nonregistration, which can render stillborn any chance for an education.

It is only in the last century that girls in rural areas were regularly given names instead of being called simply "eldest daughter" or "second kid." Some still receive names like Laidi, which means "bring a younger brother." Sons are more desirable because they carry on the family name, assume a heavier work load in the fields and because they traditionally provide a social-security safety net for elderly parents. In rural villages, men remain with their families upon marrying, while women leave home for their husband's community and are considered "water spilled on the ground," according to a Chinese proverb. In Chinese script, the characters that denote a married woman include "woman," and "broom," as the wife is expected to be a helper, obedient, quiet, respectful.

As few as 20 percent of girls attend school in poorer rural areas. Women are forced to retire at age 55, compared to 60 for men, and they are often the last hired and the first fired. Newspaper ads explicitly state that women need not apply for certain jobs or that secretaries will not be hired unless they are younger than 25. Graduates fresh from college often pour coffee in corporate offices and sales clerks are frequently fired in their 30s because they are not considered as capable (or attractive) as younger women.

Female athletes in China excel in such sports as badminton, table tennis, volleyball, gymnastics, swimming, basketball and distance running, but soccer for women did not gain acceptance until the early 1980s. Even now, the Chinese soccer federation says that only 30,000 girls and women play soccer, compared with 7.8 million in the United States. But collective statistics are unreliable, and some estimate that only 2,000 to 10,000 women participate. Soccer is still considered by many parents a rough and rude sport that only "coarse" or "wild" young women would dare to play. Many of the women on the current national team did not begin playing until their teenage years after they switched from other sports, such as track and field. Liu Ailing, the Chinese playmaker, began her career at age 18, while most American women began playing at six or seven. Liu had to make three trips home to Hubei Province, to convince her father to let her play, according to Chinese journalists, but has said she would not want her own daughter to participate. Pu Wei, at 18 the youngest player on the national team, conspired with her mother to play soccer for two years before telling her father, journalists said, and a former captain of the team, forward Sun Qing Mei, kept pursuing soccer even though her parents sometimes locked her in her room in a mining town in Hebei Province.

"People think girls should do more feminine things, piano, ballet, not running all over a soccer field," said Jun Shen, a close friend of Sun Wen's who played collegiately at Iowa State University. "With the one-kid birth control policy, parents feel soccer is too dangerous. What if their child gets injured? In the Chinese culture, people feel that education is the key to the future. It is very tough to get into college. People think that's the only way to be well off in the future."

Credit for starting a women's national team is generally given to the assistance of Deng Yingchao, the widow of former Premier Zhou Enlai who headed the state-run All-China Women's Federation. A women's national team was formed in 1982 or 1983, on a threadbare budget. Like the American women, the Chinese wore men's uniforms or the jerseys of their provincial teams. Unable to afford airfare, or even sleeping berths on trains, the players traveled by rail within the country, sitting on hard benches for up to 30 hours at a time. When the team traveled to Italy in 1987, it had no money for plane tickets so the players traveled free of charge, dressed as airline workers, said Han Zhongde, the former general manager of the women's team, adding that parents sometimes had to pay for travel costs.

"When we started the team, we had in mind foreign pictures of Chinese women with bound feet," Han said. "I wanted to portray to the world that they were not bound-feet women. Since 1949, Mao said, women hold up half the sky. They are as important as men. I wanted to portray such a picture."

The first Chinese national team set up camp on the dirt runway at an abandoned airfield in Wuzhou, Guangxi Province, in southern China. In 1985, the team endured a training camp in the isolated town of Yingde, in Guangdong Province, where there was no hot water or dining hall, and the players ate outdoors, crouched, holding their rice bowls in their hands. The resilient ability to withstand such deprivation—to eat bitterness, as it is known—has become the defining characteristic of the Chinese women's team. "They are seen as being able to endure hardships that other people can't," said Liu Chang, a Chinese journalist who wrote the script for a four-part series titled *Sunflowers Through Wind and Rain*, that was broadcast on state television. The title came from lyrics to a song written by Sun Wen, the team's high-scoring forward: "Roses are conceived in silence. They grow in wind and rains and they blossom in excitement."

China hosted the inaugural Women's World Cup in 1991, and was considered a favorite, but it did not even reach the championship game, losing to Sweden in the quarterfinals. The coach, Shang Ruihua, felt such pressure and personal responsibility for the defeat that he had to be hospitalized for drinking, according to Han, the team's general manager. Because women's soccer was not yet included in the Olympics, and because funding wavered, the national team essentially disbanded for a year.

In late 1992, Ma Yuanan was named coach of the women's national team. He is a calm, friendly man, easy with a joke, and even with a receding hairline appears younger than his 54 years. However, Chinese journalists said he suffered from hypertension, and like DiCicco, the American coach, he spent days and weeks at a time away from his wife and daughter. His wife was said to be so tense while watching matches on television, that she kept medication at her side to calm her. Ma was known in the Chinese press as a dedicated family man who bought skin-care products for his wife when he traveled abroad and carefully translated the instructions into Chinese. One newspaper story noted, "No wonder Mrs. Ma looks at least 10 years younger than her actual age."

When Ma took over the team, he lived in a dark, dank room in the stadium when the team trained in the southern city of Guangzhou, formerly Canton. Travel, financial and living conditions have since improved considerably for the Chinese women, although support appears to fluctuate wildly. In 1986, there was a record number of 36 teams in a women's league, Han said. By 1998, the number was down to four, although it doubled to eight in 1999. Playing for their provincial teams, the Chinese women make from $5,000 to $20,000 a year, Sun said. That is considerably less than the top Chinese men, who can make $125,000 to $250,000 a year according to the female players and team officials, but considerably more than the average worker and even college professors who earn $200 a month.

The top players received apartments from their provincial teams and bonuses for winning important tournaments. Several of the players on the national team have bought cars. For the Women's World Cup, each Chinese player would receive a bonus of $30,000, Sun Wen said. She would be able to purchase a house for $37,500 in Shanghai, and Wang Liping, a defender, would be able to contribute money toward a new house for her parents, who lived in a dilapidated dwelling where cardboard boxes sufficed as windowpanes.

After the World Cup, the suddenly popular women's league would outdraw the men's league in one southern province with crowds of up to 10,000 and 15,000 a game, said Wang Junsheng, general secretary of the Chinese soccer federation. Financial support would come pouring in, too, for the development of women's soccer: $1.2 million from the state-run All-China Women's Federation; $362,000 from a Hong Kong tycoon, another $1.2 million from a computer corporation. What remained to be seen was whether this was simply impulse nationalism or the beginning of regular, dependable assistance.

"It's hard to say whether the support will continue or the enthusiasm and excitement will last very long," Ma said.

Unable to match the Americans in the organized development of players, financial support or physical size, the Chinese had decided that their one advantage in an authoritarian society lay in their ability to call the players together for extended periods of training. Like the Americans, several Chinese players were married, but none had children who would be left without their mothers. In the months before the World Cup, the Chinese spent 47 consecutive days out of the country while playing in Portugal, Holland, Germany and the United States. At home, the women's national team trained in seclusion in the western hills outside Beijing, above the polluted air that was as milky as a cataract. The team lived in a modest, comfortable dormitory in a military area so lightly traveled that a visiting Western reporter arriving in a taxi encountered people playing cards and reading newspapers in the middle of a narrow ribbon of cement road.

"The training system is our advantage, guaranteeing that our 30,000 can compete with your eight million," Wang Junsheng said. However, some, including DiCicco, the American coach, thought that the Chinese team spent so much time together that its one advantage had become a disadvantage. "I believe this is a difference between the USA and China," wrote a cyber-journalist named Lei Ning. "Chinese players always live and train and play together. So they know each other well. Meanwhile, they have no rest, no holiday, no reading time. So they are often injured and tired."

If the Chinese players were tired for the final of the World Cup, they had a legitimate reason, having flown across country four times during the three-week tournament. The official Chinese media implied that tournament organizers had conspired to provide the United States an easy path to the final, requiring the Americans to traverse the country only once. This is a charge frequently made—and always denied—in soccer's various world tournaments, that the scheduling is rigged in favor of the home team.

For the 1999 Women's World Cup, scheduling decisions were based not on favoritism but "were entirely driven by marketing concerns," said Marla Messing, the tournament's chief organizer. To maximize ticket sales, the American games were set for huge football stadiums, each in a different city, and sites for potential matches in the quarterfinals and semifinals were selected well before the tournament. Normally, sites for the knockout rounds are determined by a team's finish in round-robin play at the beginning of major tournaments. The only manipulation of the schedule, Messing said, was to have China open the tournament in the Bay Area, where large numbers of Chinese-American fans lived, instead of in Foxboro, Massachusetts, as initially planned. Still, she could never convince all the teams that the pairings had not been rigged.

Less than two weeks before the tournament pairings were drawn in February of 1999 in Las Vegas, FIFA called a meeting to vote on a reconfiguration of the World Cup schedule. The world governing body was feeling pressure from European teams, particularly the Norwegians, Swedes and Germans, who were furious that the scheduling appeared weighted too heavily in favor of the Americans. But organizers had already signed contracts with stadiums and had sold more than 200,000 tickets. Messing said she threatened to resign, and after several hasty phone calls made in the middle of the night, FIFA backed down. The schedule remained the same. Even after the tournament began, however, North Korea grew upset about its travel schedule and twice threatened not to play matches, including one against the Americans in Foxboro, according to Messing. Neither threat was carried out.

"We told them it would be catastrophic," Messing said of FIFA's threat to alter the schedule. "They were blowing up the World Cup. We had contracts with stadiums. There would have been ill will with ticket buyers. Finally, they relented."

No one seemed less contentious about the 12,673 miles of enervating travel than the Chinese team. Ma said that his players had grown accustomed to the grind and the frustration of late flights and lost luggage during their pre—World Cup tour of Europe and the United States. "Imagine you are tourists," he urged his players during the World Cup. "Just see this as a pleasure." He kept the team's collective body clock set on West Coast time even when it traveled East. The players ate lunch at 3 P.M. instead of noon and slept at 2 A.M. instead of 11 P.M.

"Women's soccer is always regarded somewhat less equal than men; women are considered not to have the strength and stamina to do well," said Wang Junsheng. "But the travel back and forth twice across the country proved that women have the strength and stamina to play well in a rough schedule."

If the players did have a complaint, it was about the lack of variety of food. The Chinese preferred spicy sauces and sampling from five or six dishes at meals, dishes of chicken, beef, pork, fish and vegetables, instead of the one-entree meals provided by the World Cup organizers, who were operating without a lavish budget or a real understanding of Asian culture. The team supplemented its diet by sending out to local Chinese restaurants. One restaurateur in Portland, Oregon, sent over watermelons and dumplings for free. And Chinese-Americans also brought food to the team hotel, but, Ma joked, "You meet Chinese people, you take at least two hours to chat. It's a cultural thing. We just want the food."

The morning of the World Cup final, the players ate a breakfast of porridge, stuffed buns and deep-fried donuts sent over from the Chinese consulate in Los Angeles. The players then had their customary nap. On the way to the Rose Bowl, assistant coach Yan Zhongjian, whose work was published in newspapers, wrote a poem: "Brave soldiers of the women's soccer team / they have accomplished wonders on the battlefield in one hundred battles / Today they will fight for the world championship / they will make great endeavors in terms of courage and wisdom." The Chinese took a locker room adjacent to the Americans. "I was kind of surprised, they were very calm, I didn't feel any nervousness," said Stephen Tsih, a San Jose (California) City College professor of business who was the Chinese team liasion. "The tension among the Americans appeared a lot higher than the Chinese. They were playing around, joking around."

Only once had Tsih seen the players unnerved during the tournament. The Chinese team bus was held up for 15 minutes by a police escort before the semifinal in Foxboro, Massachusetts, while the Norwegian bus was allowed to proceed. The Chinese players began screaming, "Does that mean the U.S. highways hold only one bus at a time? If you don't want us to play, we won't play." That brushfire of emotion was quickly stamped out, and the Chinese had trampled Norway 5–0. But the veneer of calm that Tsih sensed was misleading. Before the final began coach Ma would detect more roiling unease. There was much confusion on the field. Proper warm-ups were not allowed, handshakes between the teams and FIFA officials were interrupted by the national anthems and a deafening flyover by the Navy's precision jet team, the Blue Angels, seemed to startle the Chinese players. A fourth F-15 flew over, stalled, and pulled straight up at full thrust, and the Chinese reacted with a collective flinch. After a few practice kicks, the referee's whistle blew and the game began abruptly, like a truck lurching into gear.

"There were too many irregularities," Ma said. "Things were not organized. We didn't know what to do. You had 90,000 people cheering for the Americans. We were lost in the beginning. Even Sun Wen was lost."

All the passion from the semifinal victory over Norway seemed spent. His team had remained excited for too long after the Norway game, Ma had come to believe. The Chinese had dominated, and after this perfect game some of the players could not let go of the perfection. They had difficulty sleeping and calmly preparing for the Americans, and when the emotion finally dissipated, seeping out like carbonation from a soda bottle, it could not be recovered. His team was in the final of the world championship and it was disturbingly flat and cautious.

"When we played the U.S., we should have been at our highest emotional level," Ma said. "But that was gone."

His best chance, the coach knew, might be to strike early. "The U.S. did not have very strong backs, not very fast," Ma said. "We were faster. If we could control the midfield, we thought there would be opportunities to score." The Americans had been particularly vulnerable in the opening minutes of their matches, and China immediately flared a long pass down the left wing. Nigeria had scored on the United States in the first 62 seconds, and Brandi Chastain had put the ball into her own net five minutes into a quarterfinal match against Germany.

"You're carrying the whole tournament on your shoulders, and at the beginning of every game it's like, 'Here we go,' and I think sometimes that cost us," Sobrero said. "It's not being ready. Or we were ready and anxious, not focused."

But this time the American defense did not come unraveled. Joy Fawcett calmly headed the first Chinese pass out of bounds, then she and Hamm pinched the ball loose after China tossed it back into play. Three minutes into the game, the young Chinese midfielder Pu Wei drifted down the middle of the field in an insistent jog, her right arm signaling, a semaphore wave that she was open, free to score. From 35 yards, Sun chipped a threatening pass into the penalty area but Brandi Chastain broke into a sprint as the ball lifted into its rainbow arc, her ponytail trailing like a rudder. With a dive to her hands and knees Chastain intercepted the pass with her head and flicked it back upfield to begin a counterattack.

"We set the tone right away," said DiCicco, the American coach. "We let them know, 'You aren't going to find space, not going to have the luxury of knocking the ball around. Things that worked for you all tournament are not going to work today.' Obviously I would have liked to see us more successful on the attacking side, but it was a game that was going to be determined by defenders."

7

Green Eggs and Hamm

M IA HAMM WAITED near midfield to start the counterattack, leaning back slightly to trap the pass with her chest, arms curled as if she were dancing or hugging a friend, and she wheeled to her right, dodged the flying hip of a Chinese midfielder, juggled the ball on her knee, and began a balletic slalom in the third minute. All eyes would be on Mia, the announcers had said earlier on television. "You can tell early in her game whether she's on," Wendy Gebauer, a former member of the American national team and a former team-mate of Hamm's, said in the ABC booth. "If she gets a goal early, she relaxes completely. If she gets fouled and she stays down for a long time, she's not really focused. She needs to get her shots. Against Brazil, she didn't have any shots."

Hamm accelerated past midfield now, tapping the ball once with her left foot, then twice, her ankle bent, her foot locked inward to keep the ball from straying. The crowd stirred, and as she sprinted the teenage screaming began, a collective dolphin screech, the same wild soprano shriek that once greeted the Beatles on *Ed Sullivan*. "Her acceleration is so visceral," said her college coach at North Carolina, Anson Dorrance, "when she gets the ball you hold your breath." She stepped over the ball with her left foot like a magician waving a hand over an upturned hat, and she changed direction at full speed, pivoting seamlessly, pushing the ball ahead with her right foot, fists lightly clinched, thumb touching forefinger, shoulders squared, her head up, her peripheral vision picking up the approaching rush of two Chinese defenders. This is what China did so masterfully, converging on the ball like white blood cells fighting off infection. Wen Lirong stood in front of Hamm, backpedaling, as Bai Jie moved in from Hamm's right. Two other Chinese closed in a vise from behind. The little assassin, Tony DiCicco called Bai Jie for her rough defensive style. Fan Yunjie was considered the toughest of China's defenders; she had knocked Michelle Akers out cold in the first few minutes of the 1995 World Cup and had been as immovable as a basketball pick when Hamm slammed into her and went down hard in the first two minutes of the 1999 final. This time, Hamm swiveled back to her left and Liu Ailing, the trailing Chinese playmaker, reached forward to brace herself with a hand on Hamm's back. Wen dropped to one knee, reaching in with her right leg, trying to poke the ball away, but it squirted up and Bai swung wildly with her right leg, just missing Hamm's knee. A look crossed Hamm's face, a grimace or a hint of irritation, and she hopped once but did not stop giving chase. The ball ricocheted forward off Bai's shoe or Hamm's thigh, and she was free for an instant, emerging from the scrum of Chinese players, the star-spangled crowd shrieking in hysterical anticipation, the ball bouncing inside the penalty area, the Chinese goalkeeper waiting in her crouch, only the desperate closing by a final defender to prevent a goal. Wang Liping rushed over and cleared the ball straight into the air before Hamm reached it, as much in anxiety as in triumph. Hamm kept up her bloodhound pursuit, and not until she was sandwiched between Wang and Liu, caught in a slamdance at the mosh-pit edge of the penalty area, was the ball finally kicked away from her immediate reach. "I ran into the Great Wall of China," she said.

Breathing lightly, Hamm retreated back on defense. This is what separated her, what made her the world's leading scorer—the dancer's feet and the felon's heart.

Off the field, she could seem phlegmatic, the Southern lilt in her accent lending her voice a sound near exhaustion. But on the field a fiercer countenance emerged, cheeks hollow in exertion, jaw clenched, the whisk-broom fan of her ponytail as she sprinted 40 yards to finish a fastbreak or carved a defender with a deft two-step and made an inexorable charge toward the goal. At these times, the effort was even visible in the bloodshot corners of her eyes. The passion of her game was most evident in the celebrative convulsion when she scored, the tendons in her neck like suspension cables, her mouth an open scream, the vaulting joy, the ecstatic knee slide, her arms cocked at the elbow and fists closed as if she has just lifted some enormous weight.

"If Mia leaves the field at the half and hasn't scored, she's actually agitated," Dorrance said. "She hates not scoring in a way that actually bothers her. That is a very powerful drive. Even though a lot of players talk the talk, 'I'm so disappointed I didn't score today,' a lot of them don't walk the walk. They don't come in visibly upset that they haven't scored. Mia Hamm loves to score goals in such a passionate way that when she doesn't, she's visibly upset. She's so trained before the media now, she will appear like it's okay, but it's not. That wonderful drive and passion that she has sets her apart."

In the homestretch of the century, Mia Hamm, more than anyone else, had come to represent the full opportunities hard won by female athletes, the cultural shift, the deflating of arguments that used gender to diminish skill.

Outside of tennis and golf, the most visible sporting opportunities for women historically have come in the Winter and Summer Olympics. But when the modern Olympic Games were begun in 1896, all 245 athletes from 14 nations who competed in Athens, Greece, were men. Women were expected to use their hands to applaud, not to participate. The founder of the modern Games, the French baron Pierre de Coubertin, declared that it was "indecent that the spectators should be exposed to the risk of seeing the body of a woman being smashed before their very eyes."

Four years later, at the 1900 Summer Games in Paris, a 22-year-old Chicago socialite named Margaret Abbott became the first American woman to win an Olympic gold medal when she took first in the golf competition. According to David Wallechinsky's *The Complete Book of the Summer Olympics*, Abbott had traveled to Paris with her mother, who was a novelist and literary editor, in order to study art. She won the tournament because her confused French competitors showed up to play in high heels and tight skirts, and she died 55 years later unaware that her victory was part of the Olympics.

Aileen Riggin Soule, the oldest living American gold medalist at 94, grew up in New York and learned of the ancient Olympic Games by listening to her mother read aloud from *The Iliad* and *The Odyssey* and other Greek epics. She began swimming to regain her health after she nearly died in the great influenza epidemic of 1918, training at the few public baths and hotel pools that admitted women and girls. By 1920, women's diving had become an Olympic sport in Antwerp, Belgium, but Soule was 14 years old, as was the other top American diver, Helen Wainwright. No one wanted the responsibility of chaperoning a pair of 14-year-olds on a two-week boat trip to Europe. Eventually officials reconsidered, and both Soule and Wainwright traveled to Antwerp. During the Atlantic crossing, they trained in harnesses and dived into a canvas tank filled with seawater. Soule won the diving competition and Wainwright finished second. Four years later, at the 1924 Paris Olympics, Soule became the first woman to win medals in two sports, a silver in diving and a bronze in the 100-meter backstroke. She preferred individual sports to team events, but she decided to watch her first soccer match when the Americans faced the Chinese in the Women's World Cup final.

"I thought we had come a long way," said Soule, who now lives in Hawaii and still competes in masters swimming events. "Those first Olympics in 1920 were so primitive. Girls were barely acknowledged. The American Olympic Committee wanted to keep it the way it was in ancient Greece, where women couldn't even be spectators. They thought we would be a nuisance. Only a few hundred people came to see us compete, mostly other athletes. I was fascinated to see all those people at the soccer match. I'd like to think we had something to do with it."

When six women collapsed after the 800-meter race at the 1928 Amsterdam Olympics, an alarmist account in *The New York Times* said that "even this distance makes too great a call on feminine strength." The *London Daily Mail* carried admonitions from doctors that women who participated in such "feats of endurance" would "become old too soon." The 800-meter race was discontinued, and for 32 years, until the 1960 Rome Olympics, women would run no race longer than 200 meters. Distance running by women was thought to be a violation of natural law. The common wisdom held that a woman was not physiologically capable of running mile after mile, that she would be unable to bear children, that she might grow a mustache, that she was a man, or wanted to be one. Not until 1984 was a woman's marathon added to the Summer Olympics.

On a voyage to the 1936 Summer Olympics in Berlin, where Eleanor Holm of Brooklyn was to defend her gold medal in the 100-meter backstroke, she was removed from the American team for public drunkenness and shooting craps. The United States Olympic Committee ignored the fact that Holm was a married adult and that the committee itself held nightly cocktail parties. At the same Berlin Games, Helen Stephens, a Missouri farm girl, won the 100-meter sprint and, she later recalled, was approached by Adolf Hitler, who "gets ahold of my fanny and he begins to squeeze and pinch and hug me up." Eventually, Hitler invited her to spend a weekend at his retreat at Berchtesgaden. She declined.

When Alice Coachman of Albany, Georgia, became the first black woman to win an Olympic gold medal at the London Games of 1948, she met members of the British royal family and was invited aboard a royal yacht. Back home in Jim Crow Georgia, she had been unable to train for the high jump on the same track as whites. And her welcome-home ceremony in the Albany Municipal Auditorium was segregated—whites on one side of the stage, blacks on the other. Coachman received a number of gift certificates and flowers, presumably from whites, but the accompanying cards went unsigned.

"During segregated times, no one wanted to come out and let their peers know they had given me gifts," Coachman said. "I knew I was from the South, and like any other Southern city, you had to do the best you could. I made a difference among the blacks, being one of the leaders. If I had gone to the Games and failed, there wouldn't be anyone to follow in my footsteps. It encouraged the rest of the women to work harder and fight harder."

Despite these cultural and racial barriers, women persevered in international sport. Gertrude Ederle of New York became the first woman to swim the English Channel in 1926, beating the men's record by more than two hours. Mildred "Babe" Didrikson of Beaumont, Texas, qualified for five events at the 1932 Los Angeles Olympics, but women were allowed to compete in only three. She chose the javelin, high jump and the hurdles and set world records in each of them. She would become the world's greatest golfer, winning 31 LPGA titles, and she would pitch in several major-league exhibition games. The *Associated Press* would vote her the best female athlete of the half-century.

At the 1948 London Games, Fanny Blankers-Koen of the Netherlands punctured the myth that athletics brought a physiological impediment to motherhood. A mother of two, Blankers-Koen won four of the nine track-and-field events held in London. At the 1967 Boston Marathon, which was forbidden to women, Kathrine Switzer entered as K.V. Switzer and completed the race after her boyfriend shoved aside a marathon official who attempted to remove her from the course. And on September 20, 1973, a year after the passage of Title IX, Billie Jean King defeated Bobby Riggs in the "Battle of the Sexes" tennis match that grew from campy excess into a seminal moment for female athletes in the century.

"Because Riggs was an arrogant guy, it became good versus evil, it had all the aspects of a morality play, an attempt to right wrongs and bring justice to society," said Richard Lapchick, director of the Center for the Study of Sport in Society at Northeastern University. "It signaled possibilities that some women and most men had never thought about. That women could play games in a way we just didn't think about before. Her success paralleled the success in small incremental steps that women were making in all phases of society, education, politics, but because it was sports it got so much more attention. She didn't only get a job over a man. On national television she made a statement of a woman winning on her talent over a man. It was symbolic of everything else that was going on but we were only reading about."

Three years later, Nancy Lieberman, who had grown up in Far Rockaway, Queens, with a disapproving mother who punctured her basketballs with a screwdriver, became, at 18, the youngest-ever American Olympic basketball player. Later, she became the first woman to play in a men's professional league. Anita DeFrantz of the United States won a bronze medal at the 1976 Montreal Olympics in the eight-oared shell with coxswain, having enduring harassment at the Vesper rowing club in Philadelphia, where men nailed shut the door to the women's locker room. As a 10-year-old, Dot Richardson, declined a chance to play Little League baseball in Orlando, Florida, when the coach demanded that she cut her hair and be known on the roster as "Bob." However, she kept playing softball through medical school, fashioning a batting cage in her Los Angeles apartment and was the starting shortstop for the American team that won the gold medal at the Atlanta Olympics.

Following such cultural markers, Hamm arrived at a rarefied place, perhaps unprecedented for a female athlete in a team sport. No one had told her she couldn't play. She was not slighted in comparison to men. In fact, the parenthesis of gender was almost entirely absent from qualifying remarks about her soccer skills. Little boys, as well as girls, wore her jersey. Cartoons appeared, showing boys playing soccer, one saying to the other, "Okay, I'll be Mia Hamm and you be Briana Scurry." Nike named a building in her honor at its headquarters. She earned a reported million-dollar income and could command $25,000 for corporate speeches. She appeared in a Gatorade commercial with Michael Jordan, challenging him in basketball, soccer, track and fencing, and flipping over her hip in a judo maneuver while the music asserted, "Anything you can do, I can do better."

"She was what I wanted, to let her skill be the determinant, to be what defined her," said Amy Love, who filed a federal lawsuit to be able to play soccer as a nine-year-old in northern California in 1975. "She's a role model based on the soccer field. It's totally about her as an athlete, not as a woman. That is a great step forward in the last century, to view athletes based solely on their capabilities and not on gender."

Hamm and her teammates exposed as fraudulent the arguments used in the most virulent resistance to women's team sports: That they were an unfair, unwanted trampling on the male domain. That interest was limited and success was undeserved. That theirs was a Potemkin achievement built solely on the foundation of political correctness and government mandate.

"There is a cultural expectation that sport is the inherent birthright of males, that by being born male you own sport," said Mary Jo Kane, a sports sociologist at the University of Minnesota. "Historically, the antithesis was being female. You have to demonstrate that you deserve to have access to sport. There is a belief that you are taking something that doesn't belong to you. That sense of 'How dare you?' That this is just about feminists insisting upon equality, that we have access only because the government says we must, because of Title IX, not because we deserve it. The players on the soccer team were world-class athletes. They provided empirical evidence that females can and should be taken seriously as athletes, that they were not pretenders to a male throne."

Ultimately, because she was so visible, Hamm became the symbol for what progress women had or had not achieved in the last century of athletic involvement. Harry Edwards, a professor of sociology at the University of California at Berkeley who once taught the American players Brandi Chastain and Joy Fawcett, said that he was uncertain whether the World Cup represented any real advancement or was simply a case of "marching up the down escalator." That Hamm endorsed a Soccer Barbie, he said, was another indication that women are still not taken seriously as athletes unless they conform to safe, unthreatening family-girl images and eliminate as much as possible any masculine or lesbian proclivities.

"It is the quintessential sexist symbol in Western society," Edwards said. "If a real woman was of Barbie doll dimensions, she'd be 10 feet tall and weigh 108 pounds. I'm not saying there's anything wrong with shapely, well-endowed women. But that's not the be all and end all. When you reduce them to a chunk of shapely meat, you do society a disservice. Sports has perpetuated that."

Mattel, the maker of Barbie, paid a $500,000 licensing fee to the Women's World Cup for the right to issue Soccer Barbie. Marla Messing, the chief organizer of the World Cup, argued on the lecture circuit that, beyond the issue of physique, Barbie was actually an iconic figure. That she could be anyone she wanted to be—a doctor, a paleontologist, a soccer player—and by extension, so could the girls who played with her. Hamm was endorsing a product, she said, that not only reflected society but influenced it in a positive, egalitarian manner. It was a tough sell. The audience response, she said, sometimes included boos and hisses.

"I thought Barbie was empowering," Messing said. "I think I stand alone in that."

Hamm's flipping of Jordan in the Gatorade commercial represented one of the most powerful images ever shown of female athletes, said Rick Burton, a professor of business at the University of Oregon. "If Jordan is the athletic ideal, the icon, the greatest athlete of our time, it was really a notable achievement to show, not only equality, but Mia defeating him," he said.

Doug Flutie, the quarterback for the Buffalo Bills, would say during a banquet speech after the World Cup that he had watched the commercial with his 10-year-old daughter, Alexa, and that she had asked, "Who's that guy with Mia?"

Fifteen rows behind the American bench, 12-year-old Leah Lauber of St. Petersburg, Florida, sat with her sister and her parents, wearing a red, white and blue jersey, her face painted "Go USA," keeping her seat in the broiling sun, afraid to miss some flashpoint of possibility. If much of the mainstream sporting media ignored Hamm and the American team, she had not. As the team prepared for the World Cup, Lauber wrote five stories for a kid's page in the *St. Petersburg Times*, twice traveling 100 miles from home with her father to interview players at the American training camp outside of Orlando. She and her family drove 12 hours to Athens, Georgia, to watch the United States play China in the final of the 1996 Summer Olympics, and she won four tickets to the World Cup final in a photo contest. Her parents had converted their credit cards to frequent-flyer accounts, hoping to earn enough miles to travel to the 2000 Summer Olympics in Sydney, Australia. When Hamm broke the world scoring record in Orlando in May of 1999, Lauber high-fived her as she left the field at halftime, then later interviewed her on the Citrus Bowl turf, wearing a replica of Hamm's No. 9 jersey, taking adolescent license with journalistic objectivity. After the World Cup final, she would join other reporters in the interview area of the Rose Bowl, carrying her tape recorder and her notepad.

"I like her because she wears my number," Lauber said of Hamm. "They are my gender; it's cool to have women as role models. They're so nice. When they sign autographs, they bring their own pens. And they think of themselves as sisters. They're so enthusiastic; they love playing soccer and they love playing with each other. I have posters on my wall. I can see that if I practice hard enough, maybe I can be on the team."

Every time Hamm steps on or off the soccer field, the young girls are waiting. They are wearing her No. 9 jersey. Their hair is pulled back into a replica of her ponytail. They carry signs like, "We Don't Like Green Eggs, But We Love Hamm." One after another, they say they are attracted to her for similar reasons: because she's a great player, humble, deflects attention away from herself to her teammates. The waiting girls hold out their hands for her to slap, or ask her to sign their jerseys, or thrust soccer balls toward her. She offers high-fives, an autograph, a smile, a nod, an affirming gesture that they can aspire to be everything she has become.

"She's a great inspiration for what we want to be," said 11-year-old Kelly Wepking, who waited with friends for autographs from Hamm at a practice in Milwaukee before the World Cup. "She doesn't brag. She's not a ball hog. She doesn't say she's the best. She just plays like the best."

Watching the final in Lee's Summit, Missouri, 19-year-old Cassie Cole was developing what appeared to be an obsession with Hamm. Two months later, when the American team would play a match against Finland in Kansas City, Cole would trail the team back and forth from practice in her Plymouth Laser which bore "Mia Ham" vanity plates. The car, covered with streamers and signs, seemed to be a rolling billboard of compulsion. Mia Hamm's name was stuck to the car in laminated letters, dangling on Cole's key chain, fashioned from a block of wood on the dashboard, programmed into the digital display of Cole's cell phone. A likeness of Hamm's autograph, retrieved from the Internet, was tattooed on Cole's right shoulder. She offered to show it to Hamm, but Hamm declined. Her bedroom wall, Cole said, contained a collage of Mia Hamm photographs and "I Love Mia" spelled out in glow-in-the-dark stars.

"I love her," Cole said. "She's a great team player, a great role model. She's the female Pelé. I want her to know I'm her number one fan. I've watched her forever. I know all about her. When she got married. Her birthday, her favorite food, her favorite color, her favorite TV show."

At the team hotel in Kansas City, security consultant Mike Gibbs said, Cole and a friend were removed from a hallway outside the players' rooms about 2 one morning. They had been sitting in the hallway, with several soccer balls, apparently hoping to get autographs, Gibbs said. Asked if she thought she might be frightening Hamm with her preoccupation, Cole said, "They wouldn't be anything without their fans. Why would I stalk her? I just wanted to meet her, and I've done it."

Saturday night July 10 edged into Sunday morning July 11 in Tehran, Iran, as the World Cup final began. The game was not available on state-run television. The fundamentalist Islamic regime would never tolerate pictures of women playing in public with bare arms and bare legs. The 1994 men's World Cup had been shown from the United States, but it had aired on taped delay and the actual crowd shots had been replaced by what appeared to be audiences dressed for European matches in winter.

The United States–China match was available, however, on satellite dishes that were officially forbidden but were not uncommon in Tehran. Women's soccer had flourished during the reign of the Shah, and in 1972, an Iranian club team named Taj played the Italian national team before a crowd of 25,000 in Tehran, according to Mehrdad Masoudi, a native of Iran and a London-based journalist who is a former spokesman for the Canadian soccer federation.

Mahin Gorji, a reporter for the daily sports newspaper, *Iran Varzeshi*, had followed Hamm across thousands of miles of geographical and cultural distance. She had watched satellite reports on CNN and the BBC, surfed Hamm's Web site, followed results of the matches on the wire services and had written daily accounts on the World Cup for her newspaper, considered one of the best sports publications in Iran.

"It is my duty," the 30-year-old Gorji said. "It is very interesting for players and girls who want to know about football in other countries. My editor-in-chief encouraged me." She was particularly intrigued with Hamm. "I saw when she hit the ball, and I wondered how she can do that," Gorji said. "It seems that her shot is so heavy."

Nineteen years after the Islamic revolution rebuilt Iranian society in 1979 on religious fundamentalism, the secular passion of soccer began gripping Iran again in 1998, when the men's national team qualified for the World Cup in France. Millions took to the streets in spontaneous revelry and some women celebrated by removing the head scarves mandated by Islamic custom. The size and jubilation of the mass gathering had not been seen since the overthrow of the Shah two decades earlier. And though women are barred from attending soccer matches, as many as 5,000 of them pushed into the national stadium in Tehran, against official warnings, to greet the men's team when it returned from its decisive qualifying match in Australia. Some women even knocked down a gate to join in the celebration, though they willingly sat in a segregated section. Another consuming celebration occurred after Iran defeated the United States, 2–1, during the first round of the World Cup.

These outpourings carried political overtones, signaling the strength in numbers of women and students who elected the reformist president, Mohammad Khatami, to power in 1997. It also sent a sobering message to the conservative clerics who ran Iran and who had been impotent in stopping the celebrations.

"It gave a sense of having power to the people," said Farideh Farhi, a political scientist based in Honolulu, Hawaii. "They realized when they come into the streets in numbers, the authorities can't do anything about it."

World Cup fervor led to discussions in the Iranian Parliament over whether to allow women to begin playing soccer for the first time since the 1979 revolution and whether to admit women to men's games as spectators. A women's league had been abandoned when

Ayatollah Ruhollah Khomeini came to power. Women were not allowed to attend games, soccer officials said, because they may be psychologically harmed by the emotional, crude behavior of male spectators. Some women did sneak in, however, wearing men's clothes, their hair stuffed into hats.

In April of 1998, Mahin Gorji became the first female sportswriter allowed into the national stadium since the Islamic revolution. Iran had invited Western reporters to see its men's soccer team before the World Cup. When security guards tried to prevent her from entering, she pointed out that female reporters from other countries were being allowed in. The guards relented. "I was taught in school never to take no for answer," Gorji said. Her mere presence, however, irritated some male spectators. As an American reporter interviewed her in the open press box, some fans tossed bits of food in her direction in protest.

At the time of the 1999 Women's World Cup, Iran was still convulsing in the advance-retreat of opening its isolated society with demonstrations in the streets, gestures toward the United States, the jailing of reformers, the opening and closing of reformist newspapers. Sport was caught in the same tumult. The Iranian men's soccer team would visit the United States in January of 2000, and the country's wrestling teams would make exchange visits, continuing the cultural exchanges suggested by Khatami to chip away at the wall of mistrust between the two countries. Gorji was allowed into arenas to cover men playing basketball, volleyball, badminton. Sporting clubs in Tehran had also begun indoor soccer matches for women. But there were limits. The women could wear shorts and T-shirts to play indoors, but fathers were not allowed to watch their daughters perform in such revealing uniforms. Neither were television cameras allowed in to record the matches and report them to the public.

"I hope one day I can go and see how my daughter is playing; I want to know if she has improved or not," Nasser Hejazi, who is considered the greatest Iranian goalkeeper and whose teenage daughter, Atousa, plays indoor soccer, said in an interview with the BBC. "One day I hope they will get permission from the government."

Plans were being made for a women's national team, Hejazi said. But so far, they were just plans. The head of Iran's soccer federation, a close ally of President Khatami, said he did not see the chance for a women's outdoor team anytime soon. Nor did he think that women would be allowed into the soccer stadiums. Sports for women is a complex issue in Iran. Prompted in large part by Faezeh Hashemi, the daughter of Ali Akbar Hashemi Rafsanjani, the former Iranian president, women in Iran are taking part in competitive and recreational sport in unprecedented numbers. Hashemi, who is vice president of the Iranian Olympic Committee, said in 1998 that roughly two million Iranian women participate in some form of sport, compared to 10,000 before the Islamic revolution began two decades ago. Lida Fariman, a female rifle shooter, carried the flag for Iran in the opening ceremonies of the 1996 Atlanta Olympics. Objections to women participating in sports come from a misreading of the Koran, Hashemi said, and from conservatives who fear that emboldened women may demand advances in other areas of society.

Despite increased opportunities and a victory by reformers in Parliament that would come in February of 2000, Iranian women still participate in sports in ways the Western women would find objectionable. Runners in Tehran's parks, and girls who play soccer in the schoolyards, must wear not only sneakers but also long coats and pants and scarves. The country's aspiring downhill skiers must wear bulky gear because the skintight, aerodynamic outfits worn by elite racers are considered too provocative. Women who water ski must also wear a waterproof coat and a scarf, which could be dangerous as well as cumbersome.

Sport remains relatively low on the list of priorities in an Islamic nation where women need their husband's permission to work and their fathers' written consent to marry, where they can be divorced for no reason and where, with few exceptions, they automatically lose custody of their children when a marriage fails. Nor is sport the greatest achievement for Iran's 32 million women, who enjoy the right to vote, to hold office, to work as teachers, lawyers, doctors and businesswomen. Essentially, the same sports available to Iranian men are available to women. Men and women can be seen jogging together in Tehran's parks, playing table tennis and recreational soccer, as long as they are clothed according to Islamic custom.

"Women become more self-confident, bolder, they learn how to cooperate with others and work in groups," said Hashemi, 37, president of the Islamic Countries Women's Sports Solidarity Council and a mother of two who favors lumberjack shirts, jeans and sneakers under her black chador. "It can be a very effective role in women's participation in society."

As assertive as she has been, however, Hashemi has been careful not to stray from the boundaries of Islam's traditions. She favors clothing that covers everything but the face and hands of female athletes who compete outdoors, and she criticized the "nudity" of women who competed in brief uniforms at the Atlanta Olympics. She does not believe that women should attend men's soccer matches until the "moral behavior" of men at the stadium can be improved. Since the spring of 1998, Gorji has not been allowed back into the national stadium to cover men's soccer. And the reformist newspaper she worked for at the time, named *Jameah*, has since been closed by fundamentalists. Even a newspaper run by Hashemi has been shut down.

"There are many pressures in our society," Gorji said. "The fundamentalists want to accost Khatami. They think that if women go to the stadium, there will be a riot in Islamic society. I'm a sports reporter. When I can't go to the stadium, how can I cover the match? Some of the sisters, or wives, or daughters of the players, they should have the right to go, too."

She holds out hopes that Iran will begin a women's national soccer team. "It is very important for a woman to have a chance like a man," Gorji said. "Women want to show their ability. Why not? We should have the right." But even the idea of holding indoor matches for women, and reporting on them, much less the idea of a female reporter covering men's sports such as basketball, volleyball, and badminton, has raised the ire of conservative clerics.

"I am only one to write about men's sports," Gorji said. "The fundamentalists protest, 'Why does she go to the stadium? She wants to be a fan. She wants to play football.' I don't care what they say. We have an association for sportswriters in Iran. The fundamentalists talked with the manager of that association. He told me to be cautious. 'They can ban you, suspend you.' I am ready for everything. I have the right to be a reporter."

Her persistence during the Women's World Cup would later result in a picture in her newspaper of Hamm and the American team presenting a jersey at the White House to President Clinton.

"A picture on the front page of the White House in Iran's main daily sports newspaper," said Masoudi, the former spokesman for the Canadian soccer federation. "Even four years ago, that would have been unheard of."

8

The Burden
of Expectations

SIX MINUTES INTO THE FINAL, Mia Hamm roamed back into the American penalty area, a determined excursion of 80 yards in the blistering sun, and with a sliding tackle, she stripped the mid-fielder Pu Wei of the ball. Two minutes later, she stood 30 yards away from the goal on a free kick, slipping a wisp of blowing hair behind her left ear, waiting, waiting as Kristine Lilly made a dummy run, stepping over the ball and leaving it for Hamm. Then four steps by Hamm and an economic punch, a sublime pass. How could anyone be this accurate with a foot? The ball bending toward the far goal post, a parabolic threat, curving and diving with a hawk swoop onto the foot of Michelle Akers, a slide of curls and muscle, a foot on the ball but no control, the shot skidding high and wide, the announcers saying Akers should have struck with her head, the best American chance barely missed, the coach reacting on the bench, his mouth curled into the "ohhh" of the almost.

Hamm had commanded the first two games of the Women's World Cup. In the opener against Denmark, her teammates had suffered a paralyzing nervous excitement to be playing in front of 78,972 fans at Giants Stadium in East Rutherford, New Jersey. Only the Pope had drawn a bigger audience in the stadium. At the time, it was the largest crowd ever to see a women's sporting event in the United States. Hamm alone seemed calm, assertive while many of her teammates were hyperventilating, struggling to force back tears of confirmation that their sport had arrived. Her first meaningful touch came in the 17th minute, and she chipped a ball off the chest of a Danish defender and blasted a left-footed shot over the head of a helpless goalkeeper.

"Are you kidding me?" Hamm kept saying to herself as she sprinted upfield in celebration. "I don't score goals like that."

In some ways, it was the most important goal of the Women's World Cup. Hamm was the face of women's soccer, the player the young girls squealed for, the one personality who had pushed through the scrim of invisibility in a sport still trying to broaden its appeal beyond the weekend fields of suburbia. For the Women's World Cup to succeed, especially early, Hamm had to succeed. She was the one person everybody knew if they knew anything about women's soccer. She was the one featured in the television commercials, the newspapers and magazine stories, the broadcast profiles. It was her No. 9 jersey that was being sold at the concession stands. To an uninformed and largely skeptical public, the cover-girl hyperbole needed a framing of legitimate performance. While her teammates seemed tight and reluctant in the opening minutes against Denmark, Hamm attacked immediately and threatened to score, or to put someone else in position to score, nearly every time she touched the ball. She kept serving up passes and in the 73rd minute, she delivered a hard cross from the right flank and midfielder Julie Foudy connected for another goal in the 3–0 victory by the United States.

"She is always a player that really excites you," coach Tony DiCicco said. "She twists a defender into the ground, scores a goal out of nothing, plays with skill, work, humility, emotion, passion. She does the kind of things that make you love the game of soccer."

In the second match, against Nigeria, an early defensive collapse had put the Americans behind, and Hamm had been knocked down at least three times in the first 16 minutes. When a Nigerian defender tried to help her up, Hamm turned her back, clearly furious with the hard tackling. "I'm coming after you," Hamm told the defender. "You might be taking little pieces out of me, but I'm coming after you and I'm starting right now."

Three minutes later, Hamm drove a free kick so hard and low and unmanageable that a Nigerian midfielder knocked it into her own goal. Seconds after that, Hamm rocketed a shot into the upper right corner of the net. Before halftime, she had played another perfect free kick for a goal by Kristine Lilly. What had been a dangerous beginning had become a 7–1 routing of an undisciplined and indifferent defense.

"That does nothing but turn Mia on, especially when there are dangerous tackles from behind," forward Tiffeny Milbrett said. "It makes you mad. You can't make a statement better than sticking the ball in the back of the net."

Then, as emphatically as they began, the goals stopped coming. Hamm would not score again in the final four games of the World Cup. Two days before a match against Germany in the quarterfinals, she warmed up insufficiently at practice and strained a hip muscle. It became uncomfortable to accelerate. "It was totally preventable," she said. "I didn't take enough time to prepare myself. I should have told the coaches I needed more time."

Even at its most inviting, soccer was a miserly game. Each goal was a theft, an invasion, an erosion of the protective order. As a rare and precious victory of attrition, it was to be hoarded like land snatched in a border war. Baseball players legitimized their hall-of-fame candidacies by succeeding at bat three times in every 10. Soccer players considered those to be generous odds. They had to be willing to endure much harsher unfulfillment without succumbing to self-doubt.

"For every 10 runs you make, you get the ball once," said April Heinrichs, who preceded Hamm as a star forward on the U.S.

women's soccer team. "For every 10 times you get it, you get one shot off. For every 10 shots, you might score once. There's a tremendous amount of failure."

As the tournament progressed, defenses tightened around Hamm. When she touched the ball, she attracted two, sometimes three, defenders the way magnets attract iron filings. After playing four games in 11 days, she grew tired. "Look at the men's World Cup," DiCicco said before the final. "They play two games in 11 days, maybe a third. We played four and flew cross-country. With all the travel, I think the front runners lost their legs."

Perhaps, too, Hamm grew reticent in challenging defenders one on one, as she sometimes did when her confidence ebbed. Pressure seemed to build inside her as important tournaments progressed. In the 1991 and 1999 World Cups, as well as the 1996 Summer Olympics, she had scored early and then she had not scored again, never more than two goals. In college, before national championship games, she had become so nervous that she had thrown up, as Bill Russell had frequently done during his years with the Boston Celtics.

As a team, the Americans had also grown more cautious and defensive-minded in trying to prevent defeat in the World Cup. In the final, especially, the forwards were played wide in a defensive posture and were often left isolated, out of contact with each other and with the connective support from midfield. Lauren Gregg, the assistant coach, would wonder, in retrospect, whether the American forwards had been asked to play too much defense, to cover too much ground, which sapped their legs for charging the goal.

"The way they were playing against our system, it made it difficult to attack," Hamm said of the Chinese. "Maybe out of fatigue we didn't do everything we could have on the ball. I never look at is as a negative for us to have to play defense. It's something I pride myself on, but there comes a point where the physical effort you're asked to play on defense takes away from your offense."

DiCicco believed that Hamm played solidly in the final but tracked back excessively on defense, overcompensating for her lack of scoring. "She's running herself out of the game offensively," he would say later, watching a videotape of the final. "You love the effort, but effort isn't always the best thing. Still I'd rather have her do too much than not enough."

Said Hamm: "Sometimes I thought I came back too far. I thought I was getting in the way. If you get too many people collapsing, it is really hard to distinguish which players are marking which players. Sometimes I think I should have stayed more forward. Both teams would have loved for it to be more attacking. But you couldn't have asked for more effort. Both teams put their heart and soul into that game."

Few athletes were asked to do what Hamm was during the summer of 1999. She had to be everything to everyone. A goal scorer, a savior, a spark that might ignite a professional league for women. Michael Jordan transcended professional basketball, but Magic Johnson and Larry Bird had already saved it. Tiger Woods expanded golf's color line, but he did not have to build his sport fairway by fairway. Hamm was being counted on to fill stadiums as well as little girls' hopes, to carry her team and her sport on her shoulders, to give the emerging women's game a name and a face. If she failed, would the United States team fail? Would the World Cup fail? Would the chance for a professional league fail?

"Mia doesn't see herself as the greatest in the world," Brandi Chastain said. "She knows she has a great deal of talent, but having people say you're the greatest in the world, that's a little overwhelming. It's got, in some way, to wear on your ability to be the best in the biggest tournament. I think maybe it got to her a little. When you have that kind of spotlight on you, it takes a little energy from you. At the point where Mia was not scoring goals, people were saying, 'What's happening?' She had a lot of things weighing on her. I think it did get to her. As much as you try not to let it affect you, it does."

Unfailingly honest about her game, Hamm conceded that she did not deliver her best soccer in the World Cup, just as she had not been in top form in previous big tournaments for reasons of youth, injury, the burden of expectation. But there had been no concession in her play, no frustrated pouting that had sometimes flecked her game in earlier years. If Hamm erred, it was to play overexuberantly on defense, and who could really complain about that? She continued to run hard, to offer vital serves on corner kicks and free kicks, to attract clumps of defenders, which unleashed her free-range teammates. It was a threatening sprint by Hamm in the 80th minute of the semifinals that caused a Brazilian defender to drag her down in the penalty area, providing a penalty kick by Michelle Akers and the security of a 2–0 lead.

"Her fingerprints were all over our success," Gregg said. "She carried us in the best way she could."

If this was to be her role, then Hamm would play it dutifully. If she was not scoring, then she would set up her teammates to score. If all this scrutiny of chances unfulfilled, of goals uncollected, was pressuring, it was also revealing, oddly liberating. Hamm had come to realize that she could not carry the United States by herself and that she did not have to. This was the failsafe point with the American team. Someone would step up to make the decisive pass, the breathtaking save, the elusive shot past the keeper's outstretched hand. Someone always did.

"I'm not someone who can go and succeed at an individual sport," Hamm said. "A lot of my motivation and energy comes from being responsible to other people. I care a lot about what people think of me. In that regard, I'm not as strong as a person you would need to have out there to carry a sport. I'm willing to do whatever I can to help, but the reason I've been able to do it is because I've had a lot of support."

Mia Hamm was all of three months old when, on June 23, 1972, President Richard M. Nixon signed into law Title IX of the 1972 Education Amendments Act, which prohibited discrimination on the basis of gender at institutions, both high school and college, that receive federal funds. The act was passed with the primary intent of allowing women greater access to professional careers in such fields as medicine and law, but it did not exclude athletics. Surviving vituperative legal challenges, "Title IX became the Bill of Rights for female athletes," wrote Neil Amdur, sports editor of The New York Times.

According to the National Collegiate Athletic Association, 29,977 women competed in collegiate sports in 1971–1972. By 1996–1997, that number had increased to 128,209. In 1971, one in 27 girls, or a total of 294,015, participated in high school sports. By 1998, one of every 2.5 girls participated, or a total of 2,570,333. Forty-two percent of the Americans competing at the 1996 Atlanta Olympics were women. Each of the 20 players on the American women's soccer team was a beneficiary of the Title IX's educational and financial opportunities and its legislative and judicial battering-ram against societal resistance.

"I have never been told, 'No, you can't play,' because I'm a girl," said Julie Foudy, the American co-captain.

Title IX also led to increased opportunities for women from other countries to play collegiate sports in the United States. After the World Cup, one of the Nigerian stars, Mercy Akide, would enroll at tiny Milligan College in Johnson City, Tennessee, and would lead the nation by scoring 42 goals in the fall season. She left school to prepare for the 2000 Summer Olympics, but said she would return to study communications.

"We can't play football forever," Akide said. "We can't be full-time housewives, either. We want something different. We want to work, to share our knowledge, to help support our husbands. You see some husbands smacking their wives, talking to them rudely. They respect you more if you are working. Some men are doing three jobs and the wife is doing nothing. I want to help my husband."

It would be vastly premature, however, to assume that consuming interest in the Women's World Cup meant that women had achieved overall athletic parity with men. Only two of the 16 coaches in the World Cup were women. Of 113 members of the International Olympic Committee, only 14 are women. Of the 197 countries competing in the Atlanta Olympics, 26 did not bring female athletes.

In 1994, Auburn University began a women's varsity soccer program only after it had been sued and plaintiffs had been awarded $140,000 in damages. A year later, Louisiana State University was faced with a lawsuit before it consented to upgrade women's soccer to varsity status. In January of 2000, a federal appeals court would rule that LSU intentionally violated Title IX and "fashioned a grossly discriminatory system." Trial testimony indicated that Athletic Director Joe Dean had referred to one female plaintiff as "honey," "sweetie" and "cutie," that he said the school's first women's softball team was disbanded because of the sexual preference of the players and that he preferred to start a soccer program over other women's sports because players "look cute in their shorts."

Two months after the World Cup final, female soccer players in Lake George, New York, would unsuccessfully attempt to get the local school district to begin fielding a junior high team for girls. Instead, some of the girls decided to try out for the boys' soccer team, and were forced to undergo a state-sanctioned fitness test that the boys were not required to take. The requirement that 12-year-old girls run 1.5 miles in 12 minutes was tougher than the standard for New York State Police Academy recruits. Two girls passed the test, six did not. "They just keep making it harder," Anna Crawford, who is 12 and passed the test, told the *Times Union* of Albany, New York, which reported the story.

Even with huge gains made by women in collegiate sports, an NCAA gender-equity study, released in the fall of 1999, would show that among the colleges that play big-time sports, women still account for only 38 percent of the athletes, although they make up 52 percent of the college enrollment. Male athletes still account for 70 percent of all recruiting expenses, and the disparity between what men and women receive in scholarship money has widened, from an average of $750,000 per school in 1995–1996 to nearly $800,000 in 1997–1998. In Division I-A, the average salary for coaching a women's basketball team was $100,235, and for a men's team, $164,927. The average soccer salaries were less disparate, $42,439 for men to $39,929 for women. The Women's Sports Foundation estimates that there is still a gap of $180 million between the money spent on men's and women's collegiate sports.

As the World Cup unfolded, Title IX was still facing a lack of compliance by many universities, and was under a renewed attack, based on myths that women weren't as interested in sports as men, that Title IX was causing the massive loss of men's teams in sports such as wrestling and gymnastics, that the only way to comply with the law was rigid gender quotas, that Title IX was financially damaging, and that it was only helping suburban white females while discriminating against inner-city black males.

Four months after the World Cup final, a group of male wrestlers, tennis players and soccer players from programs eliminated by Miami University of Ohio would sue the school, claiming that Title IX resulted in reverse discrimination. Curt A. Levey, legal director of the

Washington-based Center for Individual Rights, which represents the athletes, would write an op-ed column in *USA Today* shortly after the final, accusing "overzealous bureaucrats, feminist groups and confused federal judges" of twisting "Title IX's good intentions into a quota system that effectively mandates that men and women participate in college athletics at identical rates."

"Because more women can't be forced to play," he wrote, "proportionality typically is achieved by reducing the number of male athletes." He added: "The NCAA found gender quotas are denying more than 20,000 men a chance to compete in college athletics, compared to 1992 rates—yet fewer than 6,000 female athletes were added during that time. And the quotas hurt the finances of athletic departments, where men's teams typically bring in the money."

This was a common broadside that women's groups found to be rife with misinformation. True, one prong of Title IX, called the proportionality rule, says that the number of women athletes at a school should reflect the overall enrollment of women. For example, if 50 percent of a school's students are women, women should make up 50 percent of the athletes. A range of five percentage points has been found acceptable by court decisions.

But there are two less specific ways for a school to comply with Title IX without adhering to rigid quotas. One is to show "a history and continuing practice of expansion in its women's athletic program." The second is to "demonstrate that the interests and abilities" of female athletes "have been fully accommodated."

The NCAA, in releasing its gender equity study in the fall of 1999, would explicitly state that "the most recent progress in female participation did not come at the expense of males." The average number of male athletes increased by 15 per school from 1995–1996, while the average number of female athletes grew by 28 per school.

"Men's and women's sports are being added and dropped, but the net result is that women's programs are being added at a faster rate," according to Jane Meyer, the NCAA's director of Education Outreach.

Before the Women's World Cup, women's groups had grown concerned about possible attempts to dilute Title IX in Congress, noting that the Speaker of the House, Dennis Hastert, (R-Ill.), was a former high school wrestling coach. However, the vast impact of Title IX could be seen on the field during the tournament, and especially in an election year, no one would likely make an attempt to compromise the legislation, said Donna Shalala, the Secretary of Health and Human Services. The Women's Sports Foundation has repeatedly stated that no research exists to show that women are less interested in sport than men. Instead of a lack of interest, women suffer from a lack of opportunity and lack of encouragement that causes them to drop out of sports at a rate six times that of boys, the foundation said.

"I think soccer has protected Title IX for another generation," Shalala said. "That's how powerful these women were."

The Women's World Cup may accomplish in the long term something that Title IX has been unable to effect—serious reform of collegiate football, which is responsible for much of the gender inequity that exists today. If, as many women in sport believe, the World Cup doubles or triples the interest of female athletes, it will become increasingly untenable for football teams to justify 85 scholarships and 100 uniformed players when the pros need rosters of 53 and have similar turnover yearly, or to justify spending an average of $192,400 a year on recruiting or to warrant putting the players up in hotels the night before home games. Universities will find it increasingly difficult to keep cutting so-called minor sports such as tennis and wrestling; after a certain period, there will not be any sports left to cut. And the pressure to accommodate the interest in women's teams will only increase.

Football has escaped serious scrutiny because it is believed to have some greater intrinsic value than other sports, and because it is considered to be the monetary lifeline for many athletic departments. But the Women Sports Foundation issued a report in 1995 saying that 67 percent of the nation's big-time college football programs do not even pay for themselves, much less for other sports, and that 35 percent of the big-time programs operate with an average annual deficit of $1.1 million.

By reducing scholarships and lowering overhead costs from football, athletic departments would be free to offer more opportunities for women and would no longer have to play the game of divide and conquer, pitting women's sports and lesser men's sports against each other for survival. Title IX advocates do not advocate the cutting of any men's teams.

"There's still a lot of fat in high-profile men's sports," said Lynette Labinger, an attorney in Providence, Rhode Island, who represented the plaintiffs in an important case that reached the U.S. Supreme Court in 1997 and forced Brown University to comply with Title IX. "Often, the big spenders are the big money losers. They are whispering in the ears of the low-profile sports, 'The only way to save your shirts is to attack the women's sports. They're the enemy.' It's unfortunate."

"No one on the women's side wants to see men disappear," Labinger said. "Women understand the value of opportunity. We don't want to deny someone else, we just want to play. People claim women's sports are dragging men down. Women have nothing to do with it. It's a crisis of will. Schools care more about high-profile men's sports than other teams. It's an unwillingness to have a bigger pie. They pit the haves and the have-nots and say, 'You fight over the crumbs.' If the under-supported men were smart, they'd get with the women, go to NCAA conferences and vote to reduce scholarships for football."

During the Brown University case, Labinger said, an attorney representing the university suggested that Title IX largely benefited white suburban females at the expense of black urban males, adding race to the debate. Later, she noted, the university added equestrian as a sport.

"If schools are only supporting sports that require a lot of money or benefit the country club set, shame on them," Labinger said. "The schools make those decisions. To use that argument is like saying, 'Stop me before I kill again.'"

A native of Selma, Alabama, Hamm lived a road-atlas childhood in Texas, California, Virginia and Italy, where her father, Bill, an Air Force colonel, was drawn weekly to the national spasm over soccer. Mia was born with a club foot, and treatment required her to sleep in corrective shoes connected by a steel bar. When she was very young, she wore a cast, and once a week, her mother would awaken at four in the morning, put her in the tub to dissolve the plaster support, then drive 50 miles to

Montgomery, Alabama, so Air Force doctors could stretch the tendons and ligaments in her foot and turn it outward. At 15 months, Hamm and her family moved to Florence, Italy, where her father rode his bike two miles to the stadium every other Sunday to watch Fiorentina play in the Italian professional league. Mia was about 18 months old when she showed her first interest in soccer. Her mother remembers the moment as if it were a photograph: Mia in a lavender dress, white lace tights, and white corrective shoes, coming down a slide in a park, seeing a man and his son kicking a soccer ball, and running toward them.

"It was like watching a movie," Stephanie Hamm said of her daughter. "She ran until she got to the ball and she booted it. She kept kicking the ball. She wouldn't let them play. Finally, the little boy gave up and Mia and the father played for the next 25 minutes. She was no taller than a minute."

At age six, living then in Wichita Falls, Texas, Hamm played her first organized soccer. She scored one goal in the fall league, her father said, and she was like any six-year-old during a soccer match, spending as much time looking at rocks and clouds in the sky as she did looking at the soccer ball. In the spring league, though, she scored 23 goals. "No longer did they insist that she stand in one place and wait for the ball," Bill Hamm said.

Mia reminded Stephanie Hamm of her own mother, determined, competitive, the same clenched jaw, a woman who regularly beat her husband at tennis and swam expertly and stood up on roller coasters. For a shy girl whose life was frequently uprooted by military life, sport provided reliable constancy for Mia. "Ever since you're old enough to have someone make an impression on you, you're searching for an identity," she said. "How do you fit into elementary school, junior high, college? Sports is how I fit in. That was my voice. It made me feel good about myself."

When Hamm was five, her parents adopted an eight-year-old Thai-American orphan named Garrett, whose legs and arms seemed wondrously suited to propelling a ball off a bat, through a hoop, into a net. Mia followed him from one neighborhood game to the next, football to baseball to soccer, and Garrett unfailingly chose his younger sister for his team.

"I was his secret weapon," Hamm said.

Her athleticism was such that, at age 10, she joined an 11-year-old boys' soccer team and led it in scoring. As a seventh-grader in Wichita Falls, Texas, she played end and quarterback and cornerback on a junior-high football team. "Even in pads she was fast," her father said. In a desperate moment of the 1995 World Cup, the Americans made her a goalkeeper and she did not let a shot elude her. At a practice at the Citrus Bowl in Orlando, Florida, before the 1999 World Cup, someone brought a football and Hamm repeatedly knocked in field goals from 35 yards. She was also the best golfer on the soccer team.

"Growing up, I played against boys and you never had to apologize for knocking someone over or going in hard for a tackle," Hamm said. "I think guys are taught that more than girls, to compete hard and not apologize for being successful."

Even in junior high, she exhibited two traits that would define her professional career and would sometimes fall into direct conflict: a fierce passion to play and succeed and a famous reluctance to be in the spotlight. She declined to play football in the eighth grade, her mother said, because too much attention had been paid to the girl and not the team in the seventh grade.

As a young girl, Mia said, she became so frustrated over losing that she quit every game she played, neighborhood pickup games, family board games. When she wanted to play, her older sisters would ask, "Are you going to quit?" She was what she called a "screamer," a person who "reacted emotionally as opposed to thinking how a situation needed to be handled and then always going around and apologizing for things." Even after she had won an Olympic gold medal and two World Cups, losing would feel like heartburn. Following the 1999 World Cup, the Americans would lose four consecutive games to a world all-star team on an indoor victory tour. The games were only exhibitions, they meant nothing, but Hamm, spotting two reporters in an arena hallway after the fourth loss, would say in a loud voice, "I HATE LOSING!"

"The thing about emotion is, it's so unpredictable," Hamm said. "It can be my biggest strength or my biggest weakness. You never know how it's going to motivate you. I've worked on it. In college, I used to get really upset, down, every time I made a mistake. I'd take myself out of the game for five minutes. We worked on trying to turn it into positive energy by working hard defensively, or getting mad. 'You're going to take this player on again, and not let this big doubt come into your head that you're going to mess up.'"

At 15, she became the youngest player, male or female, to join the national soccer team. Hamm wrote in her autobiograhpy that Anson Dorrance, who was then the coach, pulled her aside and said, "You can become the best soccer player in the world." Taking night classes, Hamm graduated from high school in three years, and she followed Dorrance to North Carolina, where she won four national championships and met her husband, Christiaan Corry, a Marine pilot.

While her husband was in attendance at the final, her brother Garrett was not. He suffered from a rare blood disorder, aplastic anemia, and although Mia raised $50,000 for his care through a benefit soccer game, he contracted a fungal infection after a bone-marrow transplant and died in April of 1997 at the age of 28. She started the Mia Hamm Foundation in his honor for research into bone marrow diseases and to develop sporting opportunities for young women.

"He embodied what I was always reaching for in sports," Hamm said. "He never gave up. And he never made me feel I couldn't participate because I was a girl."

Donna de Varona, the chairwoman of the World Cup organizing committee, said she wondered whether her brother's death affected Mia's own struggle for self-assurance on the field. "Maybe she feels guilty about her brother," de Varona said. "She was so close to him and profoundly affected by his death. Maybe it's simply that she's alive and he's not. She gets to play and he didn't make it."

She would become soccer's all-time leading scorer, a willing pioneer but a diffident celebrity. It would be one of a number of fundamental contradictions in her personality. She was a superstar who deferred constantly to her teammates. A scorer who was a selfless passer. A forward who was as reserved with her words as she was explosive with her feet. A driven player who was impatient with failure but self-doubting about success.

"It's like these actors you see on the big screen, they put themselves up there to be criticized by everybody, but they're insecure,"

Chastain said. "I don't see how those things parallel each other. They seem opposite poles to me."

Why the insecurity alongside unsurpassed talent? "There's this kind of struggle inside herself to want to be the best and never believing she's gotten there," her mother said, "like 'I haven't done enough for my teammates, I haven't seen enough opportunities, I haven't made enough goals.' I'm sure there are games where she's not up to it physically, emotionally or psychologically, but she never wants to let down. There's never a reason not to work very hard."

As a teenager, she was out of house by 8 in the morning in the summer, practicing her shooting and dribbling and passing alone, before the sun turned from light to heat in Wichita Falls. Dorrance saw her running sprints alone one morning at North Carolina during the off-season and sent her a note: "A champion is someone who is bent over, drenched in sweat, at the point of exhaustion when no one else is watching."

"Her work ethic was above everyone else's," said Lou Pearce, who coached Hamm for two years in high school in Wichita Falls and said she was the best player on a boy's varsity team. "While the boys were sleeping till 12, she was out at 8, on the side of the high school, working for an hour and a half—30 minutes of foot drills warming up, 30 minutes of shooting, 30 minutes of running. The goal didn't have a net. She'd kick the ball where she wanted, and then she'd go get it, never walking, always jogging."

Having grown up in a military family with three sisters and two brothers, Hamm possessed a reserve, almost a sense of rank, as if she should aspire to succeed at a high level but that she should not stand out from the others or be treated differently. Even her handshake was noncommital, as if it might reveal too much. She did not want her spotlight to keep her teammates permanently in the shadows, so she spoke of them constantly, a point guard handing off verbal assists. Most of her goals were layups, she said dismissively, "harder to miss it than to make it."

Before the World Cup, she turned down a photo shoot for a possible cover of *Newsweek* magazine, she declined to appear with David Letterman, she gave few one-on-one interviews, she declined to publicize her own autobiography and she insisted that her teammates be included in Nike's advertising campaign. "I don't like the spotlight being just about me," Hamm said. "I think they had the idea of getting everyone involved anyway. That was the motivation of the whole tournament, that there was more than one athlete on the team."

Like her fellow North Carolina alum, Michael Jordan, Hamm understood the basic incongruity in what Americans wanted from their athletes, that they be educated and articulate but unwilling to offer contentious opinion. Neither she nor Jordan spoke up against Nike's sweatshop labor practices in Asia. Some reporters found Hamm to be difficult, unforthcoming, a prima donna. She was available for interviews only certain days during the World Cup. Some of her teammates wanted her to be more visible in promoting the tournament. But she had set her priorities. What she had to give she would give most of it to her team. "I didn't want it to be Mia Hamm's World Cup from the media perspective," she said. "I put enough pressure on myself. It takes me a certain amount of time to get ready for games, to focus. I don't want to put any doubt in my own head that I'm not the player right now that I want to be." If her elusiveness was frustrating for reporters, in a way it was also refreshing and fascinating. How rare to find privacy in a society where celebrity honeymoons proceed right from the bedroom to the video store. In this confessional age of scandalous tell-all, she remained a rare mystery, as effortless and guarded as DiMaggio.

"Some people love the attention," co-captain Julie Foudy said. "Mia says, 'I want to be able to have a life after soccer. I don't want to walk into a coffee shop and I'm with my husband and people are coming up for autographs.' I think that's why she stays out of the limelight as much as she can. Because she feels, 'I want a life. I don't want to have to change my life because everyone knows who I am.'"

Who could have begrudged Hamm if she had wanted most of the attention? Michael Jordan referred to his teammates as his supporting cast. Babe Didrikson used to tell other women on the golfing circuit that she deserved the publicity because she was the brightest star in the LPGA constellation. Cal Ripken Jr., baseball's ironman, could not even bring himself to stay at the same hotel as his teammates. But Hamm was so deferential that she looked downward when her face appeared on jumbo screens during the national anthem, so as not to draw undue notice to herself. She sometimes ducked her head, or stood behind teammates during photo shoots. It was her willingness to stand with the group, not apart from it, that stifled potential jealousies and allowed the idea of team to have true resonance.

"I always knew how much Mia deferred to the team, and I appreciated it, but I never realized the magnitude of it until the World Cup," Foudy said. "She said, 'I won't do any more one on one interviews because I don't want this to be the Mia show.' How many athletes in the world would do that? How many would say, 'It's not about me, it's about the team'? Look what she did for us. Look how much attention Brandi and others get now."

In more relaxed moments, Hamm could be expansive and slyly funny. She gave eloquent interviews, thanked reporters for their stories, led walks for the homeless, called high school girls out of the blue and wished them good luck in their state championship games. She had impressive analytical recall and could reconstruct a match the way golfers did, stroke by stroke. To her teammates, she was a master of accents, someone who gave as good as she got. Once, for a team video, she put on a cowboy hat and duster and, in her best Australian accent, impersonated the host of the television show, *Animal Planet*, poking at a dead bird with a stick and saying, "In the bush, we call this a 'stiffy.'"

When Foudy, in a moment of retrospection at dinner, said that she wanted to retire from soccer to do something more substantial, Hamm and Chastain dabbed at fake tears with napkins and burst into a mock Bette Midler number, singing, "Did you ever know that you're my hero?"

Nor was Hamm above pinpricking her own public image. On the box of Soccer Barbie, Hamm was pictured with a doll's freeze-dried smile and Y2K-proof makeup. "You can't tell which one is the Barbie," she said.

"I can't be Brandi, Carla, or Julie," Hamm said. "I can't be the person everyone likes. If I try, I drive myself crazy. I have to be content with who I am. I'm content with the gifts I bring to the table."

There may not be another superstar athlete who is more unflinchingly honest about his or her capabilities. When a reporter thanked her for her frankness, Hamm said, "You mean because half the time I go out there I think I suck?"

She was far more forthcoming discussing her perceived deficiencies than her achievements. Her parents learned early that she did not easily accept compliments and that she did not like to dissect games after she had played them. She seemed a bit isolated by her stardom, and she hinted in what she wrote that, despite her great success, being a soccer player was not fully sufficient. Her father had been an adviser to the commander of Allied forces in southern Europe, her mother was a ballet dancer, her eldest sister had a Ph.D. in microbiology and joined the Peace Corps. Mia, too, had thrived academically, and in retrospect, her father said, she had come to wish that she had widened her circle of friends while at North Carolina.

"I think that's normal when you focus so much of your life in one area to say, 'Gee, look what I missed,'" Stephanie Hamm said. "Sometimes when she makes a presentation, she says, 'My sister is doing this and that.' Maybe she feels, 'I wish I could have done maybe one more thing as equally interesting to me as soccer has been.'"

She was wary of the mantle of "best player in the world." It was subjective and thus vulnerable to suspicion and hyperbole. Failure, on the other hand, was as objective as mathematics. It could be divided, reduced to its primary factors, solved. She told the young girls who admired her that she experienced all of their frustrations and insecurities and that confidence, like a bed, must be remade every day.

"The thing about confidence, I don't think people understand, is it's a day-to-day issue," Hamm said. "It takes a constant nurturing. It's not something you go in and turn on the light switch and say, 'I'm confident,' and it stays on until the lightbulb burns out. I think you'd be amazed at most athletes. Someone tried to tell me that Michael Jordan doesn't have confidence problems. He's probably very selective about who he shares it with. The hardest part when you are at a high level of competition is waking up every day and saying, 'Are you ready to try to make yourself better than you were yesterday?' I don't think a lot of athletes walk around thinking they are the best. If they do, it's to hide some of the weaknesses they might have."

Before the World Cup, Hamm failed to score during eight consecutive matches. Twice during that drought, the United States lost to China, its chief rival. Hamm seemed reluctant to challenge defenders one on one, according to Tony DiCicco, the American coach. No one is better at this aspect of the women's game that is part croquet, part ballet, part bullfight. At her best, Hamm seems to release and retrieve the ball as if it were a yo-yo. But now she was hesitant. For the first time in her career, she made as much news when she did not score as when she did. Doubt crept into her game like kudzu.

"Her entire career, confidence has been a factor with Mia," DiCicco said. "Mia, because she is so hypercritical, has always had to deal at times with less confidence than she wants. She puts so much demand on herself. It's why she's the greatest scorer in history. But those high standards are hard to reach on a consistent basis. If she doesn't feel she can reach those demands, she feels inadequate. It wears on her. She's got to build herself back up. I respect how she got through the year. It was a tremendous mental battle for her. I don't think she ever felt the release she felt in other years."

During that arid period, Hamm appeared in DiCicco's office one day and tried to talk, but couldn't. She began sobbing. She kept hearing and reading that she wasn't playing her best, and the repeated suggestion of a slump had become fact.

"I want to do things as perfectly as I can," Hamm said. "Obviously it's not going to happen, but it's a good source of motivation. Sometimes it can work against me. Everything I do is tied to a tremendous amount of emotion. If I'm unhappy, it affects everything I do. I wasn't enjoying what I was doing. I was reading the newspaper a little too closely. I was worried about what people outside my support system were saying. I needed to go out and play for the reason I always played, because I loved what I do. I lost sight of that. It was my own fault. I was lost. It was all this frustration and unhappiness finally coming out. Tony was great. He told me we had a lot of time, it wasn't the end of the world. 'Quit putting so much pressure on yourself. We'll take it one step at a time.' I needed to go out and play for the reason I always played, because I loved what I do. I wasn't having any fun out there. I was critiquing every little thing I did."

Colleen Hacker, the team's sports psychologist, gave Hamm a quote attributed to Robert Hughes, the art critic, who said, "The greater the artist the greater the doubt; perfect confidence is granted to the less talented as a consolation prize."

It was Hacker, Hamm said, who counseled her to keep her priorities in line and not to "sit there and make every single living, breathing moment dependent on whether I scored a goal or not." Hamm also began talking about her struggles with family and friends, including Nomar Garciaparra, the Boston Red Sox shortstop, a soccer fan who had befriended the American team a year earlier and who had seen a few 0-for-8 moments in his own career.

"I told her that she just had to go out there and enjoy the game, and don't worry about all that other stuff," Garciaparra said. "We go through slumps all the time in baseball. I asked her if they were winning and she was playing well and she said, 'Yeah,' So I said, 'Then don't worry about it.'"

The scoring drought ended as inexplicably as it began with a steady flow of goals. On the first goal, Hamm fell backwards to the ground in relief, saying the monkey on her back had become a two-ton gorilla. She scored four goals in four exhibition games until, a month before the World Cup began, Hamm punched a shot beneath a charging Brazilian goalie for goal number 108, making her the all-time career leader, surpassing the retired Elisabetta Vignotto of Italy. It was a consummate Hamm display, one opportunity, one assertive touch, one inexorable goal.

"I just needed to go out there and play," Hamm said. "My team believed in me. I just had to give myself a break and have myself believe in me."

With 10 minutes gone against China, Brandi Chastain stood on the sideline preparing to throw the ball into play. She looked toward the goal for Cindy Parlow, the 5-foot-11 forward who had seven inches on her Chinese defender, Bai Jie, but the throw was short. Players jumping in front of the goal, rising and falling like valves on a trumpet, the ball trampolining back toward a rushing Chastain, a Ping-Pong off her chest and Sun Wen's head, and Hamm alone at the top of the penalty area, both teams caught in a tidal shift between offense and defense. Shirtless men began rising from their end-zone seats in expectation, but Hamm's idea seemed only half-formed—shoot? pass?—and her chip floated like a pop-fly to Gao Hong, the Chinese goalkeeper, who discus-hurled the ball up the right flank.

At 15 minutes, Michelle Akers poked the ball away from the Chinese playmaker, Liu Ailing. Parlow pushed the deflection ahead with her long strides, one touch, two, three, and she went around a defender with one of those cartoon moves where the truck heading for the telephone pole splits into halves and comes back intact on the other side, tapping the ball to the right of Wen Lirong and running around her on the left. Wen was beaten in the penalty area and she stabbed at the ball and Parlow went cartwheeling backward over her left shoulder. On one knee, at the end line, Parlow waited for the referee's whistle, certain that she had been taken down unfairly. *That's a penalty kick. We're going to go up 1–0.* But the whistle never blew. *I was totally taken out. She never touched the ball.* DiCicco also thought that the Swiss referee, Nicole Mouidi-Petignat had missed the call. He did not care for her refereeing—she had waited 30 minutes to issue a yellow-card warning while Nigeria viciously hacked at his players in the first round—but in watching a videotape after the World Cup, he would change his mind. Wen had touched the ball and Parlow had not been fouled. "Good non-call," he would say.

President Clinton flashed onto the stadium screen in the end zone, eating popcorn in his shirtsleeves, and the crowd booed lustily, a leatherlung reminder of Monica Lewinsky, of his reckless history with women from southern California. Marla Messing, the chief World Cup organizer, would feel ambivalent later to see Clinton later with his arms around the American players in the locker room. "I'm surprised other people didn't make more of an issue out of it," she said, adding that nonetheless she was happy he came to the game. De Varona, the chairwoman of the organizing committee, said she suggested to Clinton that he attend. "It's blasphemy for women to play a men's game in certain cultures," de Varona said. "You get the President there, annointing a women's event, it puts it in a different light."

Hamm received another pass in the 19th minute, 30 yards from the goal, turning to her left, stumbling, hand down, the ball filched by a Chinese double team. Another disconnect in a game that proceeded like a dubbed movie, the lips and voices slightly out of synch, everything a step off, passes played too hard, too soft, placed behind teammates instead of in front. Pressure, fatigue and heat whittled the final to an urgent stiffening of defense, a fierce digging in. Effort and resolve would have to prevail over tactics. There was only one thing to do, to keep running, keep working for some sliver of opportunity. The outside Chinese backs were not coming forward in attack. They were staying home, swarming, attempting to surround each American forward with two defenders. Both teams had grown cautious, still looking to score the winning goal, yes, but more desperately not wanting to surrender the winning goal.

"Each team understood that all the opposition needed was one mistake," Hamm said. "We weren't willing to give them that and they weren't willing to give it to us."

9

And the Captains Shall Lead Them

T HE NIGHT BEFORE the World Cup final, a visitor to the hotel room of Sun Wen, the Chinese captain, found it uncomfortably warm. The air-conditioning had been out for a couple of days, but Sun had not complained, said Ying Wu, a sports historian and assistant professor of physical education at Millersville University in Pennsylvania. "I went to the coach and told him that his players needed a good night's sleep, that he would need Sun the next day," Wu said. "Sun said she didn't mind the heat—she had the window open—but I requested a fan and they brought floor fans. Otherwise she would have said nothing. She is very humble, not like a big star."

At 5-foot-4, 125 pounds, with a helmet of hair cropped at her shoulders and a dusting of acne on her broad face, Sun had become the most valuable player in the World Cup with her vision, passing skills and predatory instinct for putting the ball in the net. The Chinese forward had scored seven goals in five games, including a hat trick against Ghana. The ball seemed to stay at Sun Wen's feet like a terrier nipping at a paper boy. She played with an effortless weaving as she dribbled. Each movement was precise and compact, the first touch always away from the defender, her dribbling guided by a clear, tight intent, protected by magnificent radar. The ball left her feet and came back as if attached to the string of a child's paddle toy. "She kicks the ball with her brain, not her feet," said the Chinese coach Ma Yuanan.

But order was thrown off its axis in the final. The lack of warm-ups, the Blue Angels flyover. When the game started, everything felt so hot, the sun, even the wall of sound pushing in from the Rose Bowl crowd, a noise that sounded like a metallic industrial reverberation. Sun Wen could not do anything with the ball, because she could not get it or keep it her possession. After 19 minutes, she had touched the ball only five times, half as many as Mia Hamm. The Chinese attack was being channeled toward the middle of the field and smothered by the strength, jumping ability and incautious determination of Michelle Akers. Sun was getting no support from her reluctant outside backs. And when the ball did escape into openings that might have threatened the American goal, she could not elude the anticipatory pouncing of Carla Overbeck or the muscling speed of Kate Sobrero.

"I felt we were really in a bowl, or in a noisy workshop in a big factory," Sun said. "I couldn't think clearly. It was very hot, the audience was hot. It was impossible to keep cool. We were nervous, the Americans were even more nervous. They made many mistakes, we made many mistakes. Both teams were afraid of losing. Neither the Americans nor the Chinese wanted to lose the first goal."

A student of Chinese literature, the 26-year-old Sun wrote poetry that appeared in Chinese newspapers and articles that were read in elementary schools, and she sang karaoke songs to the music of Elton John and Celine Dion. Her travels internationally had concerned her about China's polluted cities and convinced her that she wanted to become an environmentalist. Her mother, a teacher, had wanted her daughter to forego sports all along and to concentrate on her studies. Like many mothers in China, she did not approve of her daughter playing a game as rough as soccer. "Most families can't accept girls playing soccer easily," Sun said. "Girls are supposed to be shy and steady and not so active."

Her father, a retired factory supervisor, was a fan of the national sport and encouraged his daughter to play. She began as a 10-year-old in Shanghai, playing during breaks inside her elementary school, using wads of paper rolled into a ball when authentic equipment was not available. Even at dinner, Sun often ate while playing with a ball at her feet, said her close friend, Jun Shen.

"She kicked little stones on the way home from school," Shen said. "She liked to kick anything, I think."

The 1999 Women's World Cup unfolded at a time when female athletes were breaking cultural and social restraints in many developing nations. In attempting to bring the world back into the Olympic movement after the American and Soviet boycotts of the 1980s, Juan Antonio Samaranch played a game of political expediency, turning his back to chronic corruption within the International Olympic Committee and failing to take seriously the epidemic of performance-enhancing drugs. But he was pragmatic enough to realize that with the world's renewed participation, he needed to provide opportunities for the world's women as well as men.

In 1981, a year after he was elected president of the IOC, the Olympic committee named its first female member. In recent years, Samaranch had demanded that Olympic committees from each nation have at least 10 percent representation by women, with an eventual increase to 20 percent. While that may seem ludicrously low to Americans, it was a radical increase for many countries. Samaranch has also decreed that any new sport added to the Olympics must include female participation. About 40 percent of the athletes competing at the 2000 Summer Games in Sydney will be women.

Where women were once forbidden to participate in international sport, they were now making breakthroughs and becoming symbols for equal rights in Africa, Asia, the Middle East. Hassiba Boulmerka of Algeria won the 1,500-meter race at the 1992 Barcelona Olympics, defying taunts and spitting and rock-throwing at home by Islamic militants, who did not want a woman running in shorts, or running at all. Derartu Tulu of Ethiopia became the first black African woman to win a gold medal at the same Barcelona Games, taking first in the 10,000-meter run and avoiding the fate of many girls who live subsistence lives as shepherds and are sent into chattel marriages at the age of 12. Tegla Loroupe of Kenya, now the world-record holder, became the first African woman to win a major marathon when she stunned the field in New York City in 1994; returning home, Loroupe received a tract of land, 9 cattle, 16 sheep and welcoming embrace from the women in her Pokot tribe, who told her, "You showed that we are like the men—we can do things. We are not useless." At the 1996 Summer Olympics in Atlanta, Ghada Shouaa of Syria won track and field's heptathlon, overcoming a daily language barrier with her coach, who spoke only Russian and was forced to communicate via index cards and a translator. Also in Atlanta, Nova Perris-Kneebone became the first Aboriginal woman to win an Olympic gold medal as a member of Australia's field hockey team.

The sudden, dramatic dominance by Chinese swimmers and distance runners in the early 1990s, however, had caused much suspicion in the West that their record-breaking times were being achieved through performance-enhancing drugs. At least three dozen Chinese swimmers have tested positive for banned substances since testing began in 1972, including seven at the 1994 Asian Games and four at the 1998 world swimming championships in Perth, Australia. One swimmer, Yuan Yuan, was caught with 13 vials of human growth hormone—an anabolic steroid—in her luggage at the Perth championships. When Chinese distance runners delivered remarkable, shattering times in 1993, it provoked Western skepticism over the claims that the performances resulted solely from hard work and diets of caterpillar fungus and turtle blood. However, the runners did not fail drug tests, and there seemed to be little suspicion at the World Cup about possible drug use among China's soccer players.

"We have to trust that if any of that is happening in the women's game—and I don't believe it is—that it is controlled, marshaled, and cleaned up," said Tony DiCicco, the American coach. "I think the

Chinese women are wonderful, they play with class and talent and they have earned the right to be one of the best teams in the world."

As did Hamm, Sun Wen played soccer with boys, mostly in the streets of Shanghai. At school, she also played table tennis, badminton, basketball. Often she played soccer alone, kicking the ball against a wall at home. "Passers-by thought it was strange and unacceptable to see a girl kicking a ball against a wall," Sun said. "I didn't care. I took pride in the fact that they called me a pseudo-boy. I liked to score. If I could pass to other players, it gave me a sense of accomplishment. I played so much my parents had to buy me new sneakers every month."

Even though her school did not have a formal team, it won a district championship, with Sun scoring most of the goals. When she was 13, Sun traveled with her father to a local sports school to display her dribbling, passing and shooting skills in a tryout before a group of coaches. This was how China and the former Eastern bloc developed their athletes, identifying them at a young age, placing them in certain sports according to skills, speed, body type. When she saw the other girls wearing uniforms, she grew intimidated.

"Let's go home," she told her father, Sun Zhongao. "I don't think I can do this."

"We are already here, why not try it?" her father said.

Sun was selected to the sports school, but her career was nearly extinguished, first by a lack of funding for her high school team, and second, by a coach who thought Sun too small and too slow to play soccer. Just as she was about to return to a regular academic high school, Sun was selected to play for the Shanghai team in the Chinese women's soccer league. She was 16.

Sports schools offered the possibility of a career, but life could be Spartan for high school girls. Parents were allowed to visit once a week, on Wednesday night. Soccer players awakened at 5:45 A.M., went for a morning run, studied from 8 A.M. until 2 P.M., then had a second training session. Study hall began at 7 P.M., and lights were supposed to be out by 9, although players used flashlights and candles while sitting around talking and playing cards. Shen called the sports school a "concentration camp," but said it taught her independence and allowed her to begin making her own decisions at an age younger than most girls.

"At first, I missed my family a lot," Sun said. "After one or two years, I became used to it."

China hosted the inaugural Women's World Cup in 1991, but Sun was only 18 and had played in only three international tournaments. Nervous, she found it difficult even to catch her breath before the opening match. "Psychologically, the China team was inferior to the Americans," Sun said. "This time, we had more experience. Five or six players had played at least a hundred international matches. That gave us confidence."

Sun has spoken about wanting to study and play soccer in the United States, said Shen, her friend. In 1998, Sun took two months away from the national team to study English, her friend said, but soccer officials told her "don't do that again. You are a key player for the team." After the World Cup, Sun would be named to a list of players to face the Americans on an indoor tour, but she never participated. She was having some difficulty getting her passport released, Shen said, and there was some speculation that soccer officials feared if she left China, she would not return.

"She has told me she would never do that," Shen said. "She will never betray her country."

For the final against the Americans, Sun said her father went to a Shanghai television station to watch the match, while 30 reporters showed up at her house in the middle of the night to view the game with her mother. Wang Qiuyang had changed her mind about her daughter playing soccer. "If I wanted to quit, I don't think she would want me to," Sun said. But when the penalty kick phase arrived, her mother would not be able to watch, Sun said. Nervously, she would have to leave the room.

A sudden pinballing in the 20th minute and Pu Wei was free in the Chinese midfield. She chipped a long pass toward the American goal, and the two captains, Sun Wen and Carla Overbeck, accelerated into cruising sprints. If Sun retrieved the pass, she would be alone in front of Briana Scurry, the American goalkeeper, but Overbeck positioned herself between Sun and the ball, slowing for the bounce, shielding the Chinese captain, jumping and heading the ball safely toward a charging Scurry. Sun came to a dead stop in the penalty area, face to face with Scurry as if surprised to have met her in some desolate pasture. Another run had taken energy from Sun's legs and had given her nothing in return. She had not even touched the ball. Her ponytail piled on her head like a weather vane, Overbeck began walking upfield, a smile on her face. This was the most thoroughly disruptive game that her coach, her teammates, had seen her play in a long time, maybe ever.

In the 22nd minute, Overbeck deflected with her head another pass intended for Sun. Then the frustrated Chinese captain fouled her nemesis, jumping over her back to retrieve a futile pass. In the 25th minute, Sun poked the ball away from Julie Foudy, retrieved it from a teammate, fended off Foudy with a hip and an elbow and began a stutter-step charge, pushing the ball ahead, chopping her steps, her shoulders in a bugaloo-shimmy, trying to force Overbeck into an awkward lean, a unrecoverable shift of body weight, but the American captain backpedaled calmly, keeping her feet untangled and her hips balanced in angular composure. When Sun reached the top of the penalty box and darted left, Overbeck punched the ball away with a sweeping flick of her right leg. Sun threw her head back in torment and did an anguished hop of unfulfillment.

"One of the better games I've ever seen her play," DiCicco said of Overbeck.

He had considered removing her from the lineup before the World Cup. When Overbeck took risks, played on the edge of her ability, she could be an impenetrable defender. When she grew overly concerned about her lack of speed, DiCicco said, she surrendered too much room to roaming forwards. She could be vulnerable when the ball was played into open space.

"I thought about everyone not being in the lineup at one point or another, not just Carla," DiCicco said. "In some ways I have to coach to protect her a little bit, but I made up my mind that we were going to live and die with Carla in the lineup. She is very good on the ball and she's a great leader with great heart. This is a better team when she is in there."

It was Overbeck who gathered the team before the game and leaned into the circle of players, demanding their attention, her index finger jabbing the air for emphasis. "We are the best," she told them with the cameras rolling. "Look right here. We are the best." And, she later confided to her husband, Greg, that she had also said, "Norway screwed us in 1995. This one is ours. We deserve it. We are the best. It's ours to go get it. The only thing between us and the trophy is that team. Let's go fuck 'em up."

With Akers in front of her and Sobrero at her side, forming a sort of protective cocoon in DiCicco's thinking, Overbeck was free to organize the American defense. She directed the team on the field, expanding and contracting the American zone like an accordion, pulling midfielders back and rotating outside backs forward, orchestrating complex shifts and traps that required movements of Rockette precision.

"I don't care if the woman was in a wheelchair, we would never be successful unless she was on the field," Sobrero said of Overbeck. "She runs the show. She's the most calm. You hear the voice. You get the sense that no matter what happens, we're going to be okay."

When Brandi Chastain put a ball into her own goal five minutes into a quarterfinal match against Germany, the first person who reached her was Overbeck. "This game is not over," Overbeck told her in a reassuring voice. "There are 85 minutes left. We are going to win this thing. Don't worry about it. Get over it. Let's do it."

"Here we are, I've got this look of 'Oh my God, I've just passed it into my own goal,' and she trusts me," Chastain said. "It shows the true character of a person when they stand up for you in times of trouble. She gave me confidence to go forward. Sure enough, in the second half, I scored a goal, for us this time, to tie the game and we win 3–2. She could have easily looked me in the eye and said, 'You blew it.' But she gave me the courage to move forward and the trust and respect I deserved from all the years of training. For me, that was my best moment of the World Cup."

When Scurry was assigned to start her first match in goal, at a tournament in Portugal in 1994, she said that Overbeck approached her and said, "You deserve to be here."

"That really helped," Scurry said. "I wasn't sure I was ready yet. I went from number five on the list to number one in three months. I hadn't played a game. She told me I was good enough. It was hard for me to judge myself, but she obviously had faith in me. I figured that if she did, I must be good enough."

Sometimes, Overbeck did not even have to say a word to stir her teammates. Sometimes all she had to do was give a look, a nod that said, 'Let's pick it up,' or a sort of smiling smirk that her husband said was "like a hawk looks at its victim, unemotional, coldblooded."

Shannon MacMillan sometimes joked with Overbeck that it took three years just to work up the courage to say hello. "When it's serious time, you're serious," MacMillan told her. "You scare the crap out of everyone."

"She is as tough as nails," MacMillan said. "In Portugal, she jammed her neck and played through the pain. She lifted weights the day her water broke when she had her son. She's got that look that shows how intense she is. Her eyes could burn through your soul. It's the look she gives opponents, like, 'You know I'm going to kick your butt today.'"

A twig of a kid with skinny arms and legs—even now she seemed to have a body of right angles—she was called Termite by her father. Her feistiness came from being the youngest of four children and from learning quickly to stand up for herself. "They tortured me," Overbeck said with a laugh about her older brothers and sister. "Told me I was adopted, that I had the same dark, brown eyes as the dog. Board games, whatever, I was always trying to beat them."

She possessed a certain fearlessness that led her, in the fifth or sixth grade, to dangle from a ski lift in New Mexico while she switched from one side of the chair to another. Her soccer career began at age five in a park that abutted the family home in Dallas. Soccer weekends meant a break from yard work. So excited to play, she said that she slept in her uniform the nights before games. "I'd be praying for two games Saturday and Sunday," Overbeck said.

At the University of North Carolina, Overbeck won four national championships and developed the leadership skills that would make her captain of the American national team. Her freshman year, coach

Anson Dorrance said, a timid Overbeck did not win a single one vs. one drill against her teammates, the results of which were posted daily. She said she was hesitant to challenge her teammates, for fear of hurting them or their feelings. "She just wanted to get along, to be a good teammate and a good person," Dorrance said. "Her transition, basically, was learning to compete." Her senior season, Overbeck did not lose a one vs. one drill.

"Somewhere in there, she said she was sick of seeing her name posted on the bottom of the list," Dorrance said. "Those lists gave her permission to be competitive. Her senior year, I've never had another player like this. In the middle of a game, she would turn to the bench and scream at me. She would say, 'Get so and so out of here.' She would scream at me to substitute a player who was not competing. She took that leadership quality to the national team, so that even the divas like Michelle Akers, Mia Hamm and Kristine Lilly, if they weren't playing well, they knew immediately. All of a sudden, someone without any notoriety was telling the best players what to do. And they accepted it because of their respect for Carla. But Carla had the courage to make those kind of statements."

She and Dorrance are close friends, but he, too, has felt the steam-heat of Overbeck's competitive nature. In the 1992 collegiate championship game, North Carolina won 9–1 over Duke, where Overbeck is an assistant coach. She believed that Dorrance had rubbed the victory in Duke's face and, two weeks later, when Dorrance arrived at her wedding, her father greeted him with these words: "I'm surprised she let you in here."

As team captain and one of two mothers on the squad, Overbeck requested that the United States Soccer Federation provide day care for her one-year-old son, Jackson, and for the two daughters of Joy Fawcett. The Americans set up training camp outside Orlando, Florida, in preparation for the World Cup, which meant that Overbeck and Fawcett essentially were facing six months on the road, away from their husbands and relatives except for a break every four or five weeks. "We need to do something about day care," she told Fawcett before camp opened. "We don't pay for it at home; why should we have to pay for it on the road?"

Previously, Overbeck and Fawcett paid for their own nannies on the road, splitting the cost of using friends or their mothers as baby-sitters and they took care of their own flights, hotel rooms and meals. Now the federation agreed to pay $500 per month for each child to the players. In turn, the players would pay the nanny, a 19-year-old college student named Nicolette Richards. The federation budgeted $50,000 to pay for the nanny's flights and hotel rooms during training camp, although it fell behind on payments to the players. Still, said Overbeck, "We're glad they thought it was the right thing to do."

The notion that a married woman with children could be a world-class athlete gained great currency at the 1948 Summer Olympics in London. Fanny Koen of the Netherlands had been 18 when she finished with an autograph of Jesse Owens, but without any medals in the high jump and the sprint relay at the 1936 Berlin Olympics. After a 12-year war absence, the Summer Games resumed in 1948, and by this time Koen had married her coach, Jan Blankers, and had given birth to two children. Surviving a case of homesickness and nerves, she won the 100 meters, 200 meters, 80-meter hurdles and the 4x100-meter relay. She is still the only woman to have won four track-and-field gold medals in the same Olympics. When she returned home, according to *The Complete Book of the Olympics*, her neighbors gave her a bicycle so she wouldn't have to run so much.

Fanny Blankers-Koen became a counterpoint to the pre–World War II stereotype of the female athlete as masculine, a common belief reinforced by such athletes as Babe Didrikson and Stella Walsh, who won the 100 meters at the 1932 Los Angeles Olympics and was revealed upon her death in 1980 to have male sex organs. The sexual preference of female athletes was no less a hot-button topic by the end of the century. After the Women's World Cup, some feminists would criticize the media trumpeting of the soccer-mom angle, saying that it reinforced the notion that a woman must be heterosexual and attractive to be a successful and accepted athlete.

"I don't think the fact that the Women's World Cup has received publicity is a bad thing, but I do think it's negative, unrealistic and damaging that the publicity has been filtered through a heterosexist lens," Laura L. Noah, a former collegiate soccer player and coach, wrote in *The New York Times*.

A contentious issue, regarding double standards, has also arisen with athletes who are mothers having to defend themselves as working women and fit parents. Pam McGee, a former professional basketball player and Olympic gold medalist, was involved in a three-year custody battle with her ex-husband, who claimed that her career impaired her ability to care for their four-year-old daughter. Early in 2000, basketball star Sheryl Swoopes declined a spot on the Sydney Olympic team after battling with the United States Basketball Federation over the issue of a nanny for her son.

On the American soccer team, the nanny issue was viewed as a progressive, necessary securing of some of the rights that women have attained in the corporate workplace, such as maternity leave and child care. It was unique in women's team sports. The Women's National Basketball Association, for instance, has no day care provisions for its players.

"I think it was necessary for them to extend their careers," DiCicco said of Overbeck and Fawcett. "If 10 players had kids, it could turn into the *Howdy Doody Show*, but I never felt it was a negative. We were trying to build a family and the most important aspect of family is children. It was a connecting point for the women. Before, I think it was always judged on a men's team mentality."

While playing the Americans in a pair of exhibition matches before the World Cup, members of the Japanese national team seemed surprised and happy, yet a bit wistful, to find that Overbeck and Fawcett could continue their careers as mothers while their own careers would be expected to end. "I think this sends a message that in the future women can realize they can be a mom and still continue to have a career athletically," Overbeck said. "Maybe they won't have the fears or self-doubt that I had."

It was Overbeck who also set the tone for extreme fitness on the women's national team. Young players who did not buy into that culture were weeded out quickly. She grew so impatient once with the laconic fairway-promenade of golf that she began jogging after her tee shot. "What are you doing?" Greg Overbeck yelled in laughing disbelief. "You're supposed to walk the ball." Another time, she Roller-Bladed around a course on the cart path, and even though she fell and suffered the raspberries of a cement scrape, it was better than walking. "I can't imagine taking four hours out of the day to play golf," she said. "I'm thinking I should be out running or lifting weights."

She ran stadium steps and hills and exercised on a stair-stepper machine during her ninth month of pregnancy. Seven weeks after her son, Jackson, was born on August 14, 1997, she returned to the lineup. Like many working mothers, Overbeck felt conflicted during her pregnancy. "You start to wonder, 'Am I going to be able to play at that same level mentally and physically?'" she said. "The team was winning all the time after the Olympics and I wasn't part of it. I could see younger, talented, quick, fast players in the back, playing my position and being successful, and I could see myself falling farther and farther behind. I was very adamant about staying as fit as I could during my pregnancy."

Never one of the fastest players on the team, she worked exhaustively to avoid losing a step during the months before World Cup training began, doing explosive lifts in the weight room, jumping on and off of plyometric boxes to maintain the twitch-fiber burst in her legs. In the World Cup final, Overbeck's plan was to keep Sun Wen in front of her, to avoid a footrace and the sneak incursion, to anticipate the pass and the dribble and to reach in with her head or her foot and deflect the ball with a preemptive stab.

"If she didn't have the ball at her feet, she couldn't beat us," Overbeck said.

In the 26th minute, another suffocating double-team of Sun Wen, Overbeck charging and Kate Sobrero leg-whipping the ball to safety, then Overbeck intercepting another pass with her right leg and lashing it before it hit the ground, the catgut clearance of a tennis volley. Then, in the 31st minute, Sobrero jumping for a ball with Michelle Akers and the Chinese midfielders Pu Wei and Zhao Lihong, an airborne square dance, and Akers ramming forward with her left knee into Sobrero's sternum and Sobrero on the ground on all fours in dry-heave helplessness, her lungs deflated by the knee punch. Play continuing with the rush of red and white jerseys, finally the referee's whistle, Kristine Lilly crouching over Sobrero, hands on her back, wondering whether she was okay, Sobrero still in the woozy Muslim kneel on the green turf, then on her feet, blinking once, twice, three times, as if trying to restore her vision along with her breathing.

I'm done. I can't even get up. The World Cup final, way to go, typical you.

At 22, the youngest of the American defenders, Sobrero was funny, spacy-brilliant, a dean's list graduate in business-science from Notre Dame who wore a tongue stud and her hair dyed red from a lost bet with a teammate. She spoke on permanent fast-forward and had overcome bizarre injury and dispirited confidence to become a reliable, sturdy presence. Unlike Overbeck, who rushed in to poke the ball away, Sobrero relied on her speed and agility and what soccer players called "hardness," a gritty willingness for the interior scrap, the shoulder-ram and arm-slap and elbow-jostle of marking a forward, teeth biting her lower lip, a competitive fearlessness from having played with three brothers, a patient physical insistence that eventually forced her opponent to make a mistake, to turn the wrong way or to kick the ball too far to be retrieved. A self-described tomboy, she said she had been angry to learn as a girl that she would not be allowed to play competitive football. But now she had taken a hit as hard as any football collision and she was struggling to refill her lungs. For a week, every time she laughed she would feel the hammering bruise on her chest.

"Michelle was a beast, a savage warrior," Sobrero said. "Without her we definitely wouldn't have won. She laid it all on the line. I thought I got run over by a Mack truck."

She had fought so hard to overcome the fluke injury, the freakish impairment, and now it had happened again. In early 1995, her freshman year at Notre Dame, Sobrero came to her first tryout with the national team. Weakened by flu-like symptoms and lacking fitness, she passed out during a running drill. Her very first practice, playing with her heroes such as Mia Hamm, Michelle Akers, Julie Foudy, and she melted like ice cream in the Florida sun.

"This was my dream and I couldn't even pass a fitness test," Sobrero said. "It destroyed my confidence for a couple of years. These were people I worshipped, and I passed out in front of them. I wasn't fit. And I wasn't mature enough emotionally to be on the national team."

For three years, when DiCicco invited her back to the national team, Sobrero turned him down every time. "I hope you don't treat your boyfriends like that," DiCicco joked with her. "You won't have any dates."

Her sophomore season at Notre Dame, her self-doubt lingered. She quit the Irish team for a week. "I couldn't even pass the ball two feet," she said. "I was so mentally a mess. I wasn't having any fun. It all stemmed from having zero confidence. I quit, but my parents wouldn't let me. They said, 'You have a scholarship, you have to finish the season. You have a commitment.'"

Resigned that her career would soon be finished, unburdened by any pressure, Sobrero began enjoying the game again, and her competitive fires were restoked. Notre Dame kept winning, advancing to the Final Four and to a national championship in the fall of 1995. Sobrero was named most valuable player of the tournament. Still, she declined DiCicco's offer to play on the national team.

By 1997, her confidence in a sort of 12-step recovery program, Sobrero played on the American team that won an important under–20 tournament in Denmark. "She needed an environment where she could succeed," said Lauren Gregg, the assistant on the national team who coached the American youth team in Denmark. In January of 1998, Sobrero was invited back to the national team, but her second tryout was even more discouraging than her first. While attempting to score a goal in a scrimmage, she collided with the knee of goalkeeper Tracy Ducar and suffered a broken jaw. She lost a tooth and, briefly, her memory. "I must have been smoking crack, thinking I was a forward," Sobrero said. For six weeks, she had her jaw wired shut, which left her with a diet of milkshakes and mashed potatoes and with 15 pounds of new, unwanted weight. She was, she joked, the only person in history to gain weight with her jaw wired shut.

She called herself a klutz, and her teammates joked that at least once a game, she was sure to trip over herself, a teammate or the ball. They described her as amusingly eccentric, endearingly absentminded. Foudy said that Sobrero was "a few feathers shy of a duck." Before a World Cup match against North Korea, she got squeezed between the elevator doors of the team hotel and thought she had broken her wrist.

"You'll see her with her shoes untied and say, 'Tie your laces before you trip,'" Brandi Chastain said of Sobrero. "She'll say, 'I feel I'm in balance when my shoes are untied.' Sometimes you meet geniuses with no common sense. That's Kate. She reminds me of a football player. She just wants to get in there and make contact. I don't think she knows her value."

Beneath her droll exterior, though, Sobrero possessed an adamant resolve. As a young girl, she suffered from kidney problems that stymied her growth, and when she entered high school, she was not yet five feet tall. As she began to grow, she experienced problems with her knees, and her doctor suggested that she pick one sport, her mother said. Sobrero chose soccer. Quick growth can throw a body's balance out of orbit, and, in compensation, Sobrero used her speed to overcome any awkwardness in her touch on the ball. After school, on weekends, holidays, she worked out in the gym at Detroit's Country Day School, running suicide drills on the basketball court, trying to get faster as she got taller.

"It was so impressive to see her in the gym, running sprints while her mom timed her, doing anything to help herself get better," said Bob Bukari, who coached Sobrero at Country Day. "She seems a little goofy, and her verbal response to things is, 'I can't do that,' but inside, she is saying, 'I can be that good. I can do that.'"

As a kid, her mother said, Sobrero used to play a game called "butts-up" with her brothers and neighborhood boys. The losers had to bend over and stick up their behinds while the winning team strafed them with soccer balls. Once, she infuriated her brother by nipping at his heels in a pickup game and he took her out with a slide tackle, kicking her severely enough to break a bone in her leg. Sobrero kept playing, and the injury was not discovered until a year later when doctors treated her for a fractured ankle in a high school play-off game. After breaking her jaw in early 1998 with the national team, Sobrero returned to the lineup later that year and never relinquished her position.

Although she had been with the national team only two seasons, Sobrero was keenly insightful about its personalities and generational demarcations. She knew that veteran players possessed something the younger ones could not—a sense of caretaker purpose, a pioneering, ground-zero drive, that came from shoveling a team's first earth, from staying in mosquito-net hotels, from explaining important victories to blank, uncaring faces. "It's their mentality that sets them apart from the rest of us," Sobrero said. "They push themselves to the point of passing out every single practice. They kill each other. It's almost inhuman. In the beginning, I struggled with that kind of competition. But that's what makes them so good. Every practice, they go nuts. I've never been yelled at for slacking but I think that's the thing that would piss them off the most. I have never seen more competitive men or women. I wonder if we will have that mentality when they retire."

What would happen, too, she wondered, now that there was real money and celebrity in the sport? Would it bring continued success, distraction, complacency? "It's going to be interesting to see," Sobrero said. "You never played for money, because you didn't make any. Now you can make a living playing the sport. I hope the players still play for the love of the game, not for how much money they can make. That's something I get a little worried about."

On the field, her occasional clumsiness was obscured by a competitive dexterity, an affinity for the duel. In the World Cup opener against Denmark, Sobrero grew so nervous at the beginning that she could not concentrate on the game. Later she settled down and made a sliding tackle to save a goal. She wrenched an ankle the day before the second match, against Nigeria, and was carried off the practice field. But she played the first half 24 hours later, and on one nimble maneuver she backpedaled for 25 yards, adroitly switching direction, her shoulders parallel to the goal line, her feet jabbing with the fluid, coordinated blur of a sewing-machine stitch, until the Nigerian forward simply ran out of room and energy and ideas.

"She can defend anyone," DiCicco said of Sobrero. "Joy Fawcett has been the best defender on the team for a long time, but now Kate may have the edge. She's great one v. one, she reads quickly and covers for other players. She's our future. She can be recognized as one of the best defenders in the world."

Two days before the final, Sobrero began to feel the creep of nervousness again, so she spoke with Colleen Hacker, the team's sports psychologist, who told her to break the game down from a 90-minute expanse to an accumulation of two-minute blocks. During those two minutes she was to keep telling herself that she would not be tired or defeated, that Sun Wen would not get around her or score a goal. The two-minute blocks would accumulate quickly and, in increments, 90 minutes would not seem forever.

When the World Cup began three weeks earlier, Sobrero had been largely unknown to casual fans and had received modest applause during the public introduction of players. For the final, the crowd had cheered as loudly for her as for her teammates. "I looked up and saw a sign with my name on it," Sobrero said. "I got two signs the whole tournament."

The first half was more than 30 minutes old now, and Sobrero did not feel the pressure that tightened her throat, the disabling nervousness of the opening match. The pressure was gone now, the Americans were in the final, and all that was left was to play. The game seemed to reduce its speed, and everything became slow and clear and understood. Thirty-three minutes, and Sun Wen, the Chinese captain, had not even threatened with a shot.

But China kept pressing ahead and in the 34th minute the referee blew her whistle and pointed toward the American goal. A foul on the United States. Sobrero and Chastain had lightly jostled Pu Wei, the Chinese midfielder, and now China would have a free kick from 22 yards. Pu Wei clapped her hands in approval of the referee's decision. This was China's best chance of the first half. The crowd let out a muted roar of disapproval and apprehension. The game could change now with one kick of the ball. Six American players bunched into a wall, moving in a chain-gang shuffle as the referee pushed them the required 10 yards from the ball. Scurry crouched into a tuck, looking between her teammates' legs for the flight path of the kick. If she did not see the ball as it left the shooter's foot, she may not react quickly enough to make a save. She thought of Sun Wen and her threats to rain shots on the American goalkeeper and she wondered why anyone would do this, give an opponent a chance to clip an article and put it on the bulletin board, throw gasoline on a motivational fire.

What are you getting so personal for? What did I do to you?

Bouncing in her tuck, peeking through the thicket of legs, Scurry looked at Sun Wen standing over the ball, and she summoned the ritual anger and bravado that had made her impermeable for four of the six World Cup games. *You can't score. You're not going to score on me.*

Zhao Lihong, the Chinese midfielder, made a run over the ball and the American wall did a nervous jack-in-the-box jump, but Zhao's approach was a disguise, a purposeful deception. Sun Wen stepped forward and punched a shot with the inside of her left foot, trying to bend it around the wall. Perhaps she caught the white flash of a charging Mia Hamm out of the corner of her eye, or she was distracted by another pogo-stick vault of the tallest Americans, Michelle Akers and Cindy Parlow, or the moment's anxiety and urgency put too much strength in her leg. Her shot was all power, no placement or threatening banana curve, and it sailed in a harmless line drive over the crossbar. Scurry moved with a goalkeeper's crabwalk to her left, but the kick sailed so high that she felt no need to jump. She threw up her right hand with a dismissive wave.

Whatever.

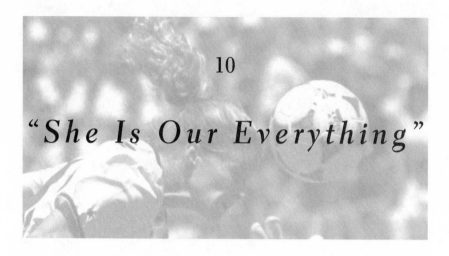

10

"She Is Our Everything"

BRANDI CHASTAIN pulled up the sleeves of her jersey, squinted toward the Chinese goal in the glare of early afternoon and lobbed a two-handed pass toward Michelle Akers. Elbows spread, Akers hooked two Chinese defenders behind her and shielded them from Chastain's throw-in. Earlier she had run onto a free kick by Mia Hamm, and she had lashed a bullwhip of a shot from 25 yards that bounced off the hands of Gao Hong, the Chinese goalkeeper. Her whole body had come off the ground in torquing effort, her legs splayed in the air as if she were jumping an invisible hurdle. This was the final match of her final World Cup, and Akers was racing against her own fatigued body as the needle on its internal tank moved steadily toward empty.

I'm going to score the winning goal. I'm going to wrap this thing up in 90 minutes. I'm not doing overtime.

Settling under Chastain's pass in the 36th minute, Akers flicked it in a high trajectory toward the Chinese goal, but the defender Wen Lirong headed the ball upward, an unthreatening floater that settled into Gao's hands. Another near miss. Akers was feeling a heaviness now, a sense of running uphill at the point where a jogger succumbs to gravity and inertia or escapes the physics of exhaustion and summons enough energy to crest the incline. Time was running out on her stamina, so she pressed on with a desperate urgency, controlling the midfield with head balls, spraying passes to her teammates, protecting her injured right shoulder as she somersaulted on the turf, sprinting forward into the penalty box, pulling the trigger on a shot at any slim availability.

Midway through the first half, she had run past the American bench and told the team doctor, Mark Adams, "This is going to be tough." Then, in the 39th minute, Akers lunged forward to head a ball out of bounds and her momentum carried her in a slam of shoulders and knees into the advertising boards that lined the field. Wincing, limping, Akers got to her feet and scrambled after the ball and headed another Chinese pass out of danger, sending it 25 yards toward midfield with a whiplash flick of hair and muscle. *This is it, this is it. I'm not going to let them shoot, I'm not going to let them score. It's not going to be from my lack of focus or effort that anything bad happens on the field.* Except in her head the words did not sound like words at all, but like the screaming "Aaaaaaaaaaaaaaaaagh" of whooshing primal fear, of inevitable galloping decline. She kept running and jumping and anyone in her way was a target with a shoulder, a clip of the foot, a flying wedge of a knee. "I think everyone was intimidated by Michelle, not only the other team," Cindy Parlow said. China was not prepared for this. It did not have the size or strength or cultural assertiveness to confront the insistent play of Akers, the rapacious intent to score the winning goal before the fog swirled in her head and the dark tunneling shuttered her vision and the whole plan of a game was reduced to the next pass, the next step, the next thought, the next breath.

"She played like a man," said Sun Wen, the Chinese forward. For her, there could not be bigger praise.

Liu Ailing, the Chinese playmaker, wore the number 10, as Akers did. She scored three goals and scattered passes with a windshield-wiper sweep in China's first five matches. The opening game, against Sweden, had fallen on Liu's first wedding anniversary. She had promised her husband that she would point toward the television cameras for him if she scored a goal. She did score, but a quick engulf of teammates had prevented any celebrative gesture. Afterward, she had called her husband, Jun Liu, only to find out later that he was out shopping for wine to celebrate his wife's achievement. There would be no celebrating for Liu in the final. She gave away five inches and 20 pounds and some frantic, immutable persistence to Akers, and without its engine, the Chinese attack stalled in midfield. Without control of the midfield, China could not get the ball ahead to Sun Wen. Without the ball, Sun could not score.

"Akers was their key player," Sun said. "If not for her, we would have been more successful getting forward."

An hour after Akers was born, the pediatrician who came to examine her told her father, "You've got a very stubborn and persistent little girl." The doctor was right, Michelle said. Stubborn as a mule. As a young girl, she wanted to play for the Pittsburgh Steelers. She wore her "Mean Joe" Greene jersey, No. 75, dreamed of playing wide receiver and catching a touchdown pass in the Super Bowl. She had to be first at everything. First to climb a tree, first down the hill on a bike, first in Monopoly, first in checkers, first in line for lunch at the cafeteria. She couldn't bear losing. If she lost, she cried, pouted, beat up boys, threw temper tantrums. She started playing soccer at age eight, and she lost and she begged her mother to let her quit. She hated not winning, hated the girly uniforms. For a parent, it was annoying, said her father, Bob Akers, a family therapist. If Michelle's day was ruined, everybody's day was ruined. Trying to calm her made it worse, he said, "like a wind hitting a fire."

As a girl, Michelle found it confusing to reconcile soccer's endorsed assertiveness with the indirect comments she heard from parents, the vague, unmistakable looks of disapproval. Why were they looking down on her when she was doing something she loved? Girls cried when she ran over them, or they were no fun to play with because they did not challenge her, so she often played with boys. Even with boys, she struggled to find a manageable way to be competitive, to accept victory with equanimity and defeat without eating herself up on the inside.

Head Coach Tony DiCicco (center) and assistant coaches Lauren Gregg and Jay Hoffman were instrumental in guiding the U.S. women to victory.

China seemed intimidated by the assertiveness of Michelle Akers, who dominated play in the midfield even as the needle on her own internal fuel tank moved steadily toward empty.

Chinese forward Sun Wen was named the best player in the Women's World Cup with seven goals and a brilliant precision in the way she shot and passed the ball.

Playing with a muscular compactness and wondrous improvisation, Tiffeny Milbrett led the Americans with three goals in the World Cup.

Cindy Parlow: The tall striker poaches a goal on a header in the semifinals against Brazil. She was the only American forward to threaten in the penalty area during the final.

With faces covered in Title IX greasepaint, girls scribbled "USA" and Mia Hamm's name on their arms like gender-equity tattoos, having found female role models they could celebrate.

Julie Foudy, making a run through midfield against China, provided the social conscience and comic relief for the American team.

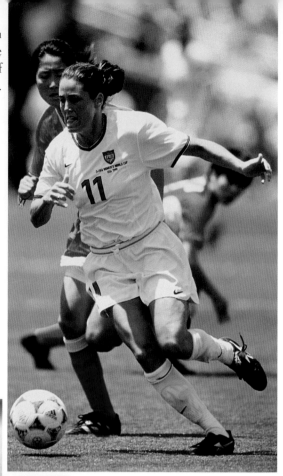

Briana Scurry pumps her fists and screams after making her penalty-kick save against China, saying to herself, *I'm a big badass.*

Shannon MacMillan, warming up before entering a World Cup match, delivered instant offense for the Americans whenever she came on in the second half with her hard, knuckling shots.

Kristine Lilly, the most experienced international soccer player in the world, man or woman, saved the World Cup final with a header off a corner kick, demonstrating again her brilliance at rudimentary skills.

A sea change in the respect for female athletes seemed to take place in the World Cup as boys began wearing Mia Hamm jerseys and writing love letters to her on their chests.

Mia's passion for soccer was most evident in the celebrative convulsion after she scored a goal.

Gao Hong, the acrobatic Chinese goalkeeper, hurls a ball upfield during the final. She would later become unnerved when her attempts to intimidate the Americans during penalty kicks by smiling at them backfired.

The graceful Joy Fawcett, shown here jostling with China's Sun Wen, played defense with a sort of tuxedoed thievery and a pickpocket's stealth.

Sara Whalen, making a run upfield against China in overtime, came on in nervous relief when Michelle Akers went down at the end of regulation.

Kate Sobrero, heading a ball away from the Chinese substitute Zhang Ouying, emerged as perhaps the world's best central defender during the World Cup.

"Sometimes I backed off and I hated myself for it," she said. "At a pretty young age, I said, 'I'm going for it. If they can't deal with it, too bad. I'm not going to play down a level because they can't handle it.'"

Hers was a family of achievers, risk takers, ignorers of conventional expectation. Bob Akers ran marathons, and he hiked the Cascades and climbed Mount Rainier and Mount Adams with his son, Mike. Anne Akers was a firefighter. Soccer was Michelle's emancipation, the sanctioned roughness, the free open running and contentment of sweaty exhaustion, the mind's-eye understanding of where everyone was and where the ball should go and the raw exultant liberation of a shot bulging into the net like a dent from a fist. She gave an interview in high school and said, "I want to play professionally and I want to be the best in the world." She forgot about the interview and came across a clipping 16 years later and she had to laugh. Who ever says anything in high school that comes true? She did. Everything happened the way she said it would.

At a price.

Her athletic success in high school in Seattle cost Michelle socially, her father said. She did not have a cheerleader's thin legs or submissive eagerness. It was not enough to please with a rhyming hooray. She was an athlete, not a supplicant. But it was a time before the magazine-cover fascination with Chastain, when muscles on girls could be as threatening as horns on a bull. "As far as dating, perhaps boys didn't want a competitive person around that could beat them," Bob Akers said. "I think it was harder on her than she would like to admit."

When Michelle was 10, her parents divorced and that led to further adolescent confusion and teenage rebellion. She said she later began skipping school, dating older guys, experimenting with drugs and alcohol. "I hated who I was becoming, what I was doing to my family," she would later write. "I was angry. I was sad. I was confused."

She became a born-again Christian and, according to her father, her faith and soccer prevented this teenage spinout from become a truly dangerous personal skid. Soccer also introduced Michelle to her future stepmother. Sue Akers was a coach and referee in Seattle in the late 1970s, the early days of Title IX when high school girls "were barely playing fullcourt basketball, like they'd fall over dead if they exerted themselves." Michelle was different, self-assured, unbound by social constriction. The first time Sue refereed one of her games, Michelle popped off and Sue hit her with a yellow warning card.

"She was a diamond in the rough, an unpolished soccer player, but as an athlete she jumped out at you," said Sue Akers, a nurse who still plays soccer in an over-50 league. "She played differently than the other girls. They tiptoed around mud puddles, she slid right into them. She set the tone: This is my ball, this is my field. It was fun to see that. It was pretty bad for women then. I'd go to a coaching school, say that I wanted to learn and take back and teach, and basically I'd get laughed out of the place. But Michelle had it in her heart. 'What do you mean I can't do this?' It takes a few of us to get out there and do that, to say, 'We need this.'"

Still, the future rested on some flimsy, uncertain hoping.

"Some day you will have a national team," Sue told Michelle.

"We will?" Michelle said. "What's a national team?"

Like Michelle's father, Sue was a single parent. She had a daughter who was two years younger than Michelle. They traveled together to tournaments, played a year of high school soccer together. "I want you and my dad to get together," Michelle insisted, playmaker and match maker. In September of 1984, Bob and Sue Akers were married as Michelle began her freshman year at Central Florida University. She would earn the first national player of the year award for women's soccer, and in 1985, she would join the first American national team, which did not win a game. A year later, the team dressed like bruised fruit, wearing purple and green sweats, but it had a new coach named Anson Dorrance, who soon brought in young players named Mia Hamm, Kristine Lilly, Julie Foudy, Carla Overbeck, Joy Fawcett, and Brandi Chastain. In these women, Akers found validation for her assertive craving. They had all played with boys and knew the rough pleasure and they did not apologize for the flexing of ambition or muscles.

At 5-foot-10, 150 pounds, Akers was a classic center forward. She could crush a ball with her sinewy legs. She could hold defenders off with a hip check and elbow lance, legs bent and arms chevroned in a parachute lean, trapping the ball with her feet and turning and whipsawing a shot or flicking an aerial serve with a seal's dexterity in her head.

"At first it was real challenge," Dorrance said. "This is a real female thing. She was so trained in passing the ball, sharing the ball, being a teammate, as opposed to saying, 'Give me the ball, get the hell out of the way, I'm taking it in on my own.' I think I helped Michelle convince herself that she was a personality player, that she could win games on her own, that every time she got the ball, she should look to shoot first."

Three months before the inaugural Women's World Cup, held in China in 1991, Akers slid into a sprinkler head during training and the wound required 35 stitches, leaving her knee resembling the seams of a baseball. A doctor cautioned that the suture might split open in another collision, but Akers kept playing. At the World Cup, she scored 10 goals in six games—five against Taiwan in the quarter-finals and two in the 2–1 victory over Norway in the championship game. Eventually, she would become one of only four women to score 100 international goals. She was the first player to create widespread acceptance of the women's game. Male superstars such as Pelé of Brazil and Franz Beckenbauer of Germany watched her and came to realize that women could play as skillfully and tactically proficient as men.

"She's the best woman that's ever played the game, period," Tony DiCicco said. "The way she heads passes. Her shot is incredibly hard with long-range accuracy. She can put a player onto the ball with 40-yard passes, right and left footed, and score a goal from 25 or 30 yards."

At Christmas of 1991, Akers seemed to have a gift-wrapped life. She had recently been married to a soccer player named Roby Stahl. She had won a world championship. She had become the first female American soccer player to receive a shoe endorsement. Her stepmother had been right. The United States did create a women's national team, and Michelle Akers-Stahl had become the star. People kept calling her Michelle Aerosol, or Michelle Anchor Steam, but that was okay. They knew her reputation even if they fumbled her name.

Then a creeping lethargy began to take hold. She dismissed it at first. Of course she was tired. She had been playing soccer non-stop for years. Maybe she needed a break. But rest didn't help. Everything she had been taught as an athlete failed her. Every truth was a falsehood. Relentless pushing, never giving in, that was her strength. Now, the harder she worked, the sicker she became. A walk around the block sent her to the couch in exhaustion. She sweated through two, three T-shirts a night. Migraines thudded in her head. She had to stand at team meetings to stay awake. The next three years, she said, were "pure hell." She often had to come out of games after 20 or 30 minutes. In late 1993, she collapsed during a soccer match in San Antonio. Her brain seemed cloudy, her thinking smudged. The unknowing was as bad as the pain. She gathered medical opinions like soccer trophies, but no one could tell her exactly what was wrong or how to get better.

"I frequently asked myself, what happened to that strong, dynamic tireless Michelle Akers?" she wrote in her journal. "Will I ever see her again?" She never considered suicide, she said in an interview, but at times she wanted to die. *God, take me now. I can't endure this. I don't want to live my life like this. Death has got to be better.*

Later, in a statement to Congress, Akers described her low moments: "I walk off, drag myself off, the field, my legs and body like lead. God, they seem to weigh so much. My breathing is labored. It is all I can do to get to the locker room, change my clothes and keep from crying in utter exhaustion and weariness. I am light-headed and shaky. My vision is blurred. My teammates ask me if I am okay—and I nod yes. But my eyes tell the truth. They are hollow, empty. Dull and lifeless. It scares me to look in the mirror when I get like this. I shake my head knowing I overdid it again. I slowly get to my truck and concentrate on the road, willing myself to keep moving, to not pull over and rest. 'Almost there,' I tell myself, 'just a few more minutes.' By the time I arrive home, I leave my bags in a pile by the door and collapse on the couch. I have no energy to eat. To shower. To call someone for help."

She did not want sympathy, her statement said, only for Congress to experience a day in the life of her illness: "Experience the pounding migraine headaches that can incapacitate me for days. The insomnia that plagues me even though I am exhausted. The overwhelming fatigue that keeps me from going to a movie or dinner with friends because I don't have the energy to talk, sit up or eat. The gastrointestinal upset that has caused me to go on an extreme—gluten-free, dairy-free, caffeine-free, sugar-free, and alcohol-free—diet in hopes of finding relief or possibly a cure. The fogginess that cause me to lose concentration, forget where I am or how to get someplace that I've been a thousand times before."

In 1994, Akers was diagnosed as having Epstein-Barr virus. After more tests, doctors amended the diagnosis to Chronic Fatigue Immune Dysfunction Syndrome, a complex, little-understood illness that brings on debilitating exhaustion and for which there is no known cause or cure. There is also no simple lab test to rule the disorder in or out. Instead, an indirect diagnosis is made by excluding other illnesses with similar symptoms such as mononucleosis, multiple sclerosis, Lyme disease, lupus and depression. Once unkindly known as "yuppie flu," chronic fatigue was formerly thought to strike primarily affluent groups, in particular white women around the age of 30. However, a recent study by a Chicago researcher found that the abnormality was more prevalent in blacks and Hispanics than whites and that it struck semiskilled workers more than professionals. A Belgian study indicated that three percent of sufferers felt altogether better over time, while 80 percent felt the same or worse. An estimated 800,000 Americans suffer from chronic fatigue syndrome, but only about 10 percent have been diagnosed, according to estimates by the Chronic Fatigue Immune Dysfunction Syndrome Association of America. Viruses that cause chronic infection and fatigue, along with bacteria, have been investigated, but no conclusive pathogen has been isolated. Some patients are diagnosed with as many as five or six interrelated problems.

"My suspicion is that it is many different things under one label, many different illnesses in combination, and until we understand the components better, it will be a confusing mix," said Dr. Peter Rowe, a chronic fatigue expert from Johns Hopkins University who has treated Akers.

Confronted with a name for her affliction, Akers continued to react the way an athlete is taught to react. She attempted to overcome chronic fatigue the way she overcame a pulled hamstring muscle. Shake it off. Play through it. No pain, no gain. The hackneyed, testosterone language that equated suffering with weakness. If she just ran more sprints, lifted more weights, surely she would get better. But she did not. Where she once trained two to four hours a day, now she could not ride an exercise bike for more than five minutes on her sickest mornings.

In the summer of 1994, Akers made it through the qualifying tournament for the 1995 Women's World Cup, playing limited minutes, scoring a flurry of goals and even being named most valuable player. But her athletic success hid a personal vacancy. She returned to Seattle and she knew she was at the end of one thing and the beginning of another. She ended her failing marriage, accepted that she would never be the same indestructable athlete again and reaffirmed her lapsed faith in Christianity.

She would treat her sickness not as a theft but as a gift to encourage and inspire. But she would encounter resistance from the same people she wanted to help, other sufferers of chronic fatigue who thought that she could not be as sick as she claimed and remain an elite athlete. They accused her of trivializing the illness by playing soccer. She felt trapped in the in-between, isolated from the healthy, unaccepted by the sick, but she would not consider herself a victim or be soured by bitterness and capitulation.

"There is tremendous grief because in a sense a part of you is dying," Akers wrote in her autobiography, *Standing Fast*. "What you thought you were is stripped away and what you are left with is something, someone, you don't recognize, don't want or don't even like. Some get mad, others sad, some feel frustration, and still others lash out or withdraw into themselves in reaction to the ravages of Chronic Fatigue Immune Dysfunction Syndrome. And then, eventually, you somehow accept it. Not give up or give in, but accept it. You accept the circumstances and the limits the illness imposes on you. You learn to rest, to have peace and still be sick. You never stop fighting and striving for recovery, but learn not to react or run from the pain. You even learn to turn into it. You choose how to respond, choose the attitude you will take. You realize you are not a victim. You choose to live."

She began going to church again and regained a sense of peace and purpose, a belief that God would mold her like spiritual clay, carry her when she could not carry herself. Her illness was a preparation for something bigger, she became convinced. Around the time of the 1999 World Cup, her father would be diagnosed with colon cancer. "If I hadn't been sick, no way would I have been prepared to be present for him during this," she said.

She worried about becoming a "spiritual nut," but, in fact, she was religious without being preachy or imperious. She created Soccer Outreach International as a ministry through sport, and she spoke with a cowboy-surfer patois that lent her public speaking the casual appeal of a lumberjack shirt. Joshua was "this young warrior guy" and Paul was a "studly dude" and God told Moses "you dummy, since you didn't believe and follow through on what I told you I would do for you, you will never enter the promised land." To affirm a statement, she often answered "Rock on," and when she faced a difficult task, it was time to "cowboy up."

Far from being morose, Akers was a funny, mischievous prankster. In college, she and a roommate, Amy Allmann, used to hide in a giant bike box at various places on the campus of Central Florida University. Once, late at night, they followed a teammate from the library, moving a few feet at a time in the box, then running after her as the teammate fled in terror. Later, the player told the whole team, "You guys are going to think this is weird, but one night when I was coming home from the library, this box started chasing me." At a tournament in Portugal with the national team, Akers was hooked up to an IV in her hotel room when she screamed, "Oh, no, an air bubble" in mock panic, sending a terrified Sara Whalen running into the hallway for help.

Her teammates teased her about her forgetfulness, sometimes telling her the wrong starting times for meetings, and they joked about her sleepwalking, and she played along in good fun. In more serious moments, they realized that she was the team's most indispensable player and that, without her, women's soccer in this country might have remained dismissed, invisible.

"She is our everything," Hamm said.

"If Mia is the Queen of soccer, Michelle is the Queen Mother," said Mark Adams, the team doctor.

As hard as it was to imagine in the summer of 1999, Akers' career nearly ended several years before the first Women's World Cup had been played. She played only two matches in 1988, having suffered a concussion from striking her head on the ground during a match in China. She spent several days in a Chinese hospital and, over the ensuing months was told by American soccer officials that she would not be allowed to play with the national team. Apparently they were concerned about medical liability issues, Akers said. Dorrance, the coach, was ordered to cut her from the team but he refused. Akers was cleared by doctors, but still faced resistance from the United States Soccer Federation. She hired a lawyer and threatened to file an injunction. Finally, a soccer official named Art Walls stood up for her in a meeting, Akers said, and she returned to the team.

"There really was no medical reason to keep me off the team," Akers said. "I think it was more a matter of a lot of people knowing a little bit about what happened, a concussion that required hospitalization, and then making a drastic decision out of panic, ignorance or incompetence. I think they thought I would go away after an initial fight and it would be over and done with, but obviously that isn't my style."

Several days before the 1995 Women's World Cup began in Sweden, Akers was told by the federation that she could not play unless she wore shoes manufactured by Nike, which sponsored the national team. Nike shoes lacked support and gave her blisters, she argued. Finally, two hours before the first match, she was allowed to wear Reebok shoes with the markings blacked out. But federation shoe politics were the least of her problems. Seven minutes into the opening match against China, the defender Fan Yunjie attempted to head a ball and struck Akers in the back of the head, a whiplashing knock of skull against skull, and Akers fell to the ground unconscious, twisting her right knee as she collapsed. She returned for the semifinals, against Norway, but her knee was an unreliable hinge, and the Americans lost 1–0, in what is considered the most devastating defeat ever for the women's team. There would be no repeat title, only the unsatisfying consolation of third place.

"I was shocked," said Tiffeny Milbrett, who had replaced the injured Akers at forward during most of the tournament. "I had never seen my teammates cry."

The 1996 Summer Olympics, and a potential rematch with Norway, were only a year away, but Akers began to wonder whether her career was finally done. Her wobbly knee needed months of rehabilitation. The chronic fatigue seemed to come at her like a boxer, jabbing and retreating, punching and covering up. From day to day, she could not predict how she would feel, whether her body would possess reliable stamina to make it through practice or a game. Should she sit out, train as hard as she could, hold something in reserve? There seemed to be not one Michelle Akers but several, one stronger or weaker than the other, faster or slower, quicker thinking or mind fogged, none of them familiar or complete or reliable.

"Each day I have to assess who will show up," she wrote in her journal on April 15, 1996, three months before the Olympics. "What is my role today, healthy or sick? And when my role changes because I cannot fulfill who I want to be, I have to be able to make the transition to the next Michelle Akers. It has to be done positively, quickly and effectively. And then I have to accept the disappointment of not being who I want to be. So who is it today? And to deal with all this stuff alone! To battle back session after session, day after day, is so very tiring. Yesterday, I cried in the shower, exhausted and at the end of myself. Lord, I can't make it through this day. Please give me the strength because I just cannot do it."

As a last resort, she consulted Dr. Paul Cheney, a chronic fatigue syndrome specialist in Charlotte, North Carolina, and she began a regimen called the Elimination Diet. If certain foods were eliminated, bacteria in the body would stop producing harmful toxins, potentially alleviating such symptoms as debilitating fatigue, migraines, neck pain, stomach problems. That was the hope of the diet. It would last 10 weeks and conclude just as the Olympics began. Akers would have to avoid dairy products, beef, pork, veal, gluten, alcohol, sugar and caffeine. She began juicing two pounds of carrots a day, and she lived on a staple of gluten-free bread, peanut butter, rice cakes, cereal and pancake mix, on vitamin supplements, tuna, energy bars, apples, rice milk, chicken, vegetables, salads, baked potatoes. She traveled with a juicer and a can opener and she carried her food in her luggage, believing her choice was a menu of creative deprivation or retirement. As she adhered to the diet, she began to feel better. The clouds lifted in her head. Her stamina and balance and peripheral vision improved. She began to remember herself. The old Michelle appeared in glimpses, like an oak in the X-ray flash of lightning.

Two months before the Olympics, Dr. Rowe diagnosed Akers as suffering from neurally mediated hypotension, or NMH, a blood pressure disorder that seems to affect many chronic-fatigue patients. When most people stand up, their heart rate increases mildly to stimulate the circulation in their bodies and maintain a normal blood pressure. Michelle's heart rate increased dramatically, due to increased pooling of blood in her legs. This eventually led to insufficient flow to the brain, causing fogginess or lightheadeness and a feeling that she was going to faint. Some of the medication available to treat NMH, such as stimulants or beta blockers, were considered performance-enhancing and were banned by the International Olympic Committee. Akers had tried other measures such as antidepressants and birth-control pills, but she said she reacted adversely to both.

Working with Mark Adams, the soccer team physician, Rowe devised a plan of re-hydrating Akers with intravenous solutions after matches, and sometimes the night before. She would also add salt to her diet. Doctors generally warned against high salt intake because persons with high blood pressure were more susceptible to further elevation in pressure and to heart disease and stroke. But for sufferers of NMH, a high salt diet could prove an effective treatment. Salt helped retain fluid in Akers' blood stream, and maintained a steady blood pressure, thus alleviating the feelings of lightheadedness. Many people, including her own teammates, wondered how an athlete could perform at an elite level while suffering from chronic fatigue. Actually, she felt better in motion than standing still. When she was on the move, the muscles in Akers' legs acted as a mechanical pump, pushing blood toward the heart, keeping her from feeling faint, Rowe said. Up to a point. The symptoms of NMH became aggravated by the prolonged standing, heat, stress, and dehydration that come with playing in a soccer match. As she became tired, the symptoms began to appear, the fog in her head, the fuzzy thinking. The big problems came when she stopped running. Her blood began to pool and everything began to go dark. After games, she often needed two or three liters of intravenous fluids to keep her alert and coherent.

"She has the luxury of being able to spend all of her waking hours focusing on her health and soccer and the resources available to her because of her stature in the sport," Rowe said.

Even though she felt better at the Olympics, the heat, the stress of competition, left her feeling the familiar depletion after matches, hooked to an intravenous tube, ice bags piled on her like blankets. A rematch with Norway occurred in the semifinals. In the second half, a foul was whistled on the Norwegians, giving a penalty to the Americans. Akers turned toward the bench with an insistent look and DiCicco pointed to her and she drove a hard ball to her left while the goalkeeper guessed wrong and dived toward empty air. A jumping-jack celebration, both arms over her head, mouth wide in jubilant scream, the leonine hair, the bulge of muscle in her thighs. Tie score at 1–1. The Americans won in overtime on a goal by Shannon MacMillan and then defeated China 2–1 for the gold medal at the University of Georgia. At a postgame party, the only liquid sustenance Akers received came through an intravenous tube. But she had pushed herself to the edge, had turned the weakness of chronic illness into the strength of perseverance.

She had managed to play the full 90 minutes in four of the five Olympic matches. The old feistiness was still there. Two years after the Summer Games, Akers went to Egypt for a religious conference. Muslim fundamentalists spat disapprovingly on the sidewalks in front of her—this was not an activity for a woman, especially a woman in shorts—but she went for her daily jogs anyway, accompanied by a friend. She was invited to play in a soccer match at the conference, and of course she did, but a woman on a soccer field was a freakish thing, and the men tested her, sliding into her legs. One man shoved her and she shoved him back. "I thought I was going to get thrown out of the country," Akers laughed. "I wasn't supposed to be starting fights at a conference."

Could she summon this determination one more time for the 1999 Women's World Cup? Could she "cowboy up" at age 33? Could she will herself through months of excruciating monotony, facing the daily toll, the draining practices, her face the color of Pepto Bismol, the enervating games, the needle-stick and camel packs and filling-station tubes of intravenous fuel, the unknowing, the internal emptiness that could not be filled no matter what she ate or drank or how much she slept, the improvements and setbacks, the rope-a-dope of extreme exhaustion?

A month before the World Cup, Akers slumped on a couch at the Milwaukee Athletic Club, holding a bottle of water, her face tartare pink, her eyes vacant, and she talked about the personal and professional costs of her career, saying, "If I had known what I would have to go through, maybe I would have chosen another path." But then she added, "I'm hanging tough. I'll get the job done."

Physically, she felt stronger than in past years. Her diet was simplified now, dairy products her only restriction. She was allergic to milk and cheese and ice cream, which gave her migraines and made her throw up. A chocolate bar was a guaranteed trip to the emergency room, she said. She maintained a moderate diet while training, 40 percent carbohydrates, 30 percent protein, 30 percent fat, eating every couple of hours, staying hydrated, taking salt and fluids to boost her blood volume and to ballast her low blood pressure. She could better anticipate her "crashes" now, the approach of the migraines and vomiting and sore neck and dehydration, the succumbing that occasionally forced her roommate and former member of the national team, Amanda Cromwell, to take her to the emergency room in Lake Mary, Florida.

"Physically, she was about the same, not any worse than the Olympics," Cromwell said. "Mentally and emotionally, it was more fatiguing. When you deal with something so long and continue to have to fight through it, it takes a toll. She thought about retiring for a while."

I need to stop. I can't call it up anymore. I can't deal with the sacrifices I have to make to be on this team and the disappointment of not being able to play, or play to my full capacity, or to enjoy the process of being with my teammates. I can't do this anymore. Eight years of living on the edge, having to call it up, here we go again, again, again, again, not only on the soccer field, but I have to call it up on the ride home, at the meals, dealing with my teammates, having a life outside of soccer. I'm constantly leaning on that will and it's very tiring.

"This year was the toughest ever," Akers said. "This year was hard as hell."

Accommodations were made. She had a compulsive personality—

"all in or all out," as she puts it—but she had to keep herself from training to the edge every day. She pulled herself out of practice when she felt a crash coming on, did not train on travel days, withdrew from exhibition matches as she became exhausted, roomed alone on the road so she could get sufficient rest, declined every endorsement opportunity and most team appearances, pared her career to essential preparation for the World Cup. On the advice of Colleen Hacker, the team's sports psychologist, Akers got away from soccer when she could by water skiing, horseback riding. At a cost of draining her physical energy, she would try to recharge her emotional battery.

She lived 10 minutes from the team's training camp outside of Orlando, and Cromwell forced her to take naps in the afternoon, and tried to keep her from reclining on the couch in the evening, taking her on walks around the block, anything to keep Michelle awake until 10 or 11 in anticipation of the World Cup night games. "I'm too tired," Akers would say, and Cromwell would answer, "You've got to stay awake, the game won't be ending yet."

Coffee before games and at halftime helped boost her blood pressure. There was a new position, too, defensive midfield, where she did not have to endure the low-post bump and grind of playing forward. After 14 years on the national team, Akers had lost count of the number of surgeries on her knees: 10, 11, 12. She sometimes played with hands wrapped like a boxer's and she had a pugilistic recklessness for leading with her face, which absorbed the banging and fractures and discolorations of jarring contact.

"She leaves her heart and soul on the field, along with a few teeth and bone chips," said co-captain Julie Foudy.

As the opener against Denmark approached at Giants Stadium, Akers knew she would be in trouble. The bus ride, the shimmer of fans, the largest crowd at the stadium than for anyone but the Pope, the confirmation of 78,972 people that women's soccer was a serious endeavor, all that went by in a blur of depletion. Her estrogen level and her blood volume dropped with the onset of her period, and that affected her blood pressure, bringing on dizziness, migraines, numbing fatigue. Even before the game started, she felt exhausted. Her breathing was labored and her game was stripped to the rudiments of effort, tackling and heading the ball and passing it to someone else. Her passes were usually crisp and accurate, but now they rolled out of bounds or were intercepted by the Danes, and Overbeck and Foudy, the captains, kept yelling at her, "Stay in it, stay in it, we need you," and she kept pushing herself but she was breathing hard, panting like a dog. The fatigue kicked up a dust storm in her head. When the game ended, she made it to the locker room and Dr. Mark Adams started the IV treatment, but everything was murky and distant, going black, and she could not see or hear and she was crying and she began screaming, "Doc, I'm going to pass out, I'm going to pass out," and Adams said, "Pass out, Mich, let it go."

She rested in the third game, a victory over North Korea, but a celebrating fan grabbed her arm as she was running off the field. She fell and braced herself with her right arm and her shoulder suffered a slight dislocation. She didn't even play and she still got hurt. *Oh, no, now I've got to go tell my father I got hurt in a high-fiving accident.* For the rest of the tournament, she sat for interviews after practice with a mound of ice strapped under her jersey and leaking down her arm.

She had hoped for early leads and cruise-control floating in the midfield, conserving her energy, but there were nervous mistakes on defense, awkward collisions, fidgety breakdowns, the Americans rolling a ball into their own net in the quarterfinals against Germany. No chance to rest. Her breathing came with gasping insufficiency again against the Germans, and at halftime the Americans were down 2–1 and Tony DiCicco yelled at his players, "If you want your dream to end in the next 45 minutes, keep doing what you're doing."

"Are you coming out, Michelle?" DiCicco asked Akers. "Are you going to be all right?"

"I'm not coming out," she replied.

An injection of inflammatories to relieve the pain in her shoulder, a determination to play to the end of herself in the second half, to find some deep inner resilience. "I vowed to take control of the game by winning every head ball, prevailing in every tackle and playmaking like I never had before and do it until I dropped, literally," she wrote in her journal. "Time to cowboy up."

A redemptive goal by Chastain, a header by Joy Fawcett on a corner kick by Shannon MacMillan. The Americans had the lead to protect, 3–2, but Akers kept running forward, pressing, pressing in her "destroy and deny" mode, taking too many adrenaline risks until Kristine Lilly yelled, "Mich, we are up a goal."

"Yeah, I know, Lil, and your point is what?" Akers said.

"Stay home," Lilly said, cautioning her to hold her position. "Stay home."

She stopped her wild roaming, the Americans won, shook hands with President Clinton in the locker room and flew cross-country the next day from Washington to Palo Alto, California. The semifinal against Brazil would be in 48 hours. The soccer federation chartered a plane for the Americans, every seat first class, and Akers slept and watched *Zorro* the entire trip. "Without that plane, I'm not sure Michelle would have been able to play," DiCicco said.

Both teams seemed tired, lethargic during the semifinal at Stanford Stadium on July 4, except for the enduring Akers and the gymnastic goalkeeping of Briana Scurry. Akers found her breathing shallow again, but the Americans scored first on a header by Cindy Parlow and a fumbled save by the Brazilian goalkeeper, and there would be no need for frantic atonement. Sissi, the Brazilian playmaker, had scored seven goals in Brazil's first four games, but she was frail and wan, with the shaved-head visage of a refugee, and she faded while trying to elude and defend the vigorous Akers. Sissi raked Akers across the face with a cleat and another collision left Akers crumpled and with a goose egg on back of her head. But she seemed to grow more forceful in the second half, and in the 80th minute, she headed a pass backward to a sprinting Mia Hamm, who was pushed down in the penalty box. A penalty kick was awarded to the Americans and Akers slammed the ball into the upper right corner. The Americans were in the World Cup final.

The morning of the final, Akers awakened early as usual and read from her Bible. In the locker room, she would write Joshua 1:9 on the tape around both of her socks, a reference to the verse that says, "I hereby command you; be strong and courageous; do not be frightened or discouraged, for the Lord your God is with you wherever you go." How much would she have to give, she wondered, alone in her hotel room. Thirty minutes? Forty-five? Sixty? Ninety? *I know I'm going to be sick afterward. I know what kind of hole I'm going to be in. Am I going to quit? Will I keep going until I drop?*

It was a relief to get to the final. No more preparation, no more wondering about her stamina, no more weeks of punishing athletic fatigue. She walked onto the field and took in the sweep of the Rose Bowl crowd, the pledge-of-allegiance faces, the Title IX war paint, the hive-buzz of 90,000 voices. Her father held up a sign that said, PIG FARMER NO. 10, a family joke about some forgettable television program. Then the game started and she ran onto a curving pass from Mia Hamm that she could not direct into the goal. *Will that be my only chance?* It would be, but she kept playing ferociously, knocking the wind out of Kate Sobrero and the Chinese attack. She asked Scurry to keep yelling at her, to keep her focused and alert, not to let her drift in the heat and the fatigue.

"Singlehandedly, she owned the midfield," Scurry said. "I've never seen her play defense like that. She was possessed."

As the first half entered its final minute, Gao Hong punted from the Chinese goal and Akers charged from midfield and headed the ball 35 yards back to the Chinese goalkeeper. Pu Wei, the teenage midfielder, ran with Akers but she offered no obstruction. At 18, she was young and thin and not yet possessed of the relentless. Gao held the ball and motioned sharply for her teammates to back up, and she punted again, but Akers stood her ground, shoulders square, feet spread, neck in a shock-absorber brace and she launched her body like the stopper on a pinball machine. Back the ball went. It stayed in the air from head to head and then it was at the feet of Akers, and she volleyed a line drive of a pass just beyond Hamm, who had sprinted behind the Chinese defense. As the referee's whistle blew for halftime, another free kick for China. Akers running and jumping and heading the ball and Zhao Lihong, the Chinese midfielder, recoiling from this muscled determination as if she were trying to protect herself from something falling off a shelf. A whole area of the midfield was being conceded like some feral, marked territory on the savannah.

"The Chinese were intimidated by Michelle in 1991; they thought she was a soccer goddess and I think that carried over," DiCicco said. "She has an aura about her. You know you're not going to stop her. Whether she's competing with her head, foot, knee, she's going to get to the ball first. She'll stick her head in there. She's not going to back down. No one wants to play against a player like that. I'm not going to say they were afraid of her, but who the hell wants to deal with a player with that kind of mentality. She brings an incredible fighting spirit and they conceded a big part of the field. When she walked on the field you could see them looking at her. They didn't want to deal with her."

11

"Coach Us Like Men, Treat Us Like Women"

HALFTIME. Michelle Akers lay on the floor of the stifling American locker room and was covered with icy towels. This was her ritual, coffee to sustain her blood pressure and alertness, a granola bar, a banana, the icy revival of towels. Tiffeny Milbrett took off her jersey to cool off, sat on the floor of the locker room, drank water and Gatorade, grabbed an ice-soaked towel, tried to relax. Having sweated through her uniform, Brandi Chastain changed clothes. Tony DiCicco did not yell as he had at halftime of the quarterfinal match against Germany. The Americans had put a ball into their own goal against the Germans, and had given up a second score in retreat. In the final, the American defense had been inviolable. China made only one serious threat in the first half, the Sun Wen free kick that sailed high. Great defense, DiCicco told his players. Keep pressuring the Chinese backs, stay wide in the zone, funnel everything inside, don't get dragged into the middle of the field. Offensively, he wanted more patience. Possess the ball with short passes, swing them in a pendulum arc, switch the attack from side to side to prevent the swarming double teams and triple teams. Look for Akers, get her the ball in midfield, let her disperse it to her teammates. Nobody could make the long pass as precisely as she could. When her head was clear and her breathing did not come in gasps and the blood was not pooling in her exhausted legs, Akers could feather her passes with such dexterity that her feet reminded DiCicco of a surgeon's hands.

Forty-five minutes from a world championship. He did not think the final would distill itself to penalty kicks. China would make a mistake, a rip would form in a defensive seam and the Americans would seize this tear with Mia Hamm's acceleration or Akers' leg-cannon or Milbrett's pouncing instinct. Of this he was confident. There had been much less certainty in 1995, DiCicco's first World Cup as head coach. He had replaced Anson Dorrance on August 22, 1994, and because the Americans were world champions, he was reluctant to make many changes in personnel or style. Still, DiCicco wanted to make his own imprint and, in retrospect, the players said they felt overtrained as the World Cup approached in Sweden. Burned out, according to Milbrett. Then Akers got hurt and the United States lost in the semifinals to Norway and change was necessary and inevitable.

After the 1995 World Cup, DiCicco scrapped the system of three defenders for a zone with four, weatherproofing against the counterattack. The Americans could no longer succeed simply on speed and talent and cultural bludgeon. The women's game was growing more sophisticated. It was not sufficient any longer for the American women to play soccer the way men played hockey, knocking the puck into the corners and digging it out. He instituted a more practical and refined attack built on short, connecting passes that swiveled the ball from one side of the field to the other. A year later, the United States won the first Olympic tournament for women.

At 51, the mustachioed DiCicco still lived in his hometown of Wethersfield, Connecticut, and he kept his office near the same school where he had listened on the radio in 1960 as Bill Mazeroski of the Pittsburgh Pirates hit the home run that put the New York Yankees out of the World Series. He and his wife, Diane, had four sons, ages 17, 14, 12, and eight, and coaching soccer with the women's team meant he often could not be home on the sidelines with his boys. Before the tournament, DiCicco had privately convinced himself that he would retire at its conclusion, and after the championship match, his eight-year-old son, Nicholas, would say, "Is this your last game, Dad? Are you going to retire?"

In 1999, DiCicco was a comfortable jigsaw fit for the American women. He had been greatly influenced as a boy by his mother, who shot baskets with him in the driveway and swam skillfully and showed by her example that women had the talent to be participants, not just spectators. He still lived a mile or two from his parents. His grandparents were so excited to have a girl after three boys that they named his mother Welcome. "I never had a bias about girls playing sports," DiCicco said. "I was always open to that. I never thought they couldn't play. We had girls in our neighborhood who were great athletes. There was a girl named Susan Tickham who was a really good sandlot baseball player. There was another girl whose parents were friends of our family. Carol Mazarella. They would come over and she was so fast, we couldn't catch her."

An all-American at Springfield College in Massachusetts, DiCicco played professionally for five years in the American Soccer League and made one appearance as goalkeeper with the men's national team in 1973. He joined the women's national team as goalkeeper coach in 1991 and, as head coach, he constructed a side that was tremendously conditioned, selfless, purposeful in attack and psychologically forceful. He also came to the important realization that a successful, veteran team of vigorous personalities would respond best to a coaching style that was inclusive, more democratic than autocratic.

During the six months of training for the World Cup, the American players lived outside of Orlando, Florida, away from their husbands, friends, relatives. Unlike the Chinese players, who remained abroad for 47 consecutive days in one stretch to play tournaments and exhibition matches, DiCicco gave the Americans a week's break every four weeks, believing that "when they disconnect from those relationships, it unsettles them." With a wife and four sons, he also felt disconnected, unsettled, after long periods away. To keep in touch with his players, he met with them individually the day of games. The captains, Carla Overbeck and Julie Foudy, served as onboard sensors, alerting him when tired bodies need refueling and when the tread on the team's cohesiveness was about to suffer a blowout.

"I have great respect for Tony," Overbeck said. "After '95, he changed the entire team, the way we played. We were naïve; our speed and talent overwhelmed people. With Tony, we went from a team that attacked at all costs to possessing the ball and being much smarter. He's a guy you can approach very easily. He listens to his captains; he has the last say and has a very good understanding of what environment we excel in. If we needed the day off, if we were getting burned out, absolutely, he'd give us the day off. If we needed more fitness, he gave us more fitness. He was all about keeping us fresh and excited about the game."

At one point during training camp, Overbeck and Foudy grew concerned about Akers' absence from such functions as the weekly team dinner on Sunday nights. "They came to me and said, 'We feel Michelle is out of the loop,'" DiCicco said. The players understood that she needed to conserve her energy, and that she sometimes had to cut practice short because of fatigue, but they did not want her drifting apart from her teammates, he said.

DiCicco and Mia Hamm had similar personalities. Both had struggled with their confidence as players and both were emotional beneath placid surfaces. On April 11, 1995, during a match between the United States and Italy in Poissy, France, they got into an argument on the field. Tiffany Roberts seemed to be playing with a blank, uncertain look in midfield, and Hamm told DiCicco that he was overcoaching her. Believing Hamm's words to be disrespectful, DiCicco yelled back at her, "Worry about your own game, it needs work." At halftime, Hamm kicked a door in the locker room. DiCicco was equally livid and wanted to bench her before Overbeck intervened.

The next day, before the Americans were to play Canada, DiCicco met with Hamm and told her that she had been right. He was overcoaching Roberts. It was a rough edge in his coaching that he was working to smooth out. Hamm apologized for yelling at him, DiCicco said.

"The look on her face when I said that, I knew I had hit a home run," DiCicco said. "I said, 'It was okay for you to be angry at me; you're probably right.' I showed my vulnerability. I learned something about coaching women, that validating their feelings is a tremendous acknowledgement. In this case her feelings were the right feelings to have. I apologized to her in front of the team and they told me they respected me even more after that."

Later that day, Hamm scored a hat trick in a 5–0 shutout of Canada.

"It was one of the things that really helped our relationship," Hamm said. "I understand how difficult it can be emotionally. I probably would have said something if I was the coach that was very sarcastic and probably would have had even more of a negative effect. The thing I appreciated from him was that we talked about it and it was over. I didn't think any differently of him and he didn't think any differently of me. It's not like he held it over my head or I held it over his head. We both reacted in a way that probably wasn't the best and it was over. We could have sat there and have it change the way we treat each other, or we could forget about it. We chose to forget about it."

It was Hamm who offered the aphorism that DiCicco hung out on his coaching shingle: "Coach us like men, treat us like women." Men and women were far more similar than dissimilar as athletes, DiCicco believed, but he had also concluded that they were motivated differently. That relationships were more important than competition for women. That they were competitive against other teams but were not naturally competitive among themselves. The women on the national team wanted to be challenged like all elite athletes, but they did not want a coach screaming in their faces or singling anyone out for criticism or behaving in a manner that might jeopardize their relationships with each other or with the coaching staff, he said.

"Most of these women would be just as happy with their best friends on the field all around them, versus the best team," DiCicco said. "That may be a little different from guys. You could be best friends, but one would say, 'You can't get it done, so I'd rather have Mick.'"

"Women internalize everything," DiCicco said. "You get them in a room together and you say, 'We have a few players who are not fit,' and they all think you are talking about them. Say the same thing to the guys and they go, 'Yeah, coach is right, I'm the only one fit. Everyone else is dogging it.'"

Just after joining the women's national team as an assistant coach in 1991, he had criticized Kristine Lilly while the team watched video of a loss in China. Several days later, word drifted back to him that Lilly was now blaming herself for the defeat. "In some ways, women are superior human beings," DiCicco said two years later in a speech at a coaching symposium. "They know that relationships are more important than competition. Girls are not wimps. But you can't just go into their face and blow them away like you do with guys or they won't respond."

His encompassing approach to coaching, and his players' reliance on teamwork, reflected a wider change in business management style in the information age. The command-and-control structure of management, typically male and symbolically represented by football, was being replaced by a more pragmatic, consensus-building style, traditionally female and represented by the operation of Internet companies. Everyone becomes a peer. Parts are interchangeable.

"These are characteristics that women bring to the game, whether it's politics, business or their families," said Charles Hess, managing director of Inferential Focus, a New York–based consulting firm that detects societal change. "The man comes in and says, 'This is the way it's supposed to be, this is the rule, my way or the highway,' and women say, 'Where are we trying to get and how are we going to get there?' The characteristic of relationships are important. It's the way Internet companies are managed. Adaptability is the key. They are constantly changing. It's counter to 'my way or the highway.' They are open to cooperating with their competitors, seeking alliances and attempting to make the whole bigger, versus getting a bigger part of the pie. They have their competitors on their boards as a way of mutually learning."

Like Internet companies and minor-league baseball franchises, Hess said, the American soccer team grew immensely popular because it focused on its customers. It catered to fans ostracized from the more entrenched and disengaged professional sports, offering relatively moderate ticket prices, a safe, welcoming environment for the family, encounters with the crowd by shaking hands and signing autographs. The Women's World Cup also occurred during a cultural shift in American values, Hess said. As television ratings for mainstream sporting events plummeted, the Dalai Lama had two books on the best-seller list, poetry readings increased tenfold and museum attendance overtook amusement park attendance, he said. In this view, as Americans reassessed what was important, the traditional attractions of professional sports—scores, ticket sales, standings, statistics, and salaries—became less relevant. And the story lines offered by the women's soccer team—sacrifice, loyalty and teamwork—became more gripping.

DiCicco's belief that women should be coached differently did not suggest a weakness in women as much as it underscored the increasing failure of methods used to coach men at the end of the century. The double-knit explosions of baseball managers who kicked dirt in sandbox apoplexy, the petulant stomping of basketball coaches, the cantilevered bellies of football coaches, unable to control their own personal excesses, much less the excesses of their players. Players had begun to rebel against this screaming, yelling, humiliating behavior, or worse, to emulate it. Latrell Sprewell choked P. J. Carlesimo, his abrasive coach with the Golden State Warriors. Former basketball players at Rutgers University filed suit against Coach Kevin Bannon who allegedly forced them to run sprints in the nude. A judge dismissed the lawsuit, saying athletes are accustomed to communal nudity. Mark Weinstock, a junior varsity basketball coach at Pardeeville High School in Wisconsin, faced a reprimand for making his players participate in a rebounding drill that required them to wear women's panties.

Clem Haskins resigned from the University of Minnesota after reporters uncovered the academic fraud of tutors who wrote term papers for members of his basketball team. Bob Knight of the University of Indiana shot an acquaintance with 16 pellets in a hunting accident and didn't bother to inform authorities; later, he was accused of choking a player. Don Nelson of the Dallas Mavericks got into a bumping match with Karl Malone of the Utah Jazz. John Chaney, the basketball coach at Temple, once threatened to kill John Calipari, the former coach at University of Massachusetts, during a heated postgame news conference. Not only male coaches were accused of mistreating athletes. An athlete named

Kathleen Peay filed a federal lawsuit against Bettina Fletcher, the former women's soccer coach at the University of Oklahoma, claiming she suffered physical and emotional abuse when Fletcher forced players in a hazing ritual to wear adult diapers and to simulate oral sex on a banana. In April 2000, her claims for breach of contract, battery and infliction of emotional distress were dismissed, but the case is still pending.

When coaches ignored irresponsible behavior, could their players be expected to act any less boorishly?

"I've seen men's coaches jump down someone's throat," Brandi Chastain said. "It doesn't work with women, but I don't think it works with men, either."

Of course, not every successful leader of women's teams subscribed to DiCicco's belief in tailoring his coaching to gender differences. Pat Summitt coached the women at the University of Tennessee to six NCAA basketball titles and more than 700 victories with an excitable style that required her to occasionally have her rings reshaped after she pounded them angrily into ovals at courtside.

Coaches should recognize that differences between players are not specific to gender but to the personalities, abilities, perceptions, socialization and life experiences of the people involved, said Jan Smisek, the first woman to receive a top-level soccer coaching license in the United States. Her remarks were made in an essay used in an instruction manual by the National Soccer Coaches Association of America. "Limiting or elevating your expectations of players simply because they are male or female can retard their development," Smisek wrote.

Colleen Hacker, the sports psychologist for the women's national team, said that individual coaching experiences should not be used to formulate gender stereotypes. Sports science indicates that there are far greater differences in psychological makeup between individual female athletes than between men and women, said Hacker, an assistant dean at Pacific Lutheran University.

"In my view, Tony is very skilled at responding to individual differences," Hacker said of DiCicco. By saying that women should be coached differently from men, he "does himself a disservice by reducing it to that," Hacker said. "I think he is much more textured and complex in his thinking."

Hamm said that she did not want a coach yelling at her and chastising her in front of her teammates. "I want someone to feel confident in being able to criticize me, but in a positive way," she said. "I'm going to give you everything I have. I want to know you're going to do the same, even when I'm not playing well. When I'm not playing well, don't abandon me. That's when I need you most. And I need you there to help me figure out how to play better. Not just tell me, 'things are going great.' Guys might have a different approach. I played with guys growing up, and it was pretty much you just told them how to do it. You just walked up and said, 'Get this done.' With girls, I think you have to take a different approach. If a coach comes up and yells at me, he might as well take me out."

Akers said that if a coach yelled at her, she would yell back and become incensed, which would motivate her to play harder. "For the most part, guys are less sensitive; you can yell at a guy and most times his game won't fall apart and he will not leave the field in tears and cry about it in a hotel room for two days," Akers said. "For the most part, if you yell at a girl, she will get all riled up and cry and it will be a big deal. I'm bent more toward the guy side. I'm going to yell back and get ticked off. If anything, I'll play harder. But that's not what motivates me in the long term. If I'm getting yelled at all the time, and not having fun, I'm going to go play for someone else. A coach has to pay attention to each person and see how they are wired."

As the 1995 Women's World Cup approached, DiCicco wanted to bring in a sports psychologist for the American team. As a former goalkeeper, he had come to believe the mental edge made the difference at the elite level of soccer, where teams were relatively evenly matched in skill and tactics. Officials at the United States Soccer Federation, most of them coaches or former coaches, laughed at him, DiCicco said. Two of them got on the floor and pushed their feet together in a spoof of a team bonding experience and told him, "What's all this touchy-feely bullshit?" His request was denied. The reason given was a lack of funding, but a lack of respect for sports psychology was just as evident.

"I made fun of it," said Hank Steinbrecher, then the executive director of the soccer federation. "Team bonding, when I played, was running. If I had a mental problem, I ran. I'm from the old school, but I fully appreciate it's a new day and new age in contemporary sport."

Before the semifinal match against Norway at the 1995 World Cup, DiCicco sensed a lack of confidence, a tentativeness, in some of his players. One of his young players, Tiffany Roberts, came to him and expressed her concern about defending against Ann Kristin Aarones, the six-foot-tall Norwegian forward.

This hesitancy seemed to infect the entire American team as the game played on, DiCicco recalled. Aarones scored the lone goal when she flicked a corner kick in with her head and the United States lost a chance to repeat as World Cup champions. Perhaps a sports psychologist would not have made a difference, DiCicco said, but he also knew that the slightest advantage could separate winning from losing. For the 1996 Summer Olympics, he obtained a grant from the United States Olympic Committee and used it to hire sports psychologist Colleen Hacker. He called her a mental skills coach, convinced that psychological training was as valuable as technical, tactical and physical training.

An ebullient motivator, Hacker possessed a certain legitimacy from also having coached Pacific Lutheran to three collegiate championships among schools belonging to the National Association of Intercollegiate Athletics. In 1988, she became the first woman to coach a collegiate soccer team to a national title.

Some members of the national team admitted to skepticism when she first arrived—"It's a little quirky; who had ever had sports psychology training before?" Tiffeny Milbrett said—but the environment was quickly welcoming. Three of the players, including Carla Overbeck, the captain, had degrees in psychology. Akers' father was a psychologist, and Lauren Gregg, the assistant coach, had a masters degree in consulting psychology.

"I've never seen anyone come in and be accepted so fast by the team," Milbrett said.

Sports psychology was first employed in team sports by the Chicago White Sox in 1932, Hacker said. At the 1988 Summer Olympics in Seoul, South Korea, the USOC had one sports psychologist. That number had grown to 100 by the Atlanta Olympics, Hacker said, and when the 600-plus members of the United States delegation were asked to name the top 10 qualities of success, mental skills ranked in the top five. She believed that she could make a three to five percent difference in an athlete's performance with what she called "the secret of the slight edge." She considered mental-skills training no different from the biomechanical training that swimmers received by having their strokes analyzed in a water flume.

"My goal isn't to fix problem athletes," Hacker said. "My ultimate goal is to take excellence and try to eek out a little more. It's not like we had head cases or problems. We were trying to take world champions and make them better."

The slight edge, Hacker believed, separated first place from second place, hall of famers from all stars, starters from bench players. She collected hundreds of thousands of pages of material written on mental skills training, scouring the literature from Australian cricket to Canadian sailing, underlining relevant passages with green and yellow markers, converting dry, inedible science into entertaining, digestible parables. The difference between golf's top money winners and the next tier of players was less than one stroke per round, Hacker told the American players. The difference between a .250 hitter in baseball and a .333 hitter is less than one hit out of 10. A .333 hitter is a candidate for the Hall of Fame, she told them, while a .250 hitter is just another face on a trading card.

"These players do not view anything other than triumph as an option," Hacker said of the American team. "Losing is not contemplated, it is not addressed, it is not one of the options. In my view they work backward from that. 'In order to make sure we win, I have to do this.' So many teams can tell you what to do. The difference is knowing what to do and doing it. Competition doesn't occur in ideal situations. Games become how you handle distractions, jets flying overhead, lack of training time, no water, penalty kicks. We were committed to planning for the unexpected. So often people point to things after the fact and say, 'This threw us off, we didn't handle this.' What we said was that we were going to plan in advance and anticipate and develop skills before we needed them to handle these types of things."

Spending five days a month with the team before the World Cup, and joining the players for the entire tournament, Hacker held individual meetings, slipped motivational notes under their doors, made motivational audio tapes, had them switch roommates on each trip to avoid cliques, served as a sounding board for personal and professional issues, set up a buffer between players and their families to avoid distractions like tickets and travel arrangements, handed out "permission" cards for the players to use to decline interviews or appearances or parental requests if they felt they were getting swamped.

"Colleen was a lifesaver," said Julie Foudy, the co-captain. "In '95, I really feel a lot of problems we had were mental. Distractions. Physically we felt totally exhausted and beat up. Mentally we had all these stupid issues we shouldn't have been dealing with. Shoe endorsements, contractual stuff. We were having to call our lawyer all the time. It was a nightmare. It would have never have happened if Colleen had been there. With Colleen it's like going to church, it's so cleansing. We had so many issues, parents wanting tickets, other things. She set up a system. Go to Carla's mom or Brandi's mom, never call your daughter and say, 'I need this or that.' The World Cup was our task and everything else was secondary. She made it okay to deal with that. With the 'permission' card, we could say, 'Check back with me after the World Cup. I don't have time to discuss this now.'"

She helped Hamm with her confidence, Akers with diversions from a life of chronic fatigue, Kate Sobrero with her nervousness before the final, Shannon MacMillan with the jarring change from starting in the Olympics to coming off the bench in the World Cup. A year after a nervous match against Norway in the World Cup, a self-assured Tiffany Roberts marked Norway's star midfielder, Hege Riise, into invisibility in the semifinals of the Atlanta Olympics. Hacker stressed the importance of sublimating individual goals for team success and she helped foster trust and dependence and competitive cooperation among the players with team-building exercises. She had players lead their blindfolded partners down a 600-foot cliff, place balloons between their bodies and ferry them without using hands, navigate courses of ropes with a partner while harnessed 20 or 30 feet above the ground.

"This was my biggest fear in life, fear of heights and falling, and, in

'96 we went to a ropes course and I had to bear my soul to the team,"
MacMillan said. "I didn't think I could do it, but my teammates were
there for me and I knew they would be there for me in everything.
When you have to go down to nothing, and rely on someone else and
they are there for you, that builds a bond that is unbreakable."

Before the semifinal match against Brazil, Hacker and the coaching staff jogged in a circle at practice in Palo Alto, California, carrying American flags and chanting Marine chants. "I don't know but
I've been told, USA is going for gold." The day before the final, the
team went to a park several blocks from its hotel in Pasadena, California, and the players chanted and carried flags and jogged to the
stage of a bandshell, where they sipped champagne and sang the
national anthem, not arrogant about victory but confident and prepared to win. As the heat and the pressure mounted in the final, as a
scoreless first half merged into a scoreless second half, and two overtimes passed without a goal, Hacker sensed an unruffled composure
among the American players.

"It wasn't, 'Gee, I hope win, I wonder if we'll win,'" Hacker said.
"We knew."

In September of 1998, with the Americans in the middle of a three-
game tournament on the East Coast, Hacker rolled a portable coat
rack into a team meeting. The coat rack was covered with a bedspread. As she spoke to the players, Hacker walked behind the coat
rack, stood in front of it, tiptoed around it, bumped into it, but did not
mention what it was or why it was there.

The World Cup was nearly a year away, but an issue had arisen
that could have splintered the team. Two months earlier, one of the
national team players, Debbie Keller, had filed a sexual-harassment
suit against Anson Dorrance, her coach at the University of North
Carolina from 1993–1996 and the former coach of the women's
national team. The national collegiate player of the year in 1996,
Keller alleged that Dorrance had used his position as coach to twice
coerce her into meeting alone with him and had made uninvited
romantic advances. She also alleged that on other occasions Dorrance engaged in inappropriate physical contact by placing his hands

on her body and that he would "constantly interrogate" members of the Carolina team about their personal lives and sexual activities.

The lawsuit said the university was "aware that it was rumored that Dorrance had resigned from his position as U.S. Women's National Soccer Coach because he had engaged in a sexual relationship with a player on the women's national team." Hank Steinbrecher, then the executive director of the United States Soccer Federation, said there was "no truth whatsoever," to the rumor. Dorrance denied all the allegations, saying he was "shocked and saddened," and filed for a dismissal of the lawsuit. As of April 2000, his motion was still pending.

Another former North Carolina player, Melissa Jennings, joined the lawsuit, alleging that Dorrance encouraged underage drinking and that he pressured her into making a $400 bank withdrawal to help pay for supplies for the team. Dorrance repaid the money and apologized. In a letter to Jennings' father sent two months before the lawsuit was filed, North Carolina athletic director Richard Baddour said that Dorrance had participated "in group discussions of a jesting or teasing nature with team members" that the university considered "altogether inappropriate." However, the university said it found no evidence of sexual harassment. The school stood by Dorrance and so did Mia Hamm and 100 other Tar Heel players, who signed a letter saying that Dorrance and his coaching staff behaved "at all times appropriately and with absolute professionalism and integrity." The players added that they would "have no reservations about our own daughters someday playing soccer" at North Carolina.

The potential for an explosive unraveling of the national team was real. Of the eventual 20 members of the 1999 World Cup team, Dorrance coached eight of them at North Carolina. He had also coached other stars as Michelle Akers, Julie Foudy and Brandi Chastain to the 1991 World Cup title. The tangle of relationships led to inevitable tension and wrenched allegiances. Tracy Ducar, a reserve goalie on the national team and assistant coach at North Carolina, was a defendant in the lawsuit. She felt betrayed being sued by one of her teammates. Kristine Lilly had played for Dorrance at North Carolina, but she was also dating Keller's brother, Steve. She believed that Keller deserved a chance to make the World Cup team, and she also understood that DiCicco had the right to name his own roster. It never was easy, sorting out this roiling ambivalence, Lilly said.

"Some things weren't handled as nicely as I'd like," Lilly said. "A lot of people spoke out when we decided not to speak out. Basically, someone got hurt. It was Debbie. Whether people agree or disagree, that's their choice. That was hard for me. Whether it was right or wrong, I guess we handled it in a way that was right for winning, for keeping the team together. No one on our team knows the truth. People wouldn't talk about it with me, but you had a feeling. It was never at rest. Whether or not she should be on the team, she should have had a chance. That's the hardest thing. Her chance was taken away. People can't forget, she didn't sue the team, she sued for something she believed in. She lost her whole soccer career because of it."

Faced with serious allegations by a player and the frayed cohesion of a team, Hacker wheeled the coat rack into a team meeting in Richmond, Virginia. The bedspread was a metaphor for Keller's lawsuit. *It's here. You cannot get rid of it. Don't deny it's here. Deal with it. You can deal with it and still do your job.*

Some players were irate over the lawsuit, some were sympathetic, some were neutral, some did not know much, others did not want to know much. Realizing that team reaction was split, and that the potentially divisive lawsuit could not be ignored, Hacker held another meeting and gave the players some guidelines for addressing the suit and each other. With a Ph.D. in exercise and movement science, she specialized in moral development in sport. Just as there were rules for playing soccer, there were rules for moral discourse, Hacker told the players, urging them to separate fact and opinion, to avoid generalizing, to speak openly about concerns and not behind people's backs. She also made herself available for individual counseling.

At an earlier meeting in suburban Boston, DiCicco said that he drew three circles on a blackboard, one representing personal feelings, one representing Team USA and one representing the lawsuit.

"You're going to have personal feelings, and they're going to be real," DiCicco told the players. "The legal entity is going to take its course. But if one circle bleeds into another, we're going to be in trouble. Remember our goal, the team, the World Cup. Let's do everything with our goal in mind." DiCicco also said that he spoke with Carla Overbeck, the team captain. She had played for Dorrance at North Carolina, and the two were close. DiCicco told her that she must put aside her personal feelings. "You're the captain," DiCicco said he told Overbeck. "You have to hold the team together."

Keller spoke up at the meeting and remembered saying, "I want everyone to know I didn't do this to hurt the team or anyone. It was something I had to do. Look at the position I'm in. I have nothing to gain and everything to lose."

Several weeks later, in October of 1998, DiCicco sent Keller a player evaluation in which he said that was concerned "that you have reached close to your full potential." He also said that he was "concerned with some chemistry issues."

"Beyond the current lawsuit, there have been brought to my attention some underlying issues with other players on the team," DiCicco wrote. "It's important that you maintain a positive and solid working relationship with all of the players on the team. You can trust that I am totally committed to maintaining a positive team chemistry."

Used mostly as a reserve, Keller still had been the second-leading scorer for the United States in 1998 with 14 goals. However, when invitations were sent out for the World Cup training camp than began in January of 1999, her name was not on the list. Alleging that she had been punished in retaliation for filing the lawsuit against Dorrance, Keller hired the powerful Washington law firm of Williams and Connolly and took the national team to arbitration, seeking to be reinstated. She alleged in her lawsuit that Dorrance still maintained enough influence with the national soccer federation and with DiCicco, a friend and former coaching assistant, to persuade them to keep her off of the national team roster.

"I think he definitely retaliated," Keller said in an interview of DiCicco. "After I filed, at that team meeting, he was uncomfortable. He barely looked me in the eyes. I had filed a suit against my former college coach. Technically, it had nothing to do with him. But I got the hint he was not supportive of me."

Her mother warned her that if she filed a suit, she would be cut from the national team, Keller said, adding that she believed her scoring ability had at least put her in a position to deserve an invitation to the World Cup training camp.

"Sure, I could have backed down and waited and played in the World Cup, but to me that would have been one ring versus doing what is right," Keller said. "I would never pick a World Cup over that. It would mean nothing to me if I couldn't stand up for what I believe in."

It was Keller's lack of scoring against powerful teams such as China and Norway, not the lawsuit, that kept her off the national team, DiCicco said. Still, he heard the swirl of nasty rumors that he was a marionette for Dorrance, and that he still relied on Dorrance to assign the American lineups. It hurts "when you hear that your morals are being challenged and basically you're being told that you're professionally dishonest," DiCicco said.

"My whole reputation rested on winning the World Cup," DiCicco said. "Was I going to keep a player off who could help us win? That's stupid." Reserve forwards such as Shannon MacMillan and Danielle Fotopoulous were greater challenges to the American defense in daily training than Keller would have been, DiCicco said. "We had other good players," he said. "How long do you keep investing in a player who you don't think is ever going to be a fulltime starter?"

Although the team issued a statement in the fall of 1998, saying it would not speak publicly about Keller's lawsuit, brushfires of disharmony flared in public remarks. Lilly told the *Chicago Tribune* that Keller should be in the World Cup training camp. Cindy Parlow, who had just completed her senior season at North Carolina, accused Keller in *Newsweek* of fabricating the allegations against Dorrance. Tiffany Roberts, also a North Carolina graduate, told *Sports Illustrated* she was "bitter" about the lawsuit.

Players with no connection to North Carolina were also divided on whether Keller should have been brought to camp. "I think anyone with that much productivity, hands down, should have been there in camp," Tiffeny Milbrett said in an interview. "It wouldn't have been a problem in my eyes. The UNC players had their say on it. They're the ones the decision catered to. They're the ones who had to deal with it. Debbie on the team or not on the team wasn't going to affect me. Tony making the decision he did was for the good of those people. If it was based on merit, she deserved to be there. To me, as Tony always said, it's a chemistry thing."

Michelle Akers said that she wrote letters of support to both Keller and Dorrance.

"I can see both sides," Akers said. "Keller is a good player, she scores goals. However, the situation she put herself in was a potential distraction and divider among the team. If I was a coach, it would weigh heavily on my decision to bring her in or not. You're not only looking at soccer skills, but how they get along with the team. As a coach, I would have had a hard time putting her on the team because it might have risked our performance. When Keller decided to go public, and the timing of it, she must have considered that this might play a part in her place on the team."

While the decision not to bring Keller in camp was based on soccer abilities, DiCicco said, he acknowledged that her presence would have left him with a house divided.

"We can guess the impact on the team," he said. "I can guarantee the team wouldn't have been as close as it was. Would that have meant not winning the World Cup? I don't know."

Soon after the American team went into training camp in January of 1999, Brandi Chastain and Mia Hamm had what Chastain described as an emotional meeting to sort out their feelings on the issue. They would be rooming together for five months, and they had feelings about Dorrance that were polar opposites. Chastain said she had written Dorrance a letter calling him a coward for not telling her face-to-face why she had not been invited to a training camp in 1994. Eventually, she was left off the 1995 World Cup team.

"Anson is the kind of person who can scare people and make them feel very uncomfortable and do it intentionally," Chastain said. "I was very uncomfortable with him."

Hamm's experience with Dorrance had been one of familial closeness. He had served for a while as Hamm's legal guardian at North Carolina, while her parents lived out of the country. She continued to serve as an assistant coach with the Tar Heels. She wrote in her autobiography that, apart from her late brother Garrett, "Anson Dorrance has probably been the most influential person in my life."

The meeting lasted about 45 minutes over ice cream at the house the two players were sharing in suburban Orlando, Florida, Chastain said.

"We knew we had to rely on each other," Chastain said. "Why put a wedge between relationships when you know in the long run those are people you're going to have to rely on? We're old enough, mature enough to know that. There was no conclusion, it was just talk, how she was feeling, where she was coming from, where I was coming from."

Sitting in her car in front of Carmichael Auditorium on the North Carolina campus several months after the World Cup, Hamm would talk at length for the first time about the lawsuit, her support of Dorrance, the national team's separation of personal feeling and professional responsibility.

"It wasn't a judgment or an indictment on anyone, no matter what they felt like," Hamm said of Keller and Jennings. "I didn't go, 'Oh, they're just not good people.' Everyone has a right to their own opinion, and you have to respect that people had different relationships with the parties involved. My experience here was wonderful and maybe someone else is going to have a different opinion and that's okay."

The open, respectful way that the players dealt with the Keller lawsuit allowed the national team to keep its focus on the World Cup instead of dividing itself internally, Hamm said.

"The thing about this team that is so strong and is one of things that helps us through times like that, is that we all have tremendous respect for each other," Hamm said. "I understood that there are certain people that don't feel the way I feel. But they aren't going to hold that against me, and I'm not going to hold that against them. We were all very open about it. We talked about it, and said, 'If you have feelings, that's understandable, but the thing we can't do is, we cannot let it divide us. We can't start forming these little factions of for and against because it will destroy us.' You just have to be adult about it and have respect for each other and know that, in real life, people are going to have a difference of opinion."

This ability to separate the personal from the professional, to keep the external distraction of the Keller lawsuit from detonating an internal fissioning, may have been the single most important accomplishment of the team off the soccer field. Kate Sobrero said that, while she could imagine Overbeck's feelings on the subject, that she never once heard the team captain express her point of view.

Still, as the American coaching staff prepared for arbitration hearings, the outward calm on the team was buffeted by inner tension. This was late April of 1999. The World Cup was less than two months away. What happened if the arbitrators placed Keller back in training camp? Who would be cut? Whom would Keller room with? Would her teammates talk to her, pass her the ball? Would DiCicco keep his job?

The tension finally spilled into the open as the Americans prepared for an exhibition match against Japan on May 2 in Atlanta. At a practice where coaches and staff members were scrimmaging against players, DiCicco blew up at MacMillan, a player with tremendous talent who, in his eyes, did not always play with enough heart. Players and staff members said he appeared stressed, near tears.

"Are you going to start scoring?" DiCicco challenged MacMillan. "Are you going to start picking up your game? Or are you just going to keep it in neutral? That's how you're going to make the team?"

Overbeck intervened, and to MacMillan's credit, she did not respond to his demeaning outburst, DiCicco said. "It was mean stuff, it hurt her," he said. On the team bus, he apologized. "I was wrong," he said. "I had no right to say that."

"I don't think we knew half of what he was going through," MacMillan said. "He apologized and I left it at that. Of course it left a scar, but you learn and grow from something like that."

A week later, DiCicco spent several days testifying before a panel of the American Arbitration Association in Chicago, where Keller lives. Then, on May 10, with the World Cup only six weeks away, the arbitrators made their ruling. Keller's attempt to rejoin the team was rejected. DiCicco could now name his roster. A potentially corrosive situation had been handled with minimal damage to the team, if not to Keller's career. Foudy gave DiCicco a necktie ornamented with the scales of justice. Not guilty, it said.

During the arbitration hearing, Keller said that she had been made to feel "like I couldn't tie my shoes." She later flew to Denmark, where she played professionally, scored the goal that put her team in the league championship match, then scored again as Fortuna Hjorring won the Danish title. She returned home before the World Cup began and attended the second United States match, against Nigeria, at Soldier Field.

"It was fun to watch them play, but it sucked," Keller said. "I didn't turn the TV on again until the final. Not that I didn't want them to win or do well. It's just not easy to watch when you didn't get a chance to try out."

She did not hold it against her former teammates for not speaking more forcefully in her favor, Keller said. "Looking at my example, if they spoke up, for all they knew they would have been cut," she said. "By no means is it any of their fault."

On the afternoon of the final, Keller would watch the match, and at its conclusion, she would go for an eight-mile run, the emotions pooling like sweat in the loneliness of having been on the outside, looking in. "You always want your country to win, but it was frustrating, disappointing, upsetting, aggravating, all combined into one," she said. "Sometimes when you're upset you tend to push a little harder on your run. I could push that day. Then I was fine. There's was nothing I could do. It was my way of letting go."

12

"My Team Needs Me"

As halftime neared its end, and the Americans left the locker room, Michelle Akers sat for a moment in the tunnel leading to the field. Sitting with her knees up to her chest, or leaning forward with her hands on her knees, was a useful way to raise her blood pressure and keep an adequate flow of blood to her brain. "I don't know if I'm going to make it," she said to Dr. Mark Adams, one of the team physicians. "Mich, you'll make it," he replied. "You're doing great. You'll be okay."

The second half began, the whole game a labor now. A chippy assertion, both teams probing for a shudder in resolve, a blinking of will. Mia Hamm down in a fetal crumpling from a collision with Bai Jie, the Chinese defender. If Bai was known as the Little Assassin to the Americans, in China she was hailed as Hero of Mine Clearance. Her mother had forbidden her to play soccer during her adolescent years and became upset when her daughter came home late and dirty after school, according to Chinese reporters. Persistent, her mother went to Bai's school in Hebei Province to bring her daughter home each day, but Bai snuck out the back door or climbed a wall to play her favorite game. Now, her mother was her biggest fan.

Akers and Jin Yan, the lithe Chinese forward, smacked together like clapped erasers. Sun Wen stole a pass at midfield, but Akers and Hamm forced her laterally, turning her until her back was to the goal, the way a roper turns a steer. Kristine Lilly tucked a pass into the penalty box, and Wang Liping kicked it over the Chinese bench to prevent an opening for Julie Foudy. A corner kick for the Americans, Tiffeny Milbrett squeezing out room among the photographers and lifting a pass toward Akers, 10 yards out, two defenders leaping, Akers jumping higher, getting her head on the ball, but the shot floating wide of the crossbar. Shannon MacMillan wearing her yellow vest on the sideline, jogging, preparing to enter as the first substitute.

This is when people dig in. This is where the battle begins. It comes down to guts, who wants it more.

Six minutes into the second half, Joy Fawcett feathered a pass from midfield to Cindy Parlow racing into the penalty box. Only Wen Lirong to beat in the Chinese defense. Brilliant instinct by Parlow, the ball bouncing to the right of Wen and Parlow cutting left, her long strides carrying her in a threatening rush. Her hand raking Wen's ponytail, a lock of arms for balance and leverage, the girls with the painted star faces on their feet, teenagers standing in their sports bras with U-S-A on their billboard bellies, a flash of hope for the deadlock broken. The hope turning to groans when Wen made a frantic recovery and kicked the ball into the first row of end zone seats.

Parlow had remained in the starting lineup despite a clamoring in the media for MacMillan. At 5-foot-11, Parlow was the tallest of the American players. Her legs gathered slowly into a sprint, but she had poached a goal against Brazil in the semifinals, and Tony DiCicco considered her to be a more reliable defender, passer and heading presence than MacMillan. The youngest of the American starters, Parlow also possessed a callow toughness. Three minutes from halftime, she had lumbered after a long pass toward the Chinese goal, sliding for the ball, forcing the defender Fan Yunjie into an evasive hopscotch, then shouldering Fan to the ground with a jostling lunge.

Born in Memphis, Tennessee, Parlow sometimes registered in team hotels as Elvis. She came to soccer as soon as she could stand up. Her oldest brother would put a ball at her feet as she learned to walk, and each step became an incipient dribble. "I'd take step and fall," Parlow said. "Sometimes, I'd hit my head on the ball and fall backward and my brother would go, 'No cry, no cry,'" Parlow said. "He didn't want me growing up to be a girly-girl." The only girl among three boys, she tried gymnastics and ballet, but her ballet career ended when her mother told her the crushing news that no one wore a tutu with cleats.

"I think that's why I dropped out of ballet, because I couldn't wear my cleats," Parlow said.

She learned to strike the ball with her head because she was tall and because it was the thing to do among the boys in the neighborhood. At the University of North Carolina, Parlow was named the collegiate player of the year in 1997 and 1998, and she excelled at heading the ball into the net, but she became unnerved when studies appeared about the potentially concussive effects of her specialty. Evidence in recent studies has suggested that heading a soccer ball can cause the symptoms of concussion—blurred vision, double vision, headaches, nausea—and can affect such functions as memory and planning. When a researcher showed up on campus to conduct a test with the Carolina women's team, Parlow refused to participate.

"It's scary; I don't want to know," Parlow said. "This is what I want to do for my career. I want to be a professional soccer player, and heading is part of that. I told the researcher I'd rather be ignorant than know the facts."

She scored twice in the World Cup on headers, torpedoing a shot against Nigeria and plunking a bobbled save by the Brazilian goalie in the semifinals. In the final, Parlow was the only American to threaten China in the penalty box. She had heard the calls for MacMillan to start, but she handled the controversy with a professional detachment.

"It was out of my hands; there was nothing I could do about it," Parlow said. "I had all the confidence in Tony. He would make the right decision. If Shannon got the call, I had confidence that she would play great. I just had to be prepared, one way or the other. Whenever there is a huge event, everyone is going to question every call the referee makes or the coach makes. That comes with the territory. You just have to deal with it and move on."

The morning of the final, Parlow retreated into what she called her own personal cave. She did not listen to motivational tapes, she did not dance around with her teammates. "I just tuned into myself and what I needed to do," she said. Rarely did she get nervous. But as the team prepared to walk onto the field, she felt tense and fidgety. Kristine Lilly put a hand on her shoulder. "It was like, 'This is what we dreamed about; it's time to express ourselves,'" Parlow said. "As soon as she did that, any nervousness in my body left and I felt fine."

Until she left the game early in the second half. Then an odd sense of apprehension returned.

"I no longer had any control, I couldn't affect the game anymore," she said. "Immediately, I got nervous."

The 57th minute now, DiCicco telling MacMillan, "You can make a difference. You deserve this. Give us a lift. Play your game." Sending her in for Parlow, a hand-slap between players at the sideline, MacMillan's name being announced over the public address system, a loud welcoming for fresh legs and a career resurrected. The decision to save her for the second half was a sound one. Her appearance always seemed to increase the American pulse rate, to bring a collective shiver of expectancy. MacMillan possessed a hard shot that knuckled and dipped and bent in wicked elusiveness. "Like a moving pea," said Briana Scurry, the American goalkeeper. In a first-round match against North Korea, MacMillan collected two assists and short-hopped a ball into the goal, and in the quarterfinals against Germany, she drove a corner kick that Joy Fawcett redirected for the winning goal. When DiCicco had called on her for the final, she wondered "Am I ready to go in?" But as she ran onto the field, the applause seemed deafening. *Oh my God, that was for me. I've proven myself. This is my chance.*

Two minutes later, China made its counter move, replacing its young midfielder, Pu Wei, with the searing forward Zhang Ouying. A former track and field sprinter, Zhang had burst past Overbeck to score the winning goal in an exhibition victory over the Americans three months earlier at Giants Stadium in East Rutherford, New Jersey. "We had to make sure she didn't get behind us," Overbeck said. "I knew I wasn't going to catch her in a footrace."

Sun Wen would now withdraw into midfield. Perhaps she could reestablish broken links in the Chinese attack. Just as Zhang entered the match, an adrenaline scare for the Americans. Sun circled on a corner kick and slashed a header across the goal mouth, Scurry coming off her line, the shot carving behind her, or over her head, but just wide of the far goal post. Sun grabbed her head with her hands, the agony of failure's slight geometry.

The whole game speeded up now, urgent, the merciless sun overhead, the field without shadows, the spectators with tiny flags stuck in their hair like birthday candles. Jin Yan in a scoring rush, Chastain heading the ball back to a charging Scurry. Zhang sprinting down the left wing, Kate Sobrero in calm pursuit, punching the ball out of bounds. A long pass in the middle for Jin and Chastain again flicking the ball out of immediate danger. Fawcett clearing the ball, unintentionally kicking it into the face of Liu Ailing, the Chinese playmaker. A rocketing pass from two or three yards away, Liu's head in a Zapruder jerk, the midfielder grabbing her face, blinking, staying on her feet in stoic recovery. Zhang charging again, Sobrero poking the ball from harm. The Americans stuck in midfield, China maintaining its defensive precision, moving like a school of fish in the unity of escape.

"As far as teamwork, the Chinese are better," Bai Jie said. "As far as individual skills, the Americans are better."

Finally, in the 66th minute, an opening. Mia Hamm chested a ball at midfield and played a left-footed pass on the ground to MacMillan's churning, untired legs. MacMillan and Wang Liping in a race now, a piston-pump of elbows and knees, the ball rolling ahead, drawing out their speed, seeming to pull them along on some invisible string. If MacMillan reached the ball first, she would have an unimpeded dash to the Chinese goal, but Wang cleverly maintained her position on the inside, taking a more direct sprint, trapping MacMillan on her outside shoulder. Gao Hong ran forward from the Chinese goal and Wang pushed the ball to her feet. By the time

MacMillan arrived in the penalty area, Gao had already diverted the ball to a third teammate, an artful triangulation of avoidance. One more step and MacMillan would have been free, one more step on a whole afternoon of one more steps.

"This was the best defensive game China ever played against us," DiCicco said.

Back in China, Coach Ma Yuanan would receive much criticism because his outside backs, Wang Liping and Bai Jie, did not go forward the way they had in previous matches, creating an advantage in numbers of Chinese attackers over American defenders. This reluctance was not his idea, Ma said. "I planned for more forward movement, but it was hot and they were very tired and they couldn't move forward and retreat quickly," he said.

Wang, whose hair dropped below her shoulders and who wore a look of melancholy that belied her friendly ease, said that, "perhaps because the Americans were very strong, we were a bit more cautious." But it was her sound caution that prevented a breakaway goal by MacMillan in the 66th minute. And, Wang noted, the Chinese were not the only reticent players.

"I think Mia was not as aggressive as she was before," Wang said. "I felt very confident."

As she did before every game, MacMillan checked the roster to see if her name was in the starting lineup. Again it was not, and she felt a small disappointment. The media had been calling for DiCicco to play her from the beginning, but she had approached him and said, "I want to play, but just so you know, I support whatever you do." Instead of becoming bitter, MacMillan had become one of the team's most vocal cheerleaders, high-fiving the starters in the locker room before games, chest-bumping them, waiting her turn without accusation. Colleen Hacker, the team's sports psychologist, told MacMillan that she played a vital role off the bench. Hacker had provided the words on an audiotape of motivational phrases, which MacMillan used in imagery exercises to envision her success.

"My team needs me."

"I'm going to run my defender into the ground."

"I'm going to make them sub her out."

"I'm going to hit my shot when I feel it."

"I have a great shot."

The reporters and television commentators had been compliment-
ing MacMillan for accepting her role as a reserve, but they had it wrong.
She had never accepted it. She had gone into every practice and every
game trying to prove she was a starter. There was always a part of her,
deep down, that kept saying, "I want a chance to start, I think I deserve
it." But she possessed a restraint that was rare in the vanity of sports. She
wanted to start, but she did not publicly complain about not starting.
The Americans had succeeded as a team, and she would not fracture
the unanimity of the team.

"It was definitely hard not starting," MacMillan said, "But if you look
at the total perspective, this is the best team in the world and I'm in the
top 20 in the world. I think one of the reasons this team was so
embraced was because it was refreshing. It wasn't like I got invited to the
all-star game and said, 'I'm not starting so I'm not going.' It would have
been so easy to turn it around in the press and be negative. But it wasn't
about money, it wasn't about playing time. It was about 20 of us who
were chasing their dreams."

She and DiCicco had a tangled relationship of contention and
respect. At the University of Portland, MacMillan had been named
national player of the year in the fall of 1995. At year's end, however,
DiCicco posted his list of players invited to training camp for the
1996 Summer Olympics and MacMillan was not on it. "Devastating," she said. "The lowest point of my career." She returned to the
University of Portland, thinking her soccer career might be over. *How
could this happen? What am I going to do now?* She sat in the office of
Coach Clive Charles, crying, cursing.

"They don't know what the hell they're doing," she said of DiCicco
and his staff.

"Are you finished?" Charles asked her.

"What do you mean, am I finished?"

"I'll give you 24 hours to mope, then get your butt back on the
field," he said. "You'll get another chance. You need to keep proving
it until they can't ignore you."

Driving home, she realized that Charles was right.

"I belong on that team," MacMillan told herself. "I know I can play with them."

Several weeks later, the chance came. A group of American players had gone on strike when the soccer federation proposed offering Olympic bonuses only for a gold medal. The team was headed for a tournament in Brazil in January of 1996 and DiCicco needed replacement players. Would she play midfield? Sure, she said, she'd play goalkeeper just to get on the team. Six months later, MacMillan led the Americans with three goals at the Atlanta Olympics and scored the game-winner in overtime of the semifinals against Norway, breaking free on a long diagonal run and tapping in a perfect pass from Julie Foudy.

"I made a mistake with Shannon," DiCicco said in retrospect.

Another period of doubt began in May of 1997. MacMillan chipped a piece of bone off the back of her kneecap in a match against England, and through the next year played without any real fitness or confidence. In all of 1998, she started 14 games and scored one goal, two fewer than she had scored in five Olympic matches. DiCicco felt she had lost some of her hardness, that she stayed on the ground too long when she went down, that she needed to play more determined, less restrained. They had words at a tournament in Portugal three months before the World Cup.

"I love Shannon MacMillan; she's the kind of player you want to hug," DiCicco said. "We had some ups and downs, some hard discussions. I told her she needed to play with more reckless abandon, more heart. Unless you're injured, you've got to get up and play. Part of that was confidence. My goal was to get Shannon back to her Olympic form, and I think we saw that in the World Cup."

Sixteen minutes remaining in regulation. Akers charged the penalty area on a free kick by Hamm, Gao rushed out of the Chinese goal and they clipped like stunt planes at an air show. Akers windmilled in an awkward somersault, and Gao dropped to the ground, grabbing her right shin. A yellow card warning for Akers. Watch the fouls, DiCicco told her as she came to the sideline for a drink of water. One more yellow card and she would be forced out of the game. Akers listening as she ran back on the field but the darkness beginning in her head. Her face was flushed, her breathing shallow. A diminishing, an emptiness inside. Her vision had begun to narrow, her thoughts had grown messy. She could not think ahead, there was no planning, only the rudimentary present. Play defense. Get the ball. Pass it to a team-mate. The staticky connection between her head and her body, the hissing, crumpled commands and fuzzy, broken responses.

"It feels like a tornado is going on in my mind," Akers said. "A rush inside. I'm trying to hold off this rush of black. You can't focus. You can't hardly think. Your ears are closing up. You can't hear, you're dizzy, you can't catch your breath, you're exhausted. I kind of become a blunt instrument after a while. It's your core. There's just nothing there, like you haven't eaten for a week. You've spent everything. Just an internal emptiness. I battle the tunnel. I've got this tunnel in my head and it's a battle to keep it from closing in on me. I just try to make it to the end without costing my team or falling down."

This is damn tough. I have nothing left, I am dying here, I want to quit, but I don't want to stop short and miss all the cool stuff God has promised to do through me if I just have the courage to keep putting one foot in front of the other. I must carry this through to the end. I cannot quit because it hurts. The deeper I must dig, the harder the quest, the greater the reward, the more I am making my life count. I can go one more minute, and one more minute, and one more minute. This is my last World Cup and it will be over soon enough and I want that sat-isfaction of knowing I spent absolutely everything and went as far as my body and mind could carry me. My team has invested everything and now I refuse to stop short. Suck it up, keep going, track my girl wherever she goes, stuff her, tackle her, dominate her, stop her, smother her with my will. She knows I will never give up. I will always be there and I will do whatever it takes to compete and win.

Fifteen more minutes. DiCicco screaming from the bench. Fifteen more minutes. A frenzied closure. The 80th minute, MacMillan on the left wing, slicing inside through three defenders, a collision, an acrobatic sprawl, a pass to Kristine Lilly at the edge of the penalty box, a trip by Liu Ailing, the Chinese playmaker. A yellow card warning. Another free kick for the Americans.

Mia Hamm, Akers, MacMillan standing around the ball, keeping China uncertain as it set up its wall 10 yards away, the shuffling leg-manacle movement of the wall, Gao shouldering the near post, lining up the presumed flight path, squinting with one eye as if looking down the sight of a rifle.

"I want this one," MacMillan told Hamm.

Hamm had always told her, "If you feel it, call me off."

"Okay," she told MacMillan.

Whoa. MacMillan had surprised herself with this assertiveness. *This is the World Cup final and I just called Mia Hamm off.*

The day before the final, Hacker had placed a piece of paper on the back of each player. From teammate to teammate the players went, scribbling admiring messages. "You amaze me how you come off the bench and make an impact every time," Julie Foudy wrote on MacMillan's back. MacMillan wrote her most personal message on the back of Joy Fawcett. "I wouldn't be here without you," it said.

In Fawcett, she had found a repaired connection to family and had discovered a sense of belonging on the team. MacMillan was estranged from her own parents. They gave little support to her soccer, she said, attending few of her matches. MacMillan said she ran away from home as a high school junior in Escondido, California, and spent soccer weekends at the home of a friend. Others helped pay her fees for club soccer, she said, and she left Escondido on a bus for the University of Portland in August of 1992 with $70 in her purse and a determination not to come home. Her parents have declined to speak to reporters about the estrangement. The final break with her parents came at Christmas after the 1996 Atlanta Olympics. They had not attended the Summer Games, MacMillan said, saying they could not afford the trip. But that left her as the only American player without family support. She said she had grown weary of making excuses to her teammates for family absences. Since that time, MacMillan said she had not seen or spoken to her mother or father.

"Sometimes, so much of dealing with something is realizing it's never going to change," said Tiffeny Milbrett, MacMillan's teammate on the national team and her college roommate at Portland. "I tried to be there for her, tried to give her some advice and a listening ear.

She was only going to come to that conclusion in her own time. She did and it set her free. She's a lighter, freer person. She's come to accept her situation."

While training for the World Cup, MacMillan lived with Fawcett and her two daughters, Katelyn, who was five, and Carli, who was two. She had become particularly close to Katie during training for the Olympics, sometimes baby-sitting for Fawcett and her husband, Walter. On a personal level, MacMillan said, Fawcett had a stable family life that "renewed my faith" and encouraged her "to want to have my own kids and break the cycle" of estrangement. On a professional level, Fawcett provided inspiration by twice resuming her soccer career at an extraordinary level after having children, by providing reassurance when MacMillan's confidence began to ebb and by providing an honest assessment of MacMillan's performance in daily training.

"I could come home and relax, but she had two full-time jobs, soccer player and mother," MacMillan said. "It was really refreshing to see someone out there, chasing a dream, getting better after she had each kid. She really wanted this. If I had a bad day, I'd be like, 'I didn't have any confidence out there,' and she'd say, 'Mac, there are some days when I don't either. I struggle with the same things you do.' She helped me believe in myself again."

Before the final, MacMillan and Fawcett went through their warm-up ritual, running back and forth across the field twice with MacMillan in the role of motivational coach. "Whaddya say, whaddya say, whaddya say?" she told Fawcett. "You're one of the best defenders in the world. I'd have you behind me any day. Go out there and own that side." Fawcett had been the cheerleader in the previous months.

"It's been tough for Tony and I," MacMillan said of DiCicco. "We went through that, 'Should she be starting or not?' We can smile at the end of the day. I know at the beginning of the year I wasn't playing my best soccer. I wasn't having fun. By the time the World Cup came around, I was. I owe it all to Joy. She was my sounding board. 'How can he do this? I don't understand,' I'd tell her and she'd say, 'You belong out there, just keep doing it.' Or she'd straight out tell me, 'You sucked today, get over it and go back out tomorrow.' I could talk to her about anything and she was honest."

At 31, Fawcett was as unassuming as the peanut butter and jelly sandwiches she ate before every game. But she played with a tough reliability at right back, never hurt, always in charge of her flank with a style so fluid that it appeared effortless. Fawcett had played every minute of every game in the 1995 World Cup, the 1996 Summer Olympics and the 1999 World Cup, moving with a courtly glide, playing defense with an elegant tuxedoed thievery. Comparing Fawcett to Akers, DiCicco said, "Joy picks your pocket and Akers hits you so everything falls out of your pocket."

It was Fawcett who assisted on the winning goal by Tiffeny Milbrett against China in the gold-medal game of the 1996 Olympics, making a long run, shielded from her teammate, hearing Milbrett's screaming for the ball, passing as much to the voice as the person. And it was Fawcett who diverted MacMillan's corner kick for the winning goal in the World Cup quarterfinals against Germany. In the 56th minute of the final, she had trapped a stolen pass with her left foot, passed the ball to Parlow and had kept scudding forward with the easy skim of cloud shadow. The play seemed to wither and die, but the ball rolled free outside the penalty area and Fawcett ran onto it, hooking a pass to the far goal post, forcing China to head it out of bounds, giving the Americans a corner kick. Hamm set her kick on top of the crossbar and Brandi Chastain chipped it back across the goal, and many players began a heads-down walk upfield, believing the ball was out of bounds. But the play was still alive and Hamm did an alert tightrope walk along the end line, slicing a shot with her left foot that approached the Chinese goalkeeper with a dangerous flutter. These menacing excursions had been the expected threat of Bai Jie, China's left outside back, who often created two-on-one fastbreaks on Fawcett's wing in previous matches. But Hamm had smothered Bai, forcing her inward, and it was Fawcett who was freed for the stiletto pierce into China's defense.

"They didn't make the runs; we were all shocked," Fawcett said. "I don't think they had one of their best games. They were so focused on defense, it took a lot away from their offense. When our forwards play great, pressuring defense, it's easier on our backs. It nullified that attack for them."

A native of Huntington Beach, California, Fawcett emerged from a family where four of the nine children earned athletic scholarships. Her brother, Eric, played two games for the men's national team in 1986. After an all-American career at California-Berkeley, Fawcett coached the UCLA women's team for five years, driving four hours roundtrip to work. When she became pregnant with her first daughter, Katey, she continued to play soccer until the fourth month of her pregnancy. "We did a legends tour, indoor, against men," Fawcett said. "Guys were like, 'No, we're not coming on the field with a pregnant woman.'" Training with suggestions from a magazine that a teammate sent her, Fawcett ran until her seventh month, then worked out on stair-climbing equipment until Katey was born. Three weeks later, she was scrimmaging with the national team. She had gone to visit the team at a training camp, she said, when Anson Dorrance, the coach, suggested that she jump into the lineup.

"Being chicken, I said okay," Fawcett said. "I didn't want to ever lose my spot. At that time you're nervous anyway about getting your spot back."

When her youngest daughter, Carli, was born in 1997, Fawcett was simultaneously coaching UCLA and a youth club team, and playing on the women's national team. "Breast-feeding at halftime, or on the sideline, that can get interesting," she said. "It's like, 'I'll be back in a minute.'" At UCLA, Fawcett used to set up cones in the parking lot and run conditioning sprints after her own team practiced, Foudy said. Now, when the national team was not together, Fawcett put her daughters to bed and went running at 9 at night.

Even with a nanny, it had not been easy for her family during the six months of World Cup training, Fawcett and her daughters on one coast, her husband, Walter, on the other, weeks between visits. He usually put the kids to bed at night, and when they wouldn't listen to their mother, Joy had to call back to California so her daughters could hear their father's voice. And she didn't know what would happen during the buildup for the 2000 Summer Olympics. Katey would be in kindergarten. It would be even more difficult to juggle training camp with her daughter in school.

"In the beginning, I questioned whether this was good for the kids," Fawcett said. "I talked to the other moms and their kids eat at 8 and sleep at 12, and it's all so regular. My kids eat when they can, sleep in the stroller. But they're adaptable. I think it's good. They get to see the world and it allows me to play soccer. Having kids puts things in perspective. You come home from a bad practice and see those faces smiling at you, and you realize the game is just a game."

Living with Fawcett, seeing firsthand her acetylene determination, had fired her own resolve, MacMillan said. "You see how badly she wants it, you see her doing it and you say, 'I'm going to do it too,'" she said.

This was her chance now, in the 80th minute, a free kick for the Americans at the edge of the penalty area, a green light from Hamm to take the kick herself. MacMillan would bend a hard shot toward Gao, the flamboyant Chinese goalkeeper who sometimes ornamented her saves with the exaggerated motions of a juggler. And like a juggler, she sometimes dropped the ball. MacMillan would drive the ball and maybe Gao would bobble it, and the shot would ricochet into the net or the rebound would deflect to a teammate. Gao stomped her foot at her teammates, calling another player into the wall, and she slid off the near post to the middle of the goal line. MacMillan struck the ball confidently, but she slipped on the slick grass and fell and the shot lost its elusive trajectory. The ball bit the air and curved sharply inward, and Gao did not have to move a step to cradle the shot. Walking back on defense, MacMillan shook her head. A few feet wider. Just a few feet.

"I slipped when I hit it and I think it threw me off," she said.

Zhang, the Chinese sprinter, threw a counterpunch, trying to outrun the tired American legs, but Kate Sobrero and Overbeck sandwiched her in the penalty box, Sobrero arching backward like someone in a wind tunnel but holding her position, kicking the ball away and muscling Zhang to the ground. Zhang got to her feet and nudged Overbeck from behind. Overbeck put a dismissive hand in Zhang's face. *Don't start with me.* The 90th minute, Zhang vapor-trailing past Overbeck on the left wing, cutting inside of Sobrero at the top of the penalty area, pushing the ball in front, trying to unload a shot, needing only slight clearance for the unholstering, but Chastain rushing in with a sliding tackle and Zhang doing a futile Superman dive, the ball stripped from her feet, no shot, no goal, no shrill whistle of rebuke from the referee.

Two minutes of extra time signaled by the official on the sideline. Akers fading now, nothing left, the dark tunnel closing in. Already exhausted, she stopped a pounding shot from Bai Jie with the side of her head. The ball sailed out of bounds. Corner kick for the Chinese. Sun Wen, the Chinese captain, stood before the American goal. She would drive the ball with the woodpecker hammering of her head and China would have the startling victory. But there was confusion, and Sun began waving her arm and screaming, "Get away, get away." A teammate had crossed into her line of fire. Zhang had walked beyond the goal line to grab a bottle of water and when she set up for the kick, she could not hear Sun yelling at her to clear out. It was too loud in the curve of the stadium, the noise pushing out, a wall of painted-face screams and waving flags, all individual voices bound into one roaring voice. The corner kick came, and Zhang still held the bottle of water in her hand. She tossed it away hurriedly, but she blocked Sun's vision and Sun never got to the ball in the tangled collision of players. "Under normal circumstances, I would have scored," Sun said.

Scurry rushed from the goal line and punched the ball away, and she also punched Akers in the head. "I got some of the ball and mostly her," Scurry said. "She was exhausted and tired but I gave her a concussion." Akers went down, then pulled herself into a wobbly crouch, leaning on her left hand, her right hand grabbing her face. "Stay down," Scurry kept telling her. "Stay down. Are you okay?" Akers did not answer and Scurry motioned to the sideline for help. *Get up, get up.* Akers telling herself to stand, but she could not. "Every time I tried to get up, I was going to pass out," Akers said. "Too dizzy. I was out of it. I couldn't find the strength to get up."

Sara Whalen, who was warming up on the sideline, reached Akers and said that she seemed a little scared. Doug Brown, one of the team doctors, got to her and found her in the condition of a boxer who had been given an eight count, face flushed, wobbly, a little confused, kind of floppy. "Her fuel tank was empty," Brown said. "She had given it everything she had." The doctor walked her to the bench, and Akers sat with an icy towel over her head like a depleted, concussed Madonna.

"We've got to have an answer, Doc, and we've got to have it now," DiCicco asked over Brown's shoulder. "Can she go in?"

"I can play, Tony," Akers responded, but her combatant's will was not supported by her unresponsive legs. How could she play if she couldn't stand up?

"No," Brown said. "No, she can't go."

13

The Most Underrated Player in the World

TWO 15-MINUTE PERIODS of overtime to unspool the tie. The first goal would win, "sudden death" to the Americans, the "golden goal" to the rest of the soccer world. Players drinking water at the bench, spilling it over their heads. Mia Hamm lying on the ground, saying, "Shake my legs," wanting a trainer to milk the lactic acid out of her calves and thighs. "Sudden victory, sudden victory," Tony DiCicco kept repeating to his players, believing that sudden death sounded too looming and ominous. He would have to face overtime without his most dominant player. Who would replace Michelle Akers? Lauren Gregg, the assistant coach, wanted Tiffany Roberts, a cardiovascular marvel, a former 400- and 800-meter runner with a quarter-miler's rabid inexhaustion. She had been tested with a heart-rate monitor in 1995, and her average rate during a game was

180 beats per minute. DiCicco chose Sara Whalen, the fastest player on the team. Roberts was a defender, incessant but not so sure with the ball. Whalen had played forward in college. She might race from the back and win the World Cup with a fresh sprint, an anaerobic inspiration.

DiCicco looked Whalen in the face.

"Are you ready?"

Hell yes, I'm ready, I've trained six months for this. Her brain letting the clutch out, but her mouth not slipping into such an impudent gear. She looked DiCicco in the eyes, knowing that if she showed the slightest doubt he would not put her in. "Yes, I'm ready," she said. "I want to go in."

"Okay, go have fun."

She had been the last player chosen to the 20-member roster, age 23, a former star at the University of Connecticut with a tongue stud, and by Akers' estimation, "45 pierced body parts." Once when the two were rooming together at a tournament, a sleepwalking Akers got up in the middle of the night and screamed, "There's a man in the room!" and looked around and went back to bed. "I scared her to death," Akers said. "She stayed up the rest of the night."

Like many young players, Whalen's career had careened through this sort of bump-in-the-night uncertainty. She tried too hard at practice, believing every fumbled pass or missed shot meant she would be cut from the team. The harder she tried, the worse she played, the more her confidence plummeted, caught in the tail-chasing of insecurity. Carla Overbeck, the captain, had calmed her, told her, "Just go out and play, we have so much faith in you."

"She made me realize it wasn't about how much playing time Sara Whalen gets, but about what can I do for the team. It was one of the most important lessons I learned," Whalen said.

She was on the field now, overtime of the World Cup final, 90,000 people looking to see who replaced Akers and the pressure closing in like the noise. "Totally overwhelmed," Whalen said. "It was awesome. It was awful." She had just entered the game and already she was exhausted. *Oh my God, please get us through this.* Sixty-five seconds into overtime, Julie Foudy swung an easy pass to her and Whalen pushed it nervously out of bounds. *Everyone's exhausted and I let the ball go out of bounds like an idiot.* Her teammates looking at her now, trying to encourage her. Overbeck giving her that smile-smirk of support and impatience, the familiar admonishment that said, "It's just a game, but let's go. You're fine. Enough of that."

After two awkward, stolen throw-ins by Whalen, Gregg was even more skeptical that she was the right choice, but DiCicco turned to his assistant and said, "Lauren it's too late. The decision has been made. Now you have to support it. I need you to help this player." Later, he came to believe that Gregg's judgment probably had been correct.

Whalen took Joy Fawcett's spot at right back, and Overbeck warned her about Zhang's speed. *I know, but I'm faster.* Fawcett moved into the position vacated by Akers, defensive midfielder, where she would track Sun Wen, China's best player, and distribute the ball to her teammates, keep it moving. Brandi Chastain sometimes played there, but in the overtime of the World Cup final, DiCicco wanted Fawcett's steady reliability instead of Chastain's yearning for the dramatic. "Brandi's challenge is to play the game simply," DiCicco said. "She's Pete Maravich on the soccer field. I needed a point guard to keep it simple." Fawcett had steadied the Americans in the second half against North Korea, but now she was tired and China began to attack down the middle. At right back, Fawcett could see the whole field in front of her and she had the sideline as a virtual teammate, a protective boundary. In midfield, Chinese players buzzed all around her in a threatening swarm. "Sun Wen could think clearly when Akers went out, and she could carry the ball anywhere she liked," said Ma Yuanan, the Chinese coach. "At that point, it seemed like we had the game." DiCicco was surprised to see Sun sprint past Fawcett on the dribble. *Get your head in it,* Fawcett warned herself. *Their best player is running past you. Pick it up. Pick it up. Slow her down a little.*

"I was never going to let that happen again," Fawcett said.

Akers began to leave the bench in an empty stagger, held up by Dr. Mark Adams and Dainis Kalnins, the equipment manager, fighting to stay awake, her eyes glassy, the blood collecting in her legs, her blood pressure dropping, her mind going lightheaded and fuzzy. Adams asking her questions, Akers almost incoherent, knowing her name, where she was, but too tired to speak more than a few words. A medical room under the stadium, her jersey sheared away with scissors, her heart beating rapidly, her temperature elevated, her breathing quite hard, the signs of heat exhaustion. Intravenous tubes in each arm to hydrate her, an oxygen mask on her face, an electrocardiogram hookup, her body packed in icy towels, fans blowing to try to rapidly drop her body temperature. Akers saying, "I'm going to pass out now," and Adams saying, "Let it go, Mich, let it go," but she could never give in to the rushing blackness in her head. She kept fighting and she began to cry with the pain of exhaustion and her arms and legs began to cramp from a lack of fluids. "When you feel this bad, there is an element of fear, 'Am I going to be okay?'" Adams said. Akers had a hazy sense of people around her in a frenzy, grabbing her arms and legs, yelling at her, yanking on her cramping limbs, Adams leaning into her face, "It's okay, Mich, you're going to be okay."

"She felt as bad this time as she had felt ever," Adams said. "She's used to feeling bad at the end, but this was a little more. She left everything she had out there. I've seen her at the end of every game for a long time. She's very depleted after most games, but this one, with all the emotion involved, she was as depleted as I've seen her. Almost gaunt in appearance. Eyes glassy. This wasn't just one emotionally packed game. This was the conclusion of weeks of building emotion."

Ten minutes into overtime, Sun Wen raced past Fawcett on an elusive dribble, touching the ball with her left foot, pushing the ball ahead with splendid precision, running onto it again in a dead sprint, and from 22 yards, she fired a shot that glanced off the hip of Carla Overbeck and flew out of bounds. Corner kick for China. Kristine Lilly took her position at the left goal post, pouring water over her head, giving her face a squeegie wipe, the top of her jersey soaked. She stood with her hip resting against the inside of the eight-foot post and reached high with her right hand and grabbed the nylon netting of the goal. At 5-foot-4, she might have to yank herself up to stop a shot with her head. She was assigned to the near post because she was left-footed, and her prevalent leg would be free to clear the ball. At the other post was Tiffeny Milbrett, who was 5-foot-2. DiCicco had his short players guarding the posts, his tall players standing in a boxy zone to divert corner kicks with their heads. But attrition had made the American strategy vulnerable. The tallest players, the ones most adept at heading the ball, were Akers and Cindy Parlow, and both were out of the game.

The most experienced international player in the world, man or woman, Lilly was playing her 186th match for the Americans. She had been with the team for 12 of her 27 years, riding the coal trains in China and blowing her nose and seeing the black exhalation, living on warm Pepsi and pound cake, flying in a Bulgarian plane with a pilot who was wearing a leather helmet, enduring the years without the rewards of significant money or public recognition. And now she was in the World Cup final, playing before the largest crowd ever to watch women play sports. Five minutes into the match, during a lull, she had had stopped and looked around and taken in the painted faces and the waving flags. *Look at all these people. I was here at the beginning. I was one of the ones at the start. This was our dream, and now it has come true. And I'm here with my friends. These are the things that matter.* She found herself smiling, and the nervousness left her stomach.

Just before overtime, she could hear her brother, Scott, yelling from the stands behind the American bench. "Come on Kris, you've got to get going. You better get fired up. Don't be a wimp." He kept yelling at her, but she would not look at him. Finally, her brother said, Kristine looked up and said, "Shut up!"

"I thought, 'Cool, she's all right,'" Scott Lilly said. "That was my affectionate way of knowing she was fired up and ready to go. I went to my mom and said, 'She's ready. She's got it in her.'"

Scott Lilly, who played collegiate soccer, was four years older than Kristine. They grew up in Wilton, Connecticut, and they played in an 8-by-10-foot basement, firing hard shots at each other between posts that held up the foundation and enclosed the electrical wiring, one of them the goalkeeper, the other the shooter. "He wouldn't take it easy on her, no way he was going to let his younger sister beat him," said their father, Steve Lilly. Five boy cousins lived a couple miles away, and they all played tackle football in the yard and they did not hold back from the thudding shoulders and the lancing forearms and the grassy roughness of towheaded collision. "Kristine was usually one of the first ones picked because I knew she could catch," Scott Lilly said. She played second base in the local Little League, and joined a boys' soccer team. At a regional tournament in Niagara Falls, New York, Lilly was forbidden from participating because she was a girl, so her whole team declined to play in protest, her father said. At another tournament, a boy who was about 5-foot-8 kept harassing her during a match, saying, "Why are they letting a girl play?" and, whether it was purposeful or accidental, she silenced him with a rapier elbow to the groin, Scott said. They grew up as fans of the New York Jets, and when the Americans played China in an exhibition match in April at the football team's home stadium in East Rutherford, New Jersey, Kristine left a phone message for her brother, telling him excitedly that the United States women were using the Jets' locker room.

"I was surrounded by guys," Kristine said. "It made me tough. It made me know there was nothing I couldn't do. They never said I couldn't play because I was a girl. My parents never said I couldn't do anything because I was a girl. My brother used to bring me along. I was a girl, but I was one of the guys."

Her parents divorced before she left home for the University of North Carolina, and soccer became a safety valve to release suppressed emotions. With a career that overlapped Mia Hamm's, Lilly won four national titles at Carolina. "For the longest time I kept everything locked inside," Lilly said in *All-American Girls*, an authorized biography of the team. "The only place I expressed my feelings was in the game. I think that's a big reason why I played so well during my college years. I had this pain inside that spilled out on the field."

Even so, she continued to play with such economical restraint that her father could remember her celebrating only twice on the field, once since high school. Her great value was that she did the ordinary in an extraordinary manner. "My favorite player," Akers said. "She does the grunt work." Lilly and Overbeck were the fittest players on the team. She excelled at drills called "suicides" and "stinkers" that left players doubled over and gasping: 40 yards out and back, three times in 55 seconds, a 45-second rest, eight to 12 repeats; a shuttle run in increments of five to 25 yards, 150 yards covered in 35 seconds, 25 seconds' rest, eight to 10 repeats. She ran in the snow in suburban Chicago, where she lived. In Connecticut, she ran the steps at the high school football stadium, 100 times up and down the bleachers, and when the weather was too severe, she ran the stairs in her father's two-story home for half an hour at a time.

"She always said, 'You never know what young players are coming up and I'm not going to lose my spot over something I can control,'" Scott Lilly said.

She played with such a succinct proficiency that her contribution was not always immediately noticed. She scored goals, but she did not have the slashing visibility of Mia Hamm. She played indefatiguable defense but she did not have the ravenous presence of Michelle Akers. Like Fawcett's, Lilly's game was best appreciated in retrospect, on the rewind of videotape, where it could be admired for the space covered, the tireless running, the fundamental pass, the elemental header, the brilliance of the rudimentary. She had been so shy as a high school freshman that she feigned an ankle injury to avoid reporters after one game, her brother said. Returning to her alma mater to give a speech, Lilly became so nervous at the podium that she passed out and was caught by Dean Smith, the Carolina basketball coach.

"She's probably the most underrated player in the world," DiCicco said.

She was one of the team's smallest players, but she generated great power through legs that seemed of perfect proportion in thigh and calf and she drove a golf ball with impressive distance for someone her size. When people told Hamm that she was the top player in the world, she often said that, no, Lilly was the best.

"Anson has this saying that excellence is doing the mundane and making it a habit," Hamm said of Dorrance. "So many people don't, because they don't think it's important. Kristine does the mundane."

How many times had she done something as basic as guard the near goalpost on a corner kick? Hundreds? Thousands? Her initial job was to stay put, as immobile as a Buckingham Palace guard, making certain that no shot squeezed between her and the post. If the corner kick sailed toward the far post, she was to move in concert with Briana Scurry, the goalkeeper. As Scurry came off the goal line, Lilly was to tuck in behind her, sliding to her left, reducing the shooter's angle. Making the goal smaller, it was called. It was a basic maneuver, but defenders not infrequently lost their concentration when they grew tired. China scored on a corner kick in its opening match against Sweden, when a Swedish player came unplugged and simply walked off the post.

Growing tired but remaining alert in overtime, Lilly lined up at the near post, grabbed a fistful of net with her right hand and placed her left hand on her chest. Liu Ying of China lifted a corner kick toward the far post. The kick appeared benign on its long, lazy arc, and Shannon MacMillan backpedaled toward the ball, but the defender Fan Yunjie outjumped her with a threatening cock of her head and struck the ball like a fist hitting a punching bag. Twice, Fan had won important matches for China by flicking headers into the net. She wore her hair in a spiky cut and shopped for Italian shoes for her boyfriend and she had a sister who played for the national team until she broke a leg. Fan headed the ball on a sharp diagonal to her left and MacMillan froze. "It was in," she said of the shot. Fan thought the same thing. "I had it," she said, shaking her head. "I thought I got it." Scurry dived to her right, and the ball sailed past her and she looked over her shoulder. *Oh, shit.* She could hear the crowd, and it sounded to her like the collective inhalation of 90,000 people. Tiffeny Milbrett stood at the other post and she could not believe the power in Fan's shot. *Oh, great, it's over, we're second.* Saskia Webber, the backup goalkeeper, watching from the bench, time slowed, each movement distinct and stop-action like slides in a Viewfinder, Scurry diving, the ball going past, her own stomach in an amusement-park plummet. Julie Foudy, too, watching the slo-mo hopelessness, the ball beyond Scurry, heading toward an empty net. *Noooooo. This is our World Cup and it's over.*

Lilly followed the corner kick's indolent trajectory and she moved unhurriedly to her left, one step, two, three, and Fan redirected the ball and gave it an abrupt, dangerous geometry. "There was no thought process," Lilly said. She jumped slightly on the goal line and a photograph caught her in clenched levitation, eyes closed, arms outstretched, neck braced, the cords in her throat as thick and raised as fingers, white socks pulled to the knees, the muscular apostrophe of her quadriceps, mouth slightly open, shoulders squared, wisps of hair like solar flares, toes pointed downward, the number 13 riding up on her jersey, gravity unbound. The ball trampolined off Lilly's forehead and the game was not over. "One time in a hundred that she had to be there, and she was," DiCicco said. "She was fundamentally perfect."

Scurry saw the rescue over her shoulder, *God was behind me*, and Webber saw Lilly sliding, too, the freeze-frame deliverance, *Oh my God, yes.* The rebound came forward and appeared to graze Scurry, and the slight deflection kept three Chinese players from an unguarded convergence. Everything happening in a frantic blur. Milbrett believing that Lilly headed the ball with her nose and bloodied her nostrils. Carla Overbeck jumping with MacMillan and helicoptering to the ground and missing Lilly's heart-stopping save until she watched the television highlights. The crowd reaction behind the goal was delayed, like the retort of a starter's pistol. A security guard, facing the crowd, back to the scramble, unaware of Lilly's saving interruption. A photographer with his camera hanging at his waist. Blank, sunglassed, cap-shaded faces. One man, a Chinese flag painted on his cheek, understanding the moment before everyone else, his mouth open in the startle of expectation or disbelief.

The ball bounded free, still in front of the goal, the paralyzing helplessness between victory and defeat, Lilly's mind yelling, "Get it out, get it out." Fan rushed forward, her mouth wide in rebuffed opportunity and redemptive insistence. Zhang Ouying charged like a bull with her waist bent and head forward, Sun Wen dropped into a sliding sweep with her leg, and Foudy, 10 yards away, ran as if in a fly-papered dream, a heaviness in her legs, her stride congealed. *Get it out of there!* Brandi Chastain followed the rebound with calm intent, tossed her right leg up, braced with her left arm like a skateboarder, and scissored her body and kicked the ball high and away. If she sometimes played with strained ostentation, she had just saved the game with necessary flamboyance. Stunned relief in the crowd, the painted faces slack with stars-and-stripes incredulity.

"Oh my God, who did that?" Scott Lilly said, missing the bang-bang header on the goal line.

"Your sister, you idiot," his fiancée said.

Kristine Lilly jogging upfield, Foudy saying something to her, Lilly smiling the alleviating smile of delayed fright. *Oh God, oh man.* Webber sensing that victory was inevitable after this near miss. *If that didn't go in, it wasn't meant to be.* DiCicco convinced now that the game would extend to penalty kicks. Joy Fawcett, too, with the assurance of the redeemed.

"That's when I felt really calm and confident about the whole game," Fawcett said. "When that ball didn't go in, I was like, there's nothing else in them."

Three days after the final, a woman claiming to be Kristine Lilly would appear at a match in Denver between the American men's national team and Derby County of the English Premier League. The woman walked along the end line of the field, waving at the crowd, when she was spotted as an impostor by Bryan Chenault, the manager of public relations for the United States Soccer Federation.

"You're not Kristine Lilly," Chenault told the woman.

"Yes, I am."

"Do you have a driver's license?"

"I must have left it in the car."

A security guard approached Chenault and put a hand on his shoulder.

"Hey, buddy, what's the problem? This is Kristine Lilly."

"No, this is not," Chenault said with a smirking smile. "This is someone impersonating Kristine Lilly."

"Who cares," the guard said. "The crowd loves her."

Michelle Akers goes up for a header against a Chinese team that was not prepared physically or culturally to handle her in midfield.

Balanced with her left hand like a skateboarder, Brandi Chastain deftly clears the ball after Kristine Lilly's header save during overtime.

Michelle Akers (#10) gets punched in the head by Briana Scurry (hidden) as they rush to deflect a Chinese corner kick at the end of regulation.

Michelle Akers winces in pain and exhaustion after her collision with Scurry. "I got some of the ball, and mostly her," Scurry said.

Akers lies like a boxer who has been given an eight-count, stunned, confused. "I can play, Tony," Akers told DiCicco, but the team doctor overruled her.

Mia Hamm gets tangled up with the Chinese defender Bai Jie, known as the Little Assassin by the Americans for her insistent, rough play.

U.S. captain Carla Overbeck leaps in celebration after scoring the first American penalty kick, a symbol of confidence that relaxes her teammates.

Briana Scurry, her body parallel to the ground, makes the winning save against China's Liu Ying during penalty kicks, sensing all along that she would block the kick.

Mia Hamm screams in loud relief at
teammate Tisha Venturini
after converting a penalty kick that
she did not want to take.

The American players, bending over in tense anticipation as Brandi Chastain prepares for her winning penalty kick.

Chastain celebrating her winning kick as the ball nestles in the net. A Rose Bowl crowd of 90,185 erupts, the largest attendance ever to watch a women's sporting event.

Brandi Chastain swings her jersey in exultant triumph as her teammates bound toward her after the winning penalty kick.

The goalkeeper Briana Scurry and Sara Whalen roll around in confetti-littered delight on the field at the conclusion of the World Cup final.

"We proved to the world that we are the best," Carla Overbeck would later say.
The American women pose with their gold medals after winning the World Cup.

Brandi Chastain—now fully clothed in victory yellow—and Kristine Lilly hold up their
medals and signal "We're No. 1."

14

"Hollywood" Confidential

A S SHE RAN UPFIELD, Brandi Chastain felt the heart-skip of her acrobatic clearance. "Like a car accident," she said. "It happens so fast, then you get scared. I definitely got scared afterward." Until the final, she had not been happy with her performance in the World Cup. She had put a ball into her own goal in the quarterfinals and she had not played with the luminous versatility of which she was capable. At left back, she had fashioned herself after Roberto Carlos, the Brazilian star, and like him, she had wanted to come forward in attack, to play a game filigreed with uncommon dexterity and sophistication. She was the only player on the team, one of the few in the world, who was equally comfortable passing and shooting with both feet. She could play defense, midfield, forward. She could put the long pass in perfect stride, doing with her feet what a quarterback did with his hands. She relished the flair of the bicycle kick and the back heel pass. Like a figure skater, she was drawn to the artistry of sport. She had tried ballet and tap-dancing, even peewee football, but it was soccer that drew her, its freedom and spontaneity, the triumph of upheaval and discord over planning and pattern. No matter what lines and arrows a coach chalked on a blackboard, no matter what words were written in a manual about tactics, concepts, philosophy, the players made the ultimate decisions in the crucible of beautiful entropy.

She loved the subtlety, the trickery, the reading of a teammate's body language without conversing, the uniforms, the accents, the contact, the rough ballet of movement around the ball, the necessity of thinking three moves ahead during the sweaty, oxygen-deprived turmoil of high speed. The anticipation of chess. That was it, she said, soccer was chess without the Russian names.

Her career had been operatic in its unceasing tug of failure and success, elimination and recovery. In the quarterfinals, against Germany, the game was five minutes old when Chastain made a pass back to Briana Scurry without making eye contact and gave embarrassed chase as the ball rolled into an empty American net. He had seen many players deflated by such a mistake, Tony DiCicco said, their confidence punctured, their careers ruined, or worse. Andreas Escobar of Colombia was killed for murky reasons shortly after putting the ball into his own goal against the United States in the 1994 men's World Cup. Chastain did not wither after the humiliating error. Four minutes into the second half, a deflected corner kick bounced six yards in front of the goal and she dropped into a slide to drive the ball into the net. She ran in celebration, a relieved smile on her face, and fell on her back, arms in the air.

"I wanted to cry," she said. "I just wanted to sit there on the ground and cry. I was disappointed in what I had done earlier in the game. All the heart and soul and everything you feel you contribute to the team, and then that happens. But I finally redeemed myself. I came back."

And now, in the taut pressured moments of the final, she had begun to play with conspicuous authority. The sliding tackle at the end of regulation. The bicycling save in the first overtime. In moments where others shriveled, Chastain possessed decisive unrestraint. She longed for responsibility of the outcome affected, the conclusive shot or the definitive pass, the dramatic extrication. After the World Cup, Chastain would sit in her backyard one evening during a party for the women's soccer team at Santa Clara University. Her husband, Jerry Smith, was the head coach, and Chastain was an assistant. "You're such a performer," one of the players would tell her, and she would answer wistfully that the buildup for the World Cup had come too slowly and the tournament had passed too quickly. "I want to be on the field," she said. In the national team's media guide, Julie Foudy had listed Chastain as her favorite actress. Her teammates knew her as Hollywood. She approached fame and celebrity in the way that the newsman Harry Reasoner said spectators approached wrecks at the Indianapolis 500. They did not necessarily crave them, but they wanted to be there in case they happened.

There was a grace, an unrestricted ease, about Chastain in public. People who just met her could feel as if they had known her for years. At a child's birthday party after the World Cup, she would talk with friends, give an interview, eat cake and autograph photos at the same time, wearing a party hat and riding a toy car. She spoke to a reporter while doing lunges and curls and pull-ups in the Santa Clara weight room, gave corporate speeches without notes, took penalty kicks at clinics against wide-eyed high school stars. She came onto the field at a San Francisco 49ers exhibition game and playfully bent into a football stance, and she threw out the first pitch at a Yankees game and pretended to shake off the catcher's sign.

"Hair! Makeup!" she said in her best mock-diva voice as she walked into the green room on David Letterman's show three days before the World Cup opener. She was still anonymous then, a consolation prize for an unwilling Mia Hamm. She sat in her dressing room as the actor Seth Green walked by, and Chastain stopped him and said how much she had enjoyed his performance in the movie *Austin Powers: the Spy Who Shagged Me*. Green listened politely and said, "What's your name?"

Three weeks later, everyone would know.

Her teammates, most of them, were enthusiastic players but indifferent fans. Chastain followed soccer the way the baseball addict needed the daily fix of the boxscore. As a six-year-old in San Jose, California, she joined a soccer team called the Quakettes, and she became enamored with the flair of the Irish forward George Best, who played for the San Jose Earthquakes of the North American Soccer League. On weekends, she watched television highlights from the German Bundesliga. She played in the yard for hours with her brother, juggling the ball on her feet, slamming it against the garage. "The garage door and my head pounded constantly," said her mother, Lark Chastain. Even now, Brandi still had a jersey won in a juggling contest when she was 11. At nine or 10, her soccer camp team played at halftime of an Earthquakes game, and she scored a goal and reveled in the cheering. "I think that's what led me to like playing in stadiums," she said.

During the 1994 men's World Cup, Chastain attended two matches in one day in different cities, one at the Rose Bowl, the other at Stanford Stadium. She postponed her honeymoon to play in the 1996 Summer Olympics and finally took it in France during the 1998 men's World Cup. She had videotapes of every match from the 1994 and 1999 World Cups, and, along with her husband, she bought a satellite dish for their office at Santa Clara to pull international matches out of the sky. When she could not sleep, she watched taped matches involving Manchester United and other European club powers. When the American women trained outside of Orlando, Florida, she eagerly jumped in a car with the coaches and drove 70 miles to Tampa to watch men's matches involving Major League Soccer.

"Brandi is a student of soccer," DiCicco said. "She has a sophistication to her game that most U.S. women don't have. She knows the savvy little things, like when we're ahead, let's not run to take a throw-in. We don't live in a soccer culture. Most U.S. women don't watch soccer. Brandi watches."

She competed at everything from soccer to Ping-Pong to crossword puzzles. As a young girl, she stepped in as a replacement one day on her brother's Little League team. A kid had gotten hurt and Brandi came out of the stands and hit a home run. Eventually, she took her brother's place on the team. In junior high, she played on a boys' soccer team, but the opposition sometimes objected to forwards who wore Dorothy Hamill hairdos.

"Are you a boy or a girl?" one player asked her one day.

"A girl," Brandi replied.

"They have a girl on their team," someone shouted to much derisive laughter.

"I was thinking that this was not going to be a good thing for them," Lark Chastain said. "The score ended up being 6-0 in our favor. Brandi scored five goals."

Her mother was a cheerleader in high school and her father was a football player, and her great uncle was Chester "Swede" Johnston, one of the oldest living alums of the National Football League. Brandi, too, felt comfortable in the saddle-shoe life of newspaper write-ups and letter sweaters and the hopeful scribbling of yearbook popularity. Sport came easily—her soccer team won three state championships—but dedication to fitness and studying did not. At California-Berkeley, Brandi scored 15 goals and had 14 assists her freshman season, and *SoccerAmerica* magazine voted her the national freshman of the year in 1986. Everything was fine and everything was about to unravel. She was away from home and decompressing from the ruler-knuckling of a Catholic school upbringing and having fun and meeting people and staying out late and falling into traps that kids fall into when they become untethered for the first time. In the spring of 1987, she tore the anterior cruciate ligament in her left knee. Her identity had come from being a soccer player and now she was hurt and she could not measure herself by goals and assists and the tidy ledger of wins and losses. The freedom of college and the self-doubt of injury were dislocating. No one but herself to make sure she showed up for her psychology class with 800 other kids in an auditorium. No one to push her and she did not push herself. Her grades suffered and her course work went incomplete and she floundered out of school.

"I struggled with the fact that I was failing for the first time," Chastain said. "I felt like I was drowning and I couldn't swim to the top."

She attempted the boot-strap pull of junior college, but her grades languished and her soccer career went dormant for two years. Jerry Smith was trying to build Santa Clara into a national power and he offered her a scholarship in early 1989 to begin playing in the fall of that year. "Why do you want Brandi?" other coaches asked.

"She'll never make it." Then, in March of 1989, she tore the anterior cruciate ligament in her right knee. She was supposed to start training with Santa Clara in five months, and she had to pass a load of junior-college courses to regain her eligibility and the other coaches seemed to be right in their skepticism. She would never make it.

"I thought it was mission impossible," Smith said. "She had to do extensive rehab and take a lot of courses to make up for lost ground academically. I thought it probably wasn't going to work out."

Six months to the day of her surgery, Brandi began playing at Santa Clara. She wore a brace from hip to ankle and scored 10 goals that season and the Broncos reached the playoffs for the first time, but she never completed a fitness drill, not one. She had a passion for soccer but no dedication to being in shape. At her biggest, she weighed 160 pounds on her 5-foot-7 inches and no one was calling her "cut" or "ripped" or anything else in the serrated vocabulary of the muscles. "I hated the fitness drills," Chastain said. "I didn't think it was necessary. I felt I was a better player than the others."

Her coach thought it was necessary. Smith was building a team on effort and Chastain believed that talent would always trump hard work. He was in his third season and he was starting to win players over and his team was successful and his star was thumbing her nose. He had a decision to make. Many coaches would avoid confronting their star athletes, self-important teenagers on whom they depended for their resumes and their livelihoods. He would not avoid it.

He called Chastain into his office. A shouting match.

"Look, you're using your knee as an excuse," Smith told Chastain. "You're not working as hard, not doing fitness, not battling out there."

"I don't need this team," Chastain fired back.

"Good, we don't need you," Smith said. "Don't come back until you're ready to play the way we're going to play."

The next day, she came back. "I was a jerk," Chastain said. She came back the next day and completed her first fitness drill, and then she returned for her senior season as the fittest player on the team. Santa Clara went undefeated and was ranked No. 1 in the polls and Chastain was voted national player of the year. The team reached the Final Four, but an odd loss occurred in the semifinals, the game prolonged to penalty kicks, Chastain's kick saved by the Connecticut goalkeeper.

A year later, she was chosen for the American team for the 1991 Women's World Cup. In the qualifying tournament, she came off the bench and scored five consecutive goals in a 12–0 rout of Mexico. The Americans won the inaugural World Cup, but Chastain played little. Anson Dorrance was the coach and he preferred the thundering, lashing muscularity of Michelle Akers and April Heinrichs to the clever, aesthetic, nifty skill of Chastain. DiCicco became the head coach in 1994, and he wasn't going to change much for the 1995 World Cup. Why should he? The team was already world champion. Heinrichs was retired, but Mia Hamm was an emerging star. DiCicco had seen Chastain at a tournament in 1993, and she did not look sharp or fit. She was playing professionally in Japan and he wondered whether her career with the national team was exhausted. *She's done, she's not going to do it..*

"It was a very hard time for me," Chastain said about being left off the team for the 1995 World Cup. "I was a soccer player. I felt myself a little lost. You lose your identity."

She sat in a sports bar and watched the Americans lose to Norway in the semifinals. A sports bar in Salt Lake City. If she ever needed a drink it was now, but she was in the one town where she couldn't get served in the middle of the day.

"I never thought it was the end," Chastain said. "I never allowed myself to think that after the knee surgeries and I didn't think about it then. 'You're good enough to play on that level,' I kept telling myself. But you have to figure out what is important in the long run. Did I want to continue on the road with the national team? Was it something I had interest in or wanted to achieve again? I decided I wanted to get there again and I decided it was my responsibility to make it happen for me, not anybody else's responsibility to give me a chance, to say, 'We feel sorry for you.' It was up to me."

In September of 1995, having lost the world title, DiCicco looked to overhaul the American team. Dorrance preferred "blunt instruments" on defense, players who won with cudgeling sinew over skill. DiCicco wanted a more sophisticated defense. He wanted athletes who could possess the ball, who could pass and dribble and build an attack, who were savvy and would not be intimidated when they felt the grip of pressure from opposing forwards. He had some defenders, he said, who were so clumsy with the ball that if he put them in midfield, it was like putting them on the moon. Chastain contacted him and said, "I'm fit, I can help your team," and he invited her in for a tryout and she was the best player in camp. He invited her back in December of 1995, when some of the American stars were on strike over proposed Olympic bonus money, and Chastain was the best player again. DiCicco told her, "I feel I have to keep you, I have put you on field, but left back is the only spot I have."

"I just want to be on the field," she said.

She believed in the inexplicable knitting of people and events, the needlepoint of chance. The team had lost and it needed her, and she was lost and she needed the team. Women's soccer would be in the Olympics for the first time in 1996, and the World Cup would come to the United States in 1999, and she would be on the American side, moving from forward to defender, moving back into the embrace of her best friends. It was the sincere earnest closeness that she longed for, the musketeer togetherness of spending more time with her teammates than her family or her boyfriend over the past decade. The international travel and the fish served with eyes and heads and the subsistence on Pop-Tarts and Snickers bars, the laughing and needling, the note in the media guide that she loved visiting animal shelters and teaching herself foreign languages and the phone calls from Julie Foudy wanting to know whether she visited the shelters and spoke French to the poodles and German to the shepherds. The vital unspoken connections, the stay-clear look of a teammate on a bad day, the implicit grammar of a body that wanted the ball, the concert of the feet, the precision of balls thrown and kicked and headed, the symphony of motion and anticipation, the satisfied sweating through of her uniform by halftime, the unleashed moments after a goal, the shirt-waving and the running and diving and piling celebration, the unswerving pioneer conviction that something huge could be built and shared, something genuine and beyond the cornfield melodrama of baseball fiction.

"I could be open and honest with people who affected my life for a long time, I could let them know what I liked about them and they could get to know me again," Chastain said. "When you know someone well, you learn how they work and how they think. You almost don't have to talk to know how they are feeling, if they need to talk, if they don't need to talk. You are willing to give more of yourself, to do it in front of your peers and best friends and the people you admire most. When you put yourself on the line for other people, it only comes back to help you. I think we were the most competitive group of women I've ever encountered in my life. It was the feeling you have about something you've built from scratch and you polish it and take care of it, but you also want to show it off, to give it to everybody else. It's the giving of yourself to the World Cup, the pressure of having to deal with failure in your own country. This tournament was put on our shoulders a long time ago. They wanted to put it in small stadiums, 5,000 to 10,000 people. We were angry. 'We can get people into these big stadiums. Give us a chance. Let us make something huge about this.' It was our obligation and responsibility to make this whole thing succeed. We went to practice knowing that no one trained harder or gave more or sacrificed more than our team did over six months, over 11 or 12 years. It's the relay paradigm. A man can run the fastest 400 meters in the world, but four men will always beat one man. That's the story of this team. Not one person made the World Cup happen, not one goal decided the tournament. The effort of 20 women did."

Just before the Atlanta Olympics, Chastain and Smith were married. He was divorced, with a young son, and after her college career, the antagonism of coach and player had become a shared passion for soccer and competition at anything from backgammon to cooking to snowboarding. Around that time, Chastain did an ad for Nike in which she and other athletes appeared tastefully nude and, because she was not famous, no one noticed or said a word in objection.

The Americans won the gold medal at the Atlanta Games, but DiCicco thought that Chastain could raise her game even higher if she committed herself as much to fitness as she did to craftiness. She could be one of the best players in the world if she trained harder, he told her. She came into training camp for the World Cup at a sculpted 130 pounds, the egg-carton abdominal muscles achieved by doing 300 to 500 sit-ups a day, the definition in her arms coming from weight training and pushups that she could speed-dial at 72 a minute. This team was built on a culture of fitness. At the 1993 World University Games in Buffalo, New York, the Americans practiced one night in a parking lot, using the headlights from vans to illuminate the training. Her own reluctance in the past, Chastain said, had come not from arrogant disregard but from the fear of red-lining herself, of extending her body to its limits. Colleen Hacker, the team's sports psychologist, helped her push beyond her perceived boundaries.

"I know I'm fit, I know I can run," Chastain said. "If someone says, 'Brandi you have to run two miles in 12 minutes,' I know I can do it. The anxiety is getting to the line." The Americans had a drill in which players were required to run 120 yards, the length of the field, in 17 seconds, with 30 seconds to return and 30 seconds' rest, then eight or nine repeats. A month before the World Cup, Chastain "blew everyone away," DiCicco said.

"Her training was at game speed, sharp, not like perpetual warm-ups," he said. "The only thing she needed to do better was to play simpler."

In the days before the World Cup opener, she appeared with David Letterman and the photos in *Gear* magazine became public and Chastain laughed that she had been oiled at the photo shoot and she had slipped off a platform, falling, her robe spilling open, everything exposed. "How's that for an ice breaker?" she had said. "Now we can start."

"I've spent 10 years of my life working on my body, and it's a picture of a confident, strong woman," she told reporters at the team's training camp in central New Jersey. "If someone can't see it that way, maybe they should look in the mirror and say, 'What am I not doing?' and concentrate on themselves."

She had not told her parents or her husband about the photo shoot. "I did it for one reason, for myself," she said. "I didn't do it for anybody else. It was a strong, athletic photo. That's all it was intended to be. A lot of people look at themselves and they're not happy. The photo gave me the okay to say, 'I'm not perfect, but I feel good.' Everybody has the potential to feel good about themselves."

By placing Chastain at left back, her husband said, DiCicco assumed some risk. In defense, problems were solved by passing, and at forward they were solved by dribbling. But Chastain had been an attacking player most of her career, and she still sometimes played defense like a forward. Early in the World Cup opener against Denmark, she tried to dribble out of pressure and was stripped of the ball. After the game, when she returned to the team hotel, Smith's first words were, "Brandi, kick the hell out of the ball."

They had not seen each other in weeks, or spoken in days.

"At least you could say hello," she replied.

The night before the second American match, against Nigeria at Soldier Field in Chicago, the team watched defending champion Norway play Canada on television. Norway won in a 7–1 rout and, after scoring a goal, the defender Linda Medalen, one of the world's top players, pulled her jersey over her head in celebration.

"She's kind of a hard-looking woman, and she had something flapping under her sports bra—it looked like a nicotine patch—and our players were going, 'Oh Linda, what are you doing?'" DiCicco said. "We were watching in the bar. I was kind of sitting near Brandi. She didn't say anything. I think the wheels were moving. I think she was saying to herself, 'I could do that. I could pull it off and make it work.'"

A night later, another nervous start for the Americans, a goal by Nigeria in the first 62 seconds, a collision between Chastain and Carla Overbeck, then a steadying and a 7–1 rout. The same early apprehension against Germany in the quarterfinals, miscommunication between Briana Scurry and Chastain, a ball in the American goal.

"I don't think I played well until the final," Chastain said. "I played average; not quite the tournament I thought I was going to have. I was nervous, excited, the other teams were good. I saved my best game for the most important game."

The day of the Germany match in suburban Washington, the players edited a video for Letterman, who had declared himself the team's owner and spiritual guru. The joke was that nothing could be done without Letterman's approval, no lineup changes, no autographs. DiCicco played along too. Chastain lay facedown on a table, wearing only a towel on her buttocks and said into the camera, "Nobody but Dave massages me." It was done in fun, but DiCicco said he was concerned that the tape might give the wrong impression of promiscuity. He suggested that the tape not be sent, then relented, as long as it was made clear that the video could never be aired. It wasn't. And after Chastain's early mistake in the game, she rebounded with the tying goal in an eventual 3–2 victory. Still, once the team had flown to the West Coast for the semifinals, DiCicco admonished his players, saying that "the laser focus had become a laser show."

At a team meeting, Chastain's inadvertent goal was replayed a handful of times. DiCicco said he was not trying to be harsh, and that either the video got stuck in a loop or the taped television broadcast showed several different angles of the goal. Some in the room said there was joking but others said the situation became uncomfortable and embarrassing for Chastain. Carla Overbeck, the captain, called the players together. "We thought we had left the meeting feeling negative," Overbeck said. "We rallied around Brandi and picked her up. We knew we would need her at her best and confident. We thought her confidence had been shattered."

By the final match against China, the matter had been forgotten. The longer the game went, the more vigorously Chastain played. The sliding tackle at the end of regulation and the bicycle clearance in overtime. When Akers went out, exhausted, punched in the head, the American players had gathered at the bench. *Who are our leaders going to be? We're going to have to do this together. We know we can pull this game out. We've practiced long enough. We've done the preparation. Let's go out and do it together.*

"You have to be willing to stand in front of the crowd and say, 'I'm the one to take on the responsibility,'" Chastain said.

15

The Jell-O Wobble
of Exhaustion

T HE SECOND OVERTIME to start, 15 final minutes, the tired
clenched faces on the American bench, Tiffeny Milbrett with a
swig of water in her mouth, the tip of her ponytail wet and clumped
like a paintbrush. A teammate giving her a hug. The drinking and
splashing of water, Saskia Webber with her flag hair, Christie Pearce
massaging the shoulders of Julie Foudy, Tony DiCicco looking at the
fidgety Sara Whalen and saying, "Calm down. Don't go out there just
to play, go out to make a difference." Sun Wen at the Chinese bench,
her feet full of blisters. *Can I hold on?* The crowd hot and nervous
and uncertain, T-shirts piled on heads against the heat, the flag bandanas and tank tops, the painted soccer-ball faces, the ball caps and
sunglasses, the cheering and restless discomfort in 105 degrees, the
inevitability of penalty kicks.

Carla Overbeck, the American captain, gathering the team for a final encouragement, walking on the field, chewing gum, always the confident jaw-set, blinking as if to adjust a pair of contact lenses, her one-year-old son asleep in her husband's lap. Briana Scurry jogging to her post, Brandi Chastain with her lips pursed in resolve, Kristine Lilly walking purposefully, head down, water dripping from her chin. "The determination driving that team was like a beating heart, almost loud enough to hear," wrote Amy Shipley of the *Washington Post*. "It was spooky, almost."

The game was a walk now, a jog, a conserved burst of enthusiasm. The crowd, too, picking its spots, clapping and standing and waving flags to start the overtime, then sitting and waiting, marathoners preserving for a final ebullient kick. "There was no sprinting left," Lilly said. *If she gets the ball, keep her in front of you, don't let her by. Hopefully, help will come.* She was the fittest player but her legs were exhausted, with the invertebrate wobble of Jell-O. "Basically all you are doing is finding somewhere in your head, and telling yourself that you can make it," Lilly said. "You don't feel it in your legs. You have to tell yourself, 'I have something left.'"

The substitutes had fresher legs, but Whalen was still nervous and unfocused and a pass from Chastain rolled under her foot and beyond the side line. Julie Foudy cradled her hands over her head as if resisting a swarm of bees. A minute later, Whalen calmer now, dribbling down the right wing, the fastest player on the team, *Oh my God, I'm going forward against China,* a step on the Chinese defender, Hamm racing into the penalty area, Whalen touching the ball once, twice, then a crossing pass to Hamm, a pass like all the other passes, a bit early, a connection barely missed. Gao Hong charged from the Chinese goal to grab the ball with her hands before it arrived at Hamm's feet.

Four minutes into the second overtime, the Chinese defender Wang Liping attempted to trap a pass with her chest, but the ball bounced awkwardly off her shoulder and it dribbled to Milbrett on the left wing, 30 yards from the goal. Milbrett tried to push the ball between Wang's legs, a nutmeg, but Wang recovered and the ball deflected out of bounds. Milbrett looked toward the bench in sly weariness. It had been a grinding afternoon for her, all running and working and chasing, no open space, one shot, a slow roller to Gao, easily scooped up. The linesman had raised her flag several times, calling Milbrett offsides for being beyond the last defender when the ball was played to her and she had screamed "Come on!" in the first overtime, disagreeing angrily, gesturing with her arm. "No!"

She had been the team's leading scorer for the year, and the World Cup, two goals against Nigeria and one against Germany, but the tense comeback against Germany, the own goal and the falling behind and the emotional rescue, had sapped her energy and she could not recover. Everything went into Germany and there was nothing left. "Do what you can," she told herself before the final, sensing that she was tired and her teammates were tired and that it would not be a pretty, attacking game. *The pressure is off. We made the final. All you have to do is go out with any energy you have left and fight and keep fighting.*

"The tournament was probably more intense than anything we had to handle in our lives," Milbrett said. "Being the U.S. team and having all that pressure, we were all exhausted. I don't think as much physically as mentally. I was surprised by how tired I thought China was, too. China didn't attack the way they can. We didn't attack the way we can. A lot has to do with the fact that we were wiped out. Touches on the ball weren't there. Technique was breaking down. You just have to fight through it. You just have to battle, battle. I don't think the teams consciously held back. But so much was at stake. And because you didn't have the energy you normally would have, you didn't take any risks. That one mistake might be the winning goal."

Seven minutes into the second overtime, Milbrett stood at the right edge of the penalty box, waving her arm, the same insistent wave she had made toward Joy Fawcett before collecting a pass and scoring the winning goal against China in the gold-medal game at the 1996 Summer Olympics. Brandi Chastain spotted Milbrett and bent a pass toward her. Bai Jie, the Chinese defender, intercepted with her head, but it bounced free and Milbrett trapped it and gathered herself and hammered the ball. It was a hasty move, a hurried wheeling made in exhaustion, and the ball slammed off the stomach of Bai Jie. The Chinese defender fell to the ground, trying to catch her breath. After the game, Bai would get a severe headache and team officials would try to revive her using the healing of qigong, moving their hands in circles near her, trying to marshal the body's intangible forces.

Milbrett wiped the sweat off her face with the front of her jersey. *This is not fun, we're just working out here, not even playing soccer, just work.* There was no more running in her legs, and her feet were hurting and she felt like she was walking even when she was jogging. She had looked at the clock in the first half and the minutes seemed to take forever and then they had begun to speed up and now there was almost nothing left, nothing on the clock, nothing in her legs.

"Some days you are going to be an incredible goal scorer, some days you are going to be the playmaker, some days you are going to dig your foot into the ground every time you try to pass the ball, and some days you are going to be a workhorse and give your team what you can," Milbrett said. "That's what I was, the workhorse, doing what I can."

Her mother was in the stands, Elsie Milbrett-Parham, and before the game, mother and daughter had made eye contact. Both had a muscular compactness, and through their own playing careers could be traced the arc of opportunity for women in sports. Elsie Milbrett-Parham grew up on a farm in Minnesota and went to high school in a lumber town in western Oregon in the early 1960s, and her school did not even offer varsity sports for girls. But she had lived on a farm and she had a farmer's resilient optimism. She kept pushing for a chance to play, and she joined a men's softball league in suburban Portland, Oregon, then helped to organize a women's league. In 1979, she was sitting in the bleachers when someone mentioned the idea of a women's soccer league, and she jumped up and said, "I'll play."

At 54, she was still playing in an over-40 league, but her team, the Hearts, had to do without her in the regional playoffs because her daughter was playing in the World Cup. Fly home between matches, her coach had implored her. *Your team is as important to you as Tiffeny's is to her.*

"I'll be there next year," Milbrett-Parham said. "The regionals don't compare to the World Cup."

Elsie Milbrett-Parham worked on an assembly line in the techtronics industry and she raised Tiffeny, and her older brother, Mark, as a single mother. She planted apple trees and pear trees, made her own apple juice and orange juice, and canned beans and beets from her garden. Beginning in the fourth or fifth grade, Tiffeny said, she took a job for several summers picking strawberries, getting up 4:30 in the morning and catching a bus while the fields were still damp, working until 1 or 2 in the afternoon, until her hands were stained red with the juice of her efforts. The money never seemed to match the hours put in. It was good, awful work, she said, what the kids did in Hillsboro, Oregon, when they were still too young to flip hamburgers or toss pizza dough. One of 11 children, her mother had done similar work as a teenager, living in a cabin with her siblings in the summers and picking green beans to pay for her school clothes.

"My dad was never a figure in my life," Tiffeny said. "I never knew him. I met him a couple of times, but he never wanted to take responsibility for what was his. My mom said, fine. She raised us by herself. It was tough, paycheck to paycheck, but my mom was responsible and organized. I wouldn't say I missed out on anything. We never had food stamps or had to go to a shelter."

On weekends, Milbrett-Parham took her kids camping and skiing on water and on snow, and Tiffeny tagged along to her mother's rec league games of softball and soccer. She began her own career at age seven, and later took a refereeing class. She served as a linesman during her mother's games, sometimes receiving payment in the form of tips from her mother's friends. If she was hesitant to call fouls, it was understandable, Elsie said, "because when you're 12 or 14, it's hard to blow the whistle on people as old as your mother."

While her mother's options were limited to intramural sports in high school, and playing basketball with the boys during recess, Tiffeny became an all-state athlete in soccer, basketball and track. In college, she tied a national record, since broken, with 103 goals at the University of Portland.

"I never had the lack of opportunity that my mother did," Tiffeny said. "She always wanted to play, she always encouraged me to play. She never said, 'Tiff, that's not what girls do.'" Unlike her mother, Tiffeny and her teammates had nearly three decades of backing from Title IX. "We were never told, girls don't play," Milbrett said. "We know we deserve to be respected and considered professional athletes."

Elsie Milbrett-Parham had scheduled her vacation during the World Cup and had flown with her husband, Warren, from Portland to the East Coast and had driven to games in East Rutherford, New Jersey, Chicago, Boston, and Washington to watch her daughter play, traveling 2,500 miles of highway in 11 days. Then she flew West again for a semifinal match in Palo Alto, California, worked for a week at home in Portland, and took a flight to Los Angeles the night before the final.

"I wish this opportunity had been there for me, but these things take time to grow," she had said before the World Cup began. "A lot of men still feel we're supposed to be cooking the meals, waiting for them to come home. At least it's falling by the wayside. We're all going to go out and have fun, then come home and cook and clean the house together."

Now, as she sat in the Rose Bowl, wearing a replica of her daughter's jersey, Elsie said she felt some small achievement in kick-starting the momentum of Tiffeny's success.

"It was like you were seeing yourself through them," she said. "We didn't hold our daughters back from doing the things we would liked to have done. I remembered vividly some of the things we used to talk about when she was younger. How people would recognize how good she was and encourage her to move to a higher-caliber team. I told her she should probably stick to soccer and use basketball and track as an outlet for soccer. That it could possibly lead to a full-ride scholarship and maybe the Olympic Games. I told her she'd find some ladies in track with long legs whose one stride would be two of hers. And in basketball she'd find ladies who'd be way too tall. Soccer was going to be her best choice. But I never thought it would bloom to this. When she was 10 or 11, she'd come to my practices and she'd bring her shoes and her ball, and if we needed someone to scrimmage, she's step in and play. She'd be a forward and I'd defend her. We played pretty hard. I always made sure we had food on the table. Sometimes it was only potatoes and eggs. It was her and Mark's job to help in the garden, to snap the beans. One time, they put them all on the floor, and I had cat hair in all my beans. I didn't think it hurt either of the two to let them work in the strawberry fields. I went to the bean fields. We stayed in a cabin. The five oldest of us, we'd go out all summer, right after school in late May or early June, and come home in August. That's how we earned our school clothes. When Tiffeny was born, she weighed five pounds, 13 ounces. When I unwrapped her for the first time, to take her home from the hospital, I said, 'Look at those feet.' They were tiny feet. Soccer feet."

Her uncommon name came from the classified ads of her mother's company newspaper. There was a cat for sale named Tiffeny. Her mother liked the name and gave it to her daughter. Her uncommon soccer success came from her explosive acceleration, a compressed sturdiness at 5-foot-2 and a deft touch in tight spaces. She had played point guard in high school and she possessed exquisite vision and anticipation in the crosswalk jumble in front of the goal, a confound-ing genius for passing when it seemed she should be shooting and shooting when it seemed she should be passing.

"She's like dynamite ready to explode," DiCicco said in hyperbolic praise. "Mia twists you into the ground, Tiff blows by you and makes you spin. She's the quickest from point A to point B. She's a goal scorer. She has a knack of not doing a heck of a lot sometimes, but the ball rolls to her and she's in front of the goal. She was our best attacking weapon."

She also had a forward's artistic need for unimpeded expression, and there was an inevitable tug between player and coach for freedom and control. Milbrett believed that soccer was not a blackboard game like basketball, that it could not be orchestrated by firm direction, that it should be felt more than coached. This is why she loved soccer, because it freed her, and the way she played was an expression of how she was feeling at the moment. Two months before the World Cup, the assistant coach Lauren Gregg brought Milbrett and DiCicco together and helped to mediate the tug of war. Milbrett wanted to be left alone, to fol-low her own unobstructed compass. DiCicco was willing to give her room but he wanted her to be in better shape and to know when it was time to be an individual and when it was time to fold herself into the team.

The World Cup came, and Milbrett led the Americans in scoring, but she did not receive the same attention that the leading scorer on a men's World Cup team would have received. She did not score a decisive goal but, in part, a double standard was at work, the familiar, harsh bias that required female athletes to be beautiful as well as talented. She was handsome, with a wide, expressive face and blond ponytail, but the same muscular compactness that made her a great soccer player did not make her a great leggy spokesperson.

"If you look at anybody who's been marketed, it's been somebody who has been drop-dead hot and gorgeous," Milbrett said. "For men, you just have to be good. It doesn't matter what the hell you look like. For women, you have to be good and you have to be gorgeous. Maybe you're not even the best one on your team. Just as long as you look good, you're marketed. People's opinions are that this team is gorgeous. That doesn't bother me. What bothers me is the double standard in society and athletics. I am not drop-dead gorgeous. I don't know what I can do, keep scoring I guess. I did get some publicity, but I don't think I got my share. Three goals in the World Cup is a solid performance, not mincemeat. I do think I am somewhat a victim of that double standard."

She spoke as directly as she accelerated toward the goal, with a blunt candor that drew her the nickname in college of No Tact Tiff. Michelle Akers, a good friend, said that Milbrett spoke with the uncensored voice of a kid who yells, "Hey, Mom, that lady is fat!" and provided release from the rigors of buttoned-down politeness required by athletes of high visibility.

"So much about the history of this team, people latch on to the 91ers," Milbrett said, referring to the players who had been around since the 1991 World Cup. "I cannot wait until the 91ers leave because there's so much more about this team than the 91ers. It's a team thing. There are people who do incredible things at any given circumstance. But it's the 91ers who are goo-gooed and gah-gahed over. They are awesome. They were trailblazing, strong, incredible, history-making women. It's not a problem. It's a great, wonderful story, but we're living in the present now, things are different."

✻ ✻ ✻

Eight minutes into the second overtime, Kristine Lilly played a pass toward the right corner and Milbrett chased it down, but her legs were gone and her crossing pass had no energy, just the slow roll of a putt. Nothing on the pass, nothing in her legs. Two more minutes and her afternoon would be done. "I had done my job," she said. "It was time for someone else to do their job."

The temperature was over 100 degrees but Joy Fawcett began to feel chilled. For two hours she had run up and down in the withering heat, drinking little water, and in the middle of summer her arms felt a chilly shiver. Raw blisters kept stinging the feet of Sun Wen, the Chinese captain. *Can I hold on? Can I hold on?* Zhao Lihong, a collision at midfield, an awkward split of her legs. She limped out, and was replaced by Qiu Haiyan, a specialist at penalty kicks. Still seven minutes until the end of overtime, but Coach Ma Yuanan had seen the game slow to a run-walk and he had begun to plan ahead. In the 10th minute, a corner kick for the Americans, Shannon MacMillan driving the ball to the far goal post and Julie Foudy jumping and colliding with a Chinese player. Foudy sitting on the ground for a few extra seconds, her face flushed, taking a couple of breaths, waiting for Chastain to help her up.

"It was like, 'I can't wait until this game is over,'" Foudy said. "Not in a bad sense, but because of all the emotions, all the things going on. I was going to be able to exhale. I always knew we were going to win. I knew. Not overconfidence, but a belief that we had put in enough work and we were going to win the whole damn thing."

The team seemed tired to Foudy the whole tournament. It was the pressure, probably, the pressure and the travel. She kept talking with Lilly and Carla Overbeck. *It's like I don't have a spark, like my legs are dead, like I can't get going into that extra gear.* Lining up in the tunnel before the Germany game was the most stressful moment. It was the quarterfinals, the knockout phase of the tournament, a lot of pressure on the Americans. If they lost and did not make the final, few people would consider the tournament a success. There was no pressure, just opportunity, the players kept saying, but underneath they felt great pressure. Foudy lining up next to the Germans in the tunnel. *Holy, shit, these women are huge.* She never thought like that. *Get that out of your head, chill, you're fine.* That was the most nervous game, the own goal and the falling behind and DiCicco saying at halftime, "If you want your dream to end in 45 minutes, just keep doing what you're doing."

"I felt like shit during the warm-ups," Foudy said. "I couldn't breathe. I had nothing. I don't know if it was nerves or I was feeling run-down. I had nothing. Every run I made, I would be breathing heavily."

The Brazil game was easier in the semifinals, and Foudy had set up the first American goal with a crossing pass to Cindy Parlow. After that, the Americans could just play. There was nothing to prove in the final, no worries about a full stadium, or the viability of a women's league, nothing to do against China but just play. But, of course, the nerves were still there and it was hot and, in the first half Foudy's legs were heavy again. *Goddamn, I've had a week off, and I'm feeling like I've just played a game.* She did not have great speed, she was a cruiser in midfield, and a change of pace was everything. She needed another gear and she did not have one. The second half was much better. She adjusted to the heat and the defense settled in, then Akers left and the game became frantic and Lilly had to save everything with her alertness on the goal line. When Fan Yunjie headed the ball, Foudy's heart sank and she remembered the emptiness after the loss to Norway in 1995 and she did not want to feel that feeling again. Then Lilly saved the ball and Foudy said, "Thank you Lord."

After that, much praying. *I swear I'll go to church again. I know I haven't been a great Catholic. Just let us win this damn game. I'll start going to church again. Please God, please God.*

"Isn't that pathetic?" Foudy said, laughing over a beer a few months later.

She was the team's comic relief and social conscience, its co-captain and its keen business mind. She was a confidant of Billie Jean King and she would be named president of the Women's Sports Foundation and she was the most visible and articulate advocate among the American soccer players for gender equity in athletics. As a girl in Mission Viejo, California, she had followed the Los Angeles Lakers and Dodgers, trying to emulate men she could never emulate. "I love Magic Johnson, but I could never dunk a basketball," Foudy said. "I think it's important for girls to see something that's more realistic to them."

The day before the final, a story had appeared in the business section of *USA Today,* in which marketing experts predicted little endorsement success for the American women because they were too much a team, not reliant enough on individual stars.

"How sad is that, that the business world believes you have to show yourself individually," Foudy said. "That's what is so wrong with professional sports today. God forbid, you're not going to make any money because you're too much of a team. It's unbelievable, sad."

She also bristled at criticism, made by some purists before the tournament, that the World Cup was too much about the celebration of women's sports and not enough about the playing of soccer. "To say this was a soccer event and we were bastardizing it, come on," Foudy said. "This was about so much more than soccer, and I'm glad. You should see the bad things that happen to women in other countries, and the hope this is going to give them. I think the biggest repercussions are going to be outside this country."

Studying in Barcelona, Spain, in 1992, Foudy had been looking for a place to train, when she and a friend heard about soccer matches being played on indoor tennis courts. The sight of any woman playing soccer, much less one skilled enough to be a world champion, was so rare in a macho society that the game stopped. People began to gather, as if to see an endangered species at the zoo. "Where are you from?" they wanted to know. The men in the game did not know what to do, and instead of becoming aggressive, they backed off. *We don't want to hurt the woman.*

"We were freaks," Foudy said.

In some places, thing had changed since then. Slowly, glacially, but they were changing. In 1996, the American women won the Olympic gold medal before 76,000 fans in Athens, Georgia, and the game was broadcast in Cairo, Egypt. Several days later, a forceful advocate named Sahar Ezzat El Hawari got women's soccer officially approved by the Egyptian soccer federation. Egypt competed in the qualifying tournament for the 1999 Women's World Cup and now had a women's league featuring eight teams across the country, El Hawari said. The World Cup only furthered the acceptance of women's soccer in Egypt. The ministry of education has agreed to begin having training centers at schools for girls beginning at age eight or nine, said El Hawari, who is a member of the women's committee of FIFA, soccer's world governing body.

"It's like introducing anything new for women and girls in this area, with its traditions and customs," El Hawari said. "They don't welcome girls and women having more power and being stars. People said this wasn't a sport for women, but I had to make them aware that it was being played all over the world. They could see it on television. It wasn't the fundamentalists saying women shouldn't be wearing shorts. We have swimming and athletics and volleyball, where the costumes show much more than soccer. It was just that it was something new. I had patience, and they saw me insisting, and the opposition started to break down."

In Morocco, 200 soccer clubs for girls and women have been formed in recent years, said Nawal El Moutawakel, who took the 400-meter hurdles at the 1984 Summer Olympics and became the first woman from a Muslim country to win a gold medal. She is now a member of the International Olympic Committee.

"It was great to see an event like the World Cup, organized by women for women," El Moutawakel said. "It showed that the women can compete as strong as the men. If I could do my career again, I think I would play soccer. I had to do something more practical in the late 1970s and early '80s. Soccer was thought of as indecent. A woman's place was in the kitchen, not in the stadium."

In late 1995, Foudy began to hear about American sporting goods manufacturers using child labor to make soccer balls in developing nations, children as young as nine or 10 working for pennies an hour, stitching as many as four balls a day by hand, working until their fingers bled. After the 1996 Summer Olympics, Reebok asked Foudy to endorse a soccer ball. First, she told company officials, she wanted to see firsthand the conditions under which the balls were made at the Reebok factory in Pakistan. She visited the village of Sialkot, at the foot of the Himalayas, where most of the world's hand-stitched balls are made by various companies, and she saw that children as young as five were working for as little as seven cents an hour, stitching the balls in homes with other members of their families. She toured villages and spoke to workers and, convinced that Reebok was using no workers under 15 years of age, she agreed to endorse the ball.

"I hope things get better, but it's a difficult process," Foudy said. "You're dealing with governments that don't care about children working. And it's hard to put our Western ideals on their situations. If you don't pay people enough so they can survive with only the father or mother working, how can they expect the kids not to work?"

In an authorized biography of Foudy, written for young readers, she criticized Michael Jordan and other athletes for not speaking forcefully on the issue of using child labor to manufacture sporting equipment. "I am very concerned about the attitude of other professional athletes," she said. "I would hope that they would begin to care and speak up."

Initially, her own intended profession was to be medicine, not soccer. Foudy was accepted into medical school after graduating from Stanford University in 1993, but she delayed her entry for one year, then two, then decided that medicine seemed more of an obligation than a conviction. "I wasn't sure I wanted it to be my life for the next 40 years," she said.

Television seemed a perfect match for her effusive personality, and Foudy received solid reviews for her studio analysis during the 1998 men's World Cup in France. She wanted to do more television commentary, and also to help counsel female athletes about the financial and social issues they face collectively, regardless of sport. "We all have the same obstacles to overcome," Foudy said. "It seems like, if you know ahead of time what the obstacles are going to be and how to avoid them, you could share that insight."

Her serious ambitions, though, were leavened with an irreverent comic sensibility. Her teammates called her "Loudy Foudy" for her voluble manner, and her family held up a sign at the World Cup final that said "Rowdy Foudy." She was an admitted junk-food junkie, and after scoring a hat trick against Ukraine in December of 1998, she attributed her success to a diet of beer and doughnuts. When she scored a goal against Denmark in the World Cup opener, Foudy struck a pose from *Austin Powers: the Spy Who Shagged Me*. And when Chastain appeared in *Gear* magazine, Foudy skewered her with an Austin Powers video satire, wearing a bikini fashioned from shin guards and crossword puzzles and rounding up Tisha Venturini to play mini-Brandi. As Chastain was preparing to get married in 1996, Foudy forged a letter on soccer federation stationery, saying that a wedding was no legitimate reason to leave training camp a day early. Then she broke up laughing as Chastain fumed on the team bus.

During the days of smothering humidity before the World Cup, as the team did fitness training in the wilting heat of Orlando, Florida, Foudy would yell out, "Is Norway doing this? No, they're home eating Sasquatch." China could not be training this hard either, she would scream at her teammates, prodding them through another sweat-dripping sprint or enervating shuttle run. But even the most willful endurance was being challenged after two hours in 105-degree heat of the World Cup final. *Stay alert, stay alert.* Warning herself every 30 seconds. *I've marked my player great the whole game, and no one will care if she slips in and gets a goal in the last five seconds.* Her attention span wandering. Slapping herself in the face. *Stay focused, stay focused.* Carla Overbeck and Chastain saying, "Come on, come on," seeing that she was exhausted, encouraging her to keep running. Her legs were dead. Not burning, just dead.

Five minutes left in the second overtime. Tisha Venturini substituting for Milbrett, the third and final American replacement allowed by the rules. Venturini had scored two goals against North Korea and had celebrated with a back flip. The photographs had captured her in digital suspension, her body arched like a human circumflex. "We only need one goal this time," DiCicco told her as he sent her in. The Americans had a corner kick and Mia Hamm waited for Venturini to run onto the field. Unlike her ponytailed teammates, she had short blond hair, and cheekbones of the fashion magazines. She had taken four shots and scored two goals in the World Cup. Aside from Akers, she struck the ball with her head as well as anyone on the team, and with one flick just below the hairline she could make the Americans world champions. Hamm stood in the left corner of the stadium, pulling a stray wisp of hair behind her ear, delaying her kick until Venturini jogged to the top of the penalty area, the crowd on its feet, clapping, the wheat-field ripple of waving arms, the heat forgotten now in the yearning for ecstatic conclusion.

Growing up in Modesto, California, Venturini and her brother used the garage as the frame of a goal and they would open the door and head the ball inside. Or they would have competitions in the entryway to the house, scuffing up the walls, contests to see how many times they could strike the ball with their heads before it touched the ground. She could do it more than a hundred times.

"I played a lot with boys," Venturini said. "Right away, I was aggressive, wasn't afraid of the ball."

Three months earlier, Venturini and Hamm had connected for a late, winning goal against China in an exhibition in Hershey, Pennsylvania. Hamm drove a low crossing pass in the 93rd minute and the ball, with its speed and spin, kicked out of the hands of the Chinese goalkeeper. The ball came free and Venturini punched it into the net. She had played with great efficiency in the World Cup, and one touch could make her the hero. Hamm struck the corner kick, but she was tired after 115 minutes and the distant accuracy was no longer in her feet. The kick drifted high and Venturini could not reach it, but she kept running after the ball, chasing, chasing, full of energy amid the walk-run of fatigue, trying to score, attempting to do in five minutes what no one else could do in two hours, running, chasing, trying to do something, anything, playing in fast forward while everyone moved in slow motion.

"I could see the exhaustion, I could tell they didn't have anything left," Venturini said. "I felt helpless. I was full of energy. I wish I could have it shared it with them. They were so exhausted. People were dragging. How much more could they fight? Two overtimes, 100 degrees, the end of the tournament. I was just trying to cover as much ground as I could. It seemed like I was out there for five seconds. I ran around in circles and boom, it was over."

For almost two hours she had watched, sitting and standing in the humid bus stop that served as a bench. The Rose Bowl was full and the painted chants of U-S-A, U-S-A had given her confidence and a kind of calmness. She was nervous and excited, she felt that, too, but 90,000 fans cheering for her and her teammates had also brought a feeling of power and calm. *This is the greatest feeling I've ever had.* She had been a starter in midfield for the gold-medal team at the Olympics, then she had fallen into a post-Olympic depression, losing weight and strength and her place in the lineup. All that seemed distant now. She had recovered sufficient weight and her career and, even though she was not playing as much, she said she had never been happier.

"It makes you realize what you have," Venturini said. "How many people would kill to be on this team? I learned that's the most important part. Not about playing time or scoring all the goals. It's being part of this in whatever way. I look at every person being just as valuable as anyone else. Everyone brings something different to the table, whether you're on the field doing it or on the bench. You need all different sources."

As with many Olympians, Venturini felt a void in her life after the Atlanta Games. The American diver Mark Lenzi became so despondent after winning the springboard competition at the 1992 Summer Games in Barcelona that he offered to sell his gold medal. Venturini had just won her own gold medal, and she thought there could be nothing better, but instead she found herself bored, lost, displaced. It was frequently that way, a life of training for the Olympics, two weeks of full stadiums and international attention and pinnacle achievement and then emptiness, anticlimax. She had graduated from North Carolina, where she had won four collegiate titles. The national team would not reconvene for almost seven months. There was no school, no official training, nowhere to be, nothing to do. She could not get a fulltime job because soccer would start again, yet the World Cup was still three years away. A life full of structure then no structure at all. "You win a gold medal and then what?" she said. She began to exercise obsessively, she said, worrying about staying fit, working out for up to four hours a day, running seven or eight miles, not eating properly, losing 20 pounds.

"I missed being around my teammates, I missed being around school, soccer, I really got myself down," Venturini said. "I got really skinny, lost my strength. I got down pretty low. I was home with my parents, I didn't have a job. I was just working out, scared I wasn't going to be fit. I did myself in. I was getting depressed. I was extremely bored and sad. I would run, play, whatever. I didn't have anything to shoot for right away. I wasn't training for anything in particular. I had a rough time."

Her boyfriend had teased her about post-Olympic depression before the Atlanta Games. He had heard about it, read about it. She didn't know what he was talking about. "Afterward, I was going, 'Oh my God, that's what happened,'" Venturini said.

When the national team began training again in February of 1997, Venturini said that Foudy, Overbeck, Hamm, and Lilly confronted her in a sort of intervention. *You need to do something. You're too thin, not happy. We're worried about you.* The meeting was emotional, she was crying, they were crying, and she felt an unburdening. She had never been really open or sad or depressed, and she was hoping the sadness and depression would simply go away, like a cold, but they did not leave. Now she knew that something had to be done.

"We told her we cared," Lilly said. "I had a funk as well. I felt lost, didn't have a regimen every day, wasn't around my friends constantly. We told her that if she needed anything, we were here. It's hard to see someone go through that when they're not really happy. She needed that little comfort."

She was put on a diet of 3,200 calories a day, given counseling, a weight-lifting program and a minimum weight limit for reporting to each training camp. She listed everything she ate and sent the list to David Oliver, the team's conditioning coach. She stepped on the scale at the beginning of each camp, and if she did not meet the required weight she was not allowed to train. Tough luck. We will give you some time, DiCicco told her, and when she began to lapse he became more insistent, she said. *Look, you either get it done or you're not going to be here.* Her teammates began to write her letters. *We need you.* The urging helped. She began sustaining a proper diet, and lifting weights and getting stronger, and her weight climbed to 125 pounds and she calmed her personal maelstrom.

"It would have been easy to say, 'That's it, I don't need this,'" Venturini said. "I would say that, then someone would write me a note or say something. 'Come on, we need you.' You get a second chance and you say, no way I can let this go. I've been given this gift. Here I am on this team, I'm not going to piss it away. I got a second chance. A lot of people don't get second chances. I'm not going to blow it."

Three minutes remaining in the second overtime. Many players walking now, the rote door-to-door of commuters. A final threat by China, a pass from midfield, a header to Zhang Ouying near the penalty box, a clever chip over the head of Overbeck. An urgent sprint toward the goal, a jockey-whip desperateness in the homestretch legs, Zhang trying to win and Overbeck trying to prevent losing, Zhang faster but Overbeck gifted with the physics of elbow leverage and angle of pursuit, poking the ball to a charging Scurry as Zhang spun and tumbled down. Scurry one-hopped the ball and clutched it to her chest with gloved hands, as if it were hazardous, radioactive. Zhang lay face down on the trampled grass, her last chance exhausted, her hands on the painted white line six yards from the goal, a mime gymnast clutching the high bar.

A final summoning of will, fresh runs by Venturini and Whalen, Kate Sobrero racing Zhang down the sideline, Overbeck pushing forward and taking a somersaulting foul. One last free kick for the Americans. Overbeck limping slightly and breathing heavily. Hamm bent over in exhaustion, then placed the kick dangerously near the goal. Chastain ran toward the ball and jumped but her calves seized up and she did an awkward bicycling through the air. Gao Hong punched the ball away and Chastain sat on the ground and grabbed her right leg, trying to stretch the knot out of her muscles. "I felt like shit, I was hurting," she said. "The last 10 minutes I was cramping." *Oh my God, don't make a mistake. This could be the game. Don't be stupid and run forward when you know you might not get the ball, because you know you have to run back.* A minute remaining, a final substitute for China, Xie Huiling, whose father owned four factories and was one of the country's new rich. Then, after two hours, it was over. The game would go to penalty kicks. Brian Glanville, one of England's most eloquent soccer writers, wrote in reference to the 1994 men's World Cup that penalty kicks were a "dire, disgraceful, dishonorable conclusion to the game's greatest competition."

"It didn't seem right to end with penalty kicks," Fawcett said. "All that running, all that playing and it comes down to something like that."

Some would have preferred to keep playing, perhaps removing a player from each team after a certain period, then another, like power plays in hockey, until someone scored. Others would have liked to replay the entire game a day or two or three later, but both proposals would have played havoc with the schedules of spectators and broadcasters. So it was penalty kicks, universally hated but unsurpassed in dramatic consequence.

"I knew after the second overtime, I couldn't go anymore," Fawcett said. "No way I could have played another overtime."

The American players walked toward the bench, and Foudy drank from a bottle of water and clapped her hands and said, "Let's go, we're still fine, we're still fine."

"As a captain, you want to emit that confidence," Foudy said. "Inside, you're going, 'Oh my God, I can't believe we're in penalty kicks.'"

16

Fly in the Milk

B RIANA SCURRY sat on the Rose Bowl turf, away from her teammates, drinking a bottle of water, her eyes staring far across the
field but not really seeing the painted faces, the flag people, everything drawn inward, her own face a mask of concentration. The look
of death, she called it. Years after high school in suburban Minneapolis, her former classmates told her they had been afraid of that look in
the hallways. She was black and the majority of them were white. No
one picked on her, she said, or made kid-cruel racial remarks, just the
opposite, they left her alone, thought she was unapproachable
because of the withdrawn look on her face. *We were afraid of you. We
thought you were going to kick our ass. You looked so scary. You looked
pissed off at someone all the time.* She hadn't been mad at anyone at
all. She was just walking down the hallway, lost in thought or late for
class, but not angry. "My mom said I look like I'm going to kill someone when I'm playing," Scurry said. This was her game face, as ath-

letes called it, a heightened moment beyond spoken words, a shutting out, a feeling of calm and confidence and imminent prevailing. *This is my time. I can win this thing for my team. This game is going to penalty kicks for some reason and I'm supposed to be the one to deliver. Just save one. I've just got to save one. That's all I gotta do.*

"I felt really good," Scurry said. "I felt I was the best in the world at penalty kicks. I felt like I was going to stop one and Gao was not."

Tony DiCicco, himself a former goalkeeper, spoke with Scurry, asked if she were comfortable, if she needed anything. Sun Wen, the Chinese captain, would likely shoot to Scurry's right, he told her. She would disguise the kick, make it appear that she was going to Scurry's left, then she would go the other way. There was not much information on the other four Chinese shooters.

"You've had a tremendous tournament," DiCicco told Scurry. "Now you can put another stamp on it. We've been in this before. The pressure is on the shooter. There's no pressure on you, Bri. You can only be the hero, never the goat. If you don't save any, no one is going to blame you. If you save one, you'll be the hero."

The best a goalkeeper could hope for was to block one kick and have a nervous shooter miss the goal entirely on another kick. If you save one you are a hero, DiCicco joked with reporters, and if you save two, they build a monument in your hometown. Don't guess and dive one way or the other, he told Scurry. Don't stand still and react after the ball is kicked, either. It took only half a second for a penalty kick to cross the goal line. Half a second was not enough time to react. A goalkeeper had to travel too much distance in too little time. He wanted her to wait patiently and to pick up a cue when the shooter planted her foot, some unintended giveaway when the swing leg was a yard or a foot or two inches from the ball, a betrayal of the eyes, face, feet, hips. Read the shooter and there would be some revelation. There was another option, too. Before one of the penalty kicks, Scurry might have a strong hunch about the direction of the ball, a moment of prescience, a feeling that could not be articulated but was no less convincing in its clarity. If she had that assured feeling, she should go with it. DiCicco had experienced these intuitive moments in his own career, where he knew where the ball was going before it was kicked. "You don't know how you know, you just do," he said.

Goalkeeping is where women were at their greatest physical disadvantage compared to men. Women had to defend the same goal area—eight feet high, eight yards wide—but female goalkeepers were generally six or more inches shorter than men, had smaller hands and did not jump as high. Scurry believed that she did have one advantage over a male goalkeeper in detecting the intended trajectory of a shot: Because women's hips were wider, the hips opened up sooner as the shooter approached the ball. "With most women, you can see their intentions much earlier than with men," she said.

Through the years, goalkeepers had tried any number of psychological tricks during penalty kicks. DiCicco wanted Scurry to take her time walking into the goal on each kick, to adjust her socks, or pretend to tie her shoes. Make the shooter wait. Interrupt her rhythm. Maybe some small uncertainty would seep into her concentration. One of the most flamboyant attempts at intimidation occurred during the 1972 Pan American Games, a warm-up for the Munich Olympics. The United States held a 5–4 lead in penalty kicks over El Salvador in the semifinals. A save, or an errant kick, and the game would be over. As the Salvadoran forward readied himself, the ostentatious American goalkeeper, Shep Messing, paced back and forth, muttering, cursing, then he charged out of the goal, ripped off his shirt and began swinging it wildly over his head.

"I ranted in pidgin Spanish and obscene English: 'Simon Bolivar is a puta. Your mother sleeps with burros,'" Messing wrote in his autobiography, *The Education of an American Soccer Player*. "I spat, I snarled, I ran at the El Salvador player and I took a few licks at him with my jersey, screaming all the while. Then it was over. I was proud of myself. I had shown him I was crazy and that any fool had better think twice about scoring on me."

Messing walked calmly back to the goal and set up in his crouch. The kick sailed high over the crossbar.

DiCicco's favorite bit of penalty-kick chicanery occurred during the quarterfinals of the 1986 men's World Cup in a match between Belgium and Spain. As the Spanish player, Eloy, prepared to take his penalty kick, the Belgian goalie Jean-Marie Pfaff walked to the top corner of the penalty area, DiCicco said.

"The Spanish player came up there, he was confident, he put the ball down and he looked up and there was no keeper," DiCicco said. "And now he's waiting. Pfaff was down on his knees, tying his shoes, just looking at him." Disrupted, Eloy took the kick, and Pfaff dived to his right for the save.

According to the current rules, goalkeepers were allowed to move laterally on penalty kicks but not forward until the ball was struck. The rule was seldom enforced, and many goalkeepers came forward, just as in professional basketball, where players traveled and carried the ball and the referees did not blow their whistles. DiCicco believed that it was essential for Scurry to charge forward, reducing the shooter's angle. Otherwise, he did not think a goalkeeper had any fair chance of stopping a penalty kick. She had been reluctant to follow his instruction, preferring her own methods, and at a tournament in Portugal several months before the World Cup, DiCicco had sent his replacement goalkeeper, Saskia Webber, to warm up on the sideline during a match. But he had not put her into the game, fearing it might damage Scurry's confidence.

"At some point, I came to the realization that we were going to win or lose this thing with Briana Scurry," DiCicco said.

If coming off the line violated the letter of the rules, he believed the tactic remained within the spirit of the rules. If a goalkeeper could not come forward, how could she protect an area the size of a two-car garage?

"In baseball, a player sliding into second base is doing everything he can to interfere with the player covering the bag," DiCicco said. "That's against the rules, but in the spirit of the game, a guy goes in hard, upends the second baseman or the shortstop, and we say, 'Hey that's good baseball.' The written rule says the keeper can't move off the line. The spirit of the game says you've got to move. If you don't move, you don't have a chance."

In December of 1961, Ernest Scurry left Galveston, Texas, for Houston with $50 in his pocket and said he spent $47 on a train ticket to Minneapolis. Don't look back, his father had told him as he boarded the Rock Island Railroad. Don't look back and you won't feel tempted to return anytime soon. He wouldn't return, not for 19 years. He boarded the train carrying $3 and a picture of his dream home from a magazine or an advertisement or some such place. On September 11, 1961, Hurricane Carla had blown through Galveston, with winds reaching 173 miles per hour, raising tides as much as 12 feet, and leaving the Scurry home unlivable. There did not seem much reason to stay on the Gulf Coast anymore. These were Jim Crow days, segregated drinking fountains, blacks upstairs at the movies, whites downstairs, and he had three children to support and no real education, and there were few encouraging prospects beyond summer work on the beach and winters driving a cab and the fry-cook subsistence of separate and unequal. He worked until there was nothing but working and sleeping and eating, and he still never get ahead. He had a cousin in Minneapolis, and a picture of his dream house, and he would head up there first, and his wife, Robbie, a practical nurse, would follow in a couple of months.

"People were beginning to get tired," Robbie Scurry said. "They were picketing Woolworth's. People got tired of paying money and having to go to the back of the bus, the back of everything. We were hearing about Martin Luther King. Having been raised the way I was, I didn't believe anyone telling me what I could or couldn't do."

Ernest Scurry arrived in Minneapolis in the cold of December, and he remembered the snow was so tall, piled on the edges of sidewalks, that people seemed to be walking through tunnels. His cousin offered her home until he could get on his feet. He worked two custodial jobs, then four, and having been in the army, he was eligible for funding from the GI Bill. By the time his wife arrived in February of 1962, he had bought a home, one that looked just like the picture he had been carrying with him. Eventually, he took a job as a machine operator at International Telephone and Telegraph, went to night school and became a supervisor. The family moved 20 miles to the suburb of Dayton, right on the Mississippi River, a town where it was safe enough to leave the car unlocked at night. Eventually, he would have nine children from two marriages, and eight of them would have college educations.

"I wanted something out of life, that's why I came up here," said

Ernest Scurry, who was now 71. "I'm a firm believer, always try to be the best. I got four jobs. You know what? If you want something bad enough, you'll go over, under, around the mountain until you figure out which way to get there. That's what I did."

His youngest child, Briana, would become a soccer star and Dayton would name a park in her honor. Her first love had been football. She scored nine touchdowns one season as a wide receiver in a youth league and also played cornerback, drawn to the tackling because she could "hit people and it being legal and you would not get into trouble." Her football career ended when she moved into a weight class that her parents considered dangerous. "Unless I lost seven pounds, I couldn't play in the lower division," Briana said. "I could not lose seven pounds, so I quit. Bummer."

When she was 11 or 12, a flyer was passed around the classroom, mentioning tryouts for soccer. She was placed at goalkeeper because she was a girl on a boys' team and the coach thought that she would be protected in the harbor of the net. Somehow, it didn't seem so safe diving in front of people's feet and getting upended while rushing out to smother a crossing pass. "Bri used to get hurt, and we'd have to wrap her up like a mummy," her father said.

She saw a movie called *Victory*, which featured Pelé, the Brazilian star who was considered the greatest player in the history of the game, and, according to her father, she begged her parents to get a satellite dish so that she could watch soccer matches from around the world. "She'd watch that movie over and over, and she'd watch games, and she'd learn things, how to kick, how to fake people out of position and go the opposite way," Ernest Scurry said. "I thought it was a man's game. But these young kids are something else, so we let her play. I couldn't give them everything, but I could give them a chance."

By high school, Scurry had grown to 5-foot-8, and she had become an all-state forward in basketball. As a track-and-field star, she had qualified for the Minnesota state meet as a sprinter and long jumper. Scurry's soccer team won the state championship in 1989, and she was voted the state's top female athlete. She received a partial scholarship to the University of Massachusetts, and her father came out of retirement to help make up the difference in tuition.

Her parents had wanted her to become a doctor or a lawyer, and she made the dean's list and received a degree in political science. But she wondered if she would ever receive a chance to play soccer for the women's national team. In the summer of 1992, at a camp for goalkeepers, DiCicco tapped Scurry on the back and said, "I'll be watching you today." It made her so nervous, she said, "I almost peed my pants." She gave up three goals in 15 minutes. She had never been shellacked like that in her life. Would he ever take another look at her? She returned to UMass for her junior season, and by 1993, Scurry had become the country's top collegiate goalkeeper. Her team reached the Final Four, where it faced North Carolina and its star, Mia Hamm. North Carolina won 4–1, and Hamm scored on a penalty kick against Scurry. At the postgame press conference, Hamm told her, "Keeper, nice game," and Scurry looked toward Anson Dorrance, who was coaching both North Carolina and the women's national team. "Tell him that."

"He already knows," Hamm said.

A week later, Scurry was in training camp with the national team.

DiCicco took over as head coach in 1994, and, while he was impressed with Scurry's reflexes and her athleticism, he was particularly drawn to her calm demeanor. The more roiled the game seemed to get in front of her, the more placid she became in goal. "Her mental skills are her best quality," DiCicco said. "She's incredibly athletic and has a natural competitiveness. But her greatest strength is the fact that she focuses so well in the intense part of games. As the intensity goes up, Bri seems to get calmer. The game seems to slow down for her."

He had not found her the easiest player to coach. Goalkeeping has an individual, solitary aspect, and Scurry had her own ideas about how the game should be played. Her own style had served her well. As the World Cup final extended to penalty kicks, she had collected 53 shutouts in 84 career matches. But, in the past, DiCicco had been concerned that she hung too much on the goal line, a sort of soccer Wallenda, tightroping the white paint, uncertain of what might happened if she strayed into the penalty area. That had changed in 1999, and Scurry had been more assertive patroling the box in front of the goal. Fifteen minutes into the World Cup opener against Denmark, she collided heavily with a Danish forward, and the shot to her ribs knocked the wind out of her. She fell to the ground, climbed wobbly on all fours, then went down again. Still woozy in the 17th minute, she deflected a corner kick and smothered a header that was played dangerously near the goal.

"I'm not back there smoking cigarettes, like everybody thinks," she said.

Sometimes signals still got crossed, and her teammates weren't quite sure when she was coming out of the goal and when she was staying in. This confusion was partly responsible for the own goal against Germany, Scurry coming forward for the ball and Chastain passing it back to her without looking. The stadium scoreboard flashed a close-up of Scurry's face and she had the molten look of a prosecutor, but she never said anything to Chastain, who felt bad enough already. It was all she could do to hold back, but she did. "There's no need for me to make myself feel better by making her feel worse," Scurry said. In the men's game, a goalkeeper would have been flapping his arms like some incensed crane, pointing, turning the whole stadium against the offending teammate. Scurry was not one for the gratuitous gesture. She never wanted the other team to know that she was upset. "I want them to think I'm like ice," she said.

She had sensed that something would go wrong in the Germany game, some storm-cloud dread, a plummet of her internal barometer. She didn't even want to play, she said, well not that exactly, she was afraid of something. A fear of losing. As calm as she felt before penalty kicks, she had felt scared against Germany. Then the game started and everything went wrong. Five minutes, and the Americans put the ball into their own goal. *Please God, don't do this to me again. Not like Norway in '95.* Then her teammates rallied and the Americans won and the fear was gone. If they hadn't lost that game, they were never going to lose.

Three days later, the semifinals against Brazil, nothing got past her. She came forward and smothered a breakaway with her face and she backpedaled and palmed a shot over the crossbar and she dived like a shortstop to push another shot wide. The Americans won 2–0, and Scurry called it "the best game I ever played." Afterward, she tapped her chest twice and pointed at the crowd toward her parents. Her father had suffered several strokes and now walked with a cane, and he sat in the section for disabled spectators, but he and her mother had made the long trip from Minnesota. When she was younger, he used to give her $25 if she could shut a team out for an entire tournament, then it was $100. "I bet you can't do it," he would tell her, and then she would. Now he didn't give her money anymore. "Just a big kiss," she said.

She called herself "the fly in the milk" on the American team. The only black starter on a lily-white side. "I've been comfortable being the only one, probably because I've been the only one," she said. When she was young, her parents had talked to her and said, "Bri, there are not going to be many people that look like you, but you can be better than the best." By her estimation, her family was the only black family in a radius of three or four towns around Dayton, Minnesota. There had been few racial incidents, she said. Her father liked to joke that the n-word he most often heard was neighbor. But when she was younger, older boys sometimes picked on her at the bus stop, call her chocolate, chocolate chip, blackie, and her parents put her in karate classes. They didn't want her to start any fights, but they wanted her to be able to protect herself. "We didn't want it to get out of hand," Ernest Scurry said. Her sister, Daphne, who was nine years older, sometimes walked her to the bus stop, or picked her up after school, and one time, when a kid was calling her a racial name, Daphne "scratched the crap out of his arm," Briana said. Five or six years later, she said, the kid still had scars from the scratches.

"After she scratched that kid, I guess he told everyone, and everyone left me alone," Scurry said. "No one ever bothered me. Everyone was afraid of me, from what I understand, through high school. The look I have when I play, I guess I had it when I was just walking around, going to class. People liked me, I was real athletic. I never really had too many close friends. I wasn't down with the drinking scene."

Before the World Cup, people approached her in airports, and sensing she was an athlete, asked whether she played basketball or ran track. Never soccer. "That's what they see African-Americans involved in," Scurry said. Interviews with black soccer players from elementary school to the professional level indicated that soccer is often considered a "white-girl sport," an elitist activity. Danielle Slaton, a standout player at Santa Clara University and a member of the American team that won the unofficial 1999 world youth championship, has one white parent and one black parent. When she was younger, she said, some of her black friends would ask, "Why aren't you playing basketball or running track or hanging with us more?'" After the World Cup, Slaton boarded a plane for a cross-country flight, and when she moved into first class, the flight attendants assumed she must be Scurry because she was black and played soccer. "I didn't convince them otherwise," Slaton laughed. She was headed for a training camp in Philadelphia in preparation for the world youth tournament. At the same camp, Lakeysia Beene, the all-American goalkeeper at Notre Dame, was practicing one afternoon, when a group of young boys walked by and began screaming in mistaken admiration, "Scurry! Scurry!" If she was a goalkeeper and she was black, it must be her.

Tiara and Tory Wilson, 10-year-old twins from Fairfax, Virginia, said that black kids sometimes felt inadequate playing a sport to which they had little exposure and were frequently discouraged when they tried to learn the game. "I play at my school, and some kids say, 'You stink, you can't do anything,'" Tiara Wilson said. "I saw Briana succeed, and it makes me think I can succeed. She gives me courage."

There were only two African-Americans on the World Cup team, no field players, both goalkeepers, Scurry and Saskia Webber. At the time of the World Cup, there were no black administrators in the hierarchy of the United States Soccer Federation. A study conducted by the *Orange County* (California) *Register* after the World Cup indicated that there was one black woman coaching a women's collegiate team at the Division I level. Webber, who grew up in the privilege of Princeton, New Jersey, with a mother who is Dutch and a father who is black, said "it was hard to relate" at times when she gave clinics to kids in the inner city.

Patricia Caldwell Wilson, whose daughter Staci, was a defender on the 1996 Olympic team, said she could count only five black field players in the 15 years of the existence of the national team. She has formed an organization called "Off the Bench" to address this scarcity. "It just seems the face of soccer in America is blond and blue-eyed," Wilson said. "As far as exposure, and glory on the field, black kids are never

afforded that kind of opportunity." She noted that her daughter, a former all-American at North Carolina, had played sparingly during the
Olympics and had been called to camp with the national team only
once in the past three years.

"I feel black players are perceived as having less skills," Staci Wilson said. "What's usually said is, 'You're good, fast, quick, but your
skills aren't up to par.' Or they say something about 'chemistry.' I
think we're not looked at as thinking players."

The only time she had seen evidence of racism in her career, Scurry
said, came when she was 14 or 15 and never seemed to be chosen for
the Olympic Development Program, which fast-tracks the top country's
top young players. "I went in the back door to get on this team," she said.
"You never know how you are going to get where you need to go. Sometimes you have to make your own path." Unlike much of the rest of the
world, where soccer was primarily a game of the urban poor, in the
United States it was a sport of the suburban middle class and upper middle class. The paucity of black soccer players, as Scurry saw it, was a matter of socioeconomics and opportunity. Fees for playing on club teams
could cost from $200 to $6,000 a year. She could recall only one soccer
field in the entire inner city of Minneapolis.

"I've had a few girls say I've inspired them and they see they can
go somewhere in soccer, where, before, they didn't really know if they
could or really didn't care," Scurry said. She added: "The best thing
you can do for any kid, especially African-American kids, is give them
choices. For a long time, soccer has not been there."

She hoped the World Cup would broaden that availability. She
drew encouragement from the fact that the University of Florida won
the 1998 collegiate championship with five black players, that France
won the 1998 World Cup with a roster than was an ethnic rainbow,
and that the American men's national team could put half a dozen
black players on the field at one time. The women's under-21 team
that won the 1999 unofficial world championship also featured several black players and a Hispanic high school star. When she gave
clinics in the inner city, Scurry told kids they should try soccer, that,
like licorice, they might not like it, but it was worth a taste.

"If African-Americans can have great inner city kids playing basketball, football and baseball, why can't they play soccer, too?" she said. "Why is it any different? I'm not sure how much the soccer federation is looking into the nooks and crannies for players. I think there needs to be more focus on that. Not just assuming kids will find their way to the sport eventually. Soccer is expensive. For me, it was $200 a year to play with my club team. That's insane. Inner-city kids don't have that kind of money. You need more players going to the inner city so kids can see them. Eventually, we'll get there. It will happen. It happened in tennis with Venus and Serena Williams. It happened with Tiger Woods in golf. It happened with hockey."

The American soccer federation, which has long lacked vision for the sport, has admittedly done a poor job in developing large numbers of black and Hispanic players. Slowly, that is changing as the Americans look to build the men to international respectability and to keep the women from rappelling from the peak of the sport. The federation created a foundation with a $60 million surplus from the 1994 men's World Cup and is dedicated to building 500 soccer fields across the country in the next five years. About 25 percent of the $2 million in grant money for fiscal 1999 was earmarked for underprivileged neighborhoods, according to Alan I. Rothenberg, past president of the soccer federation.

"Eventually it's going to catch up to us," Rothenberg said. "To me, soccer players around the world, men and women, it's a street game. If kids go to school, the minute they come home, they're playing until they get dragged in because it's dark. It's no different from inner-city kids who play basketball in this country. I think soccer is going to eventually be that way in the U.S. as well. It isn't so much a racial thing as a socioeconomic thing. It's going to have to change for us to make it on the men's side and to keep our edge on the women's side. If you take our two biggest ethnic groups we are targeting, you've got two different problems. The Hispanics obviously know and love the game and are playing the game, but they tend to be in their own leagues not directly affiliated with the federation. We have to seek them out and get them either to join or at least let us recruit their players. When you look at African-American players on the national teams, or in Major League Soccer, their socioeconomic background is basically the same as the

257

white players. They are middle-class suburban kids, not inner city kids. We've got to get the inner-city kids. There are two problems. One is introducing the game. The other is field development. Because it is more crowded, you don't have the space. We have to help. It's a challenge and I think we are taking the long-range view. Nobody thinks it is going to turn around in a year or two. Role models are important, too. It's important to have role models like Briana Scurry, so kids can say, 'Hey, I want to do that, too.'"

Because she was a black player, visible enough now to play in front of 40 million television viewers and to appear on a box of Wheaties, Scurry was also asked to appear before various African-American groups. Some causes she found noble and worthwhile, others did not fit her schedule or her beliefs. After the World Cup, she would feel a chilly tension when she declined an overture to make a speech or an appearance. What were her obligations? She already gave her time to AIDS matters. Because she was black, did she have to become a leader of black causes?

"People think you owe them," she said. "Sometimes people get downright nasty. You tell them, 'No, this is not what I want to spend my time on, that I'm not saying it's a bad thing, it's just not right for me.' People take it personally. Even my friends say, 'Bri, we don't see you as this big soccer thing.' They still feel the need to tell me that. I've never accused them of seeing me that way. That's what I do. I play soccer. You can perceive me in a soccer sense to some degree. I know my friends were there before this thing got out of control. I think they're validating themselves. They're great people, but I find it odd."

Gao Hong, the Chinese goalkeeper, was confident of victory in the penalty-kick shootout. The Americans had never seemed particularly assured on penalty kicks. "Not only did China think it would win, but the Americans thought China would win," Gao said. Four months earlier, China had defeated the United States 2–1 at a tournament in Portugal when Brandi Chastain clanged a penalty kick off the cross-bar. Gao had developed an intimidating tactic of smiling at shooters before they kicked the ball. When she smiled, four creases formed in her face, like brackets that held photos in a scrapbook. "Many years ago, my smile was natural," she said. "Later, I discovered that smiling would be a threat to the kicker."

Chastain prepared to take the penalty kick in Portugal and she looked at Gao, and the goalkeeper was staring at her. She gave Chastain a weird look, maybe she winked or wrenched a smile, something, but Chastain couldn't get the look out of her head. *What's going on?* Then she approached the ball and struck it too high and it hit the crossbar and the Americans lost. "She totally rattled me," Chastain said. "She was in my house and I couldn't get her out."

Don't look at Gao, DiCicco had instructed his players in the days leading to the World Cup final. *Find the spot where you want to place the ball, surreptitiously, but don't make eye contact with her.* He had been planning for this moment for a year, knowing that China or Norway would likely be the opponent if the Americans reached the World Cup final. Gao had come to the United States in the summer of 1998 to work at one of DiCicco's soccer camps. She was the most gregarious of the Chinese players, always joking, and they communicated through a third goalkeeper from Japan, where Gao had once played professionally. Still, Gao would likely be an opponent in the World Cup and, even in the relaxed atmosphere of a summer camp, there were strategies to put into place a year in advance. DiCicco did not want her to become overly confident in her ability to keep a shot out of the net. Each day during the camp, he made a point of scoring a goal on her. And if he was not going to be there in person, he telephoned to make sure that someone else scored on her. He did not want Gao to have any perfect mornings or afternoons, no shutouts, no reason to believe that she was invincible.

"I was really concerned that she would get a lot better at that camp," DiCicco said. "I didn't want her to think she had figured out the game all of a sudden."

At 32, Gao was the oldest of the Chinese players. She had surrendered only two goals during the tournament, which led the Chinese media to refer to her as semi-unemployed. Invariably, she was described as acrobatic, although she sometimes had trouble holding onto the ball and the Americans had hoped to take advantage of a rebound off her uncertain hands. Like many of her teammates, she had come to soccer from another sport. She had played basketball at a textile factory in Inner Mongolia, but when women's soccer was introduced to the plant, her boss had issued an ultimatum. *If you don't play soccer, we will not let you play basketball.* At first she refused, then she gave in. "Under such circumstances, I was compelled to play," she said.

Sometimes, before a match, or even during a game, Gao let out a scream that seemed to roil her competitive juices. But most of the time she was smiling, whispering into someone's ear and giggling or breaking her teammates up in laughter. On occasion, she made poems out of her answers to journalists' questions. "Another athlete who wants to be a rapper," her interpreter said at one press conference before the World Cup. When an American reporter visited with Gao at the Chinese training camp in Beijing, she went around to her teammates, collected their autographs on a postcard and presented it as a token of friendship. She was a Christian in a country that was officially atheist but allowed government-controlled churches with followings of 15 million Protestants and 5 million Catholics (along with 50 million Buddhists). Unlike followers of the Falun Gong spiritual movement, which the Chinese government harshly suppressed in the fall of 1999, Christians in approved churches were free to practice their faith privately, as long as they did not proselytize and try to sell Bibles on the streets. As the Chinese and American players stood in the tunnel, awaiting entry onto the field for the final, Gao spotted Michelle Akers, thumped her fist to her chest and pointed up to the sky. She had been an atheist as a young girl, Gao said, but the deaths of millions from Mao's disastrous industrialization movement called the Great Leap Forward had taught her that it was "dangerous to believe that the power of human beings was superior."

She had a visa that would allow her to immigrate to Canada, she said, and she would have a decision to make after the World Cup. Should she stay and try to win a gold medal at the 2000 Summer Olympics, or should she get on with "more important aspects of my life," finishing her undergraduate degree and perhaps attempting to enter graduate school in the United States? Eventually, she would decide to give the Olympics another try before retiring, her friends said. But these decisions were far from her mind as the penalty kick phase began. She had not thought much about whether she liked or disliked penalty kicks, Gao said.

"It's a cruel way to decide who wins and who loses," she said. "But it is a good test of the psychology and confidence and skill of a team."

A month before the World Cup started, Scurry had sat in the lobby of a sporting club in Milwaukee and she had talked about her idea of a perfect tournament. "Being bored out of my tree, the ball nowhere near me," she said. "Then, the final penalty kick, me making a save, the whole team jumping on me. That'd be cool."

Two days before the World Cup final, she was standing in the lobby of the team hotel, when she heard a man and a woman discussing the upcoming match. "The U.S.'s defense doesn't look as good as China's," the man had said. "I think China is going to win." Scurry had assumed everyone in the United States was rooting for the Americans. *How can he say that? Now this guy's going to the game, and he thinks China is going to win. No way.*

The night before the match, Scurry thought of the 1995 game against Norway as she always did, the Norwegians scoring on a header that tucked into the goal just inches from her fingers. For four years she had thought of that goal, when she lifted weights, before she went to sleep at night. Four years. Sometimes it is not your time, she had convinced herself. The 1999 World Cup would be her time.

Then the final came, and play extended for two hours, and still nobody had scored. China had managed only four shots during regulation. *Come on, come on.* Scurry found herself growing impatient when the Americans played the Chinese, who seemed to pass incessantly but were reluctant to shoot. *Come on.* She could not understand China's tactics. Why was it not trying to attack more fiercely?

"Why in God's name would you do that?" she said, "Why give up what you have been doing so well in the tournament to prevent us from scoring, when you prevent yourself from scoring, too?"

It was time for penalty kicks. She sat there, alone on the sideline, staring ahead, and Kristine Lilly came over and they slapped hands. "Catlike reflexes," Lilly told Scurry. "Catlike reflexes."

"I'll get one," Scurry told her. "I'll save one. You do the rest."

17

A Moment of Temporary Insanity

T HE AMERICAN PLAYERS at the bench awaiting penalty kicks, Mia Hamm on her back for a massage, hands behind her head, having the blood and lactic acid kneaded out of her engorged legs. Brandi Chastain lying on her stomach, eyes closed, a towel around her shoulders as if in a sleepy park. *I don't know if I can kick this ball. My leg is cramping. I hope I don't cramp up when I go to hit it.* Julie Foudy slapping high-fives, her hair wet from a dousing of water, anxious players standing in a huddle, shifting weight from one leg to the other, drinking from frosted plastic bottles, Joy Fawcett walking around, afraid to sit because she might not be able to get up. Carla Overbeck walking, too, not wanting anyone to touch her tired legs. *We're better than they are. No way they're feeling good now. We're tougher than they are. We're going to win this thing.*

Michelle Akers, the most assured taker of penalty kicks for the Americans, was unavailable, cramping, hooked to an oxygen mask and IV tubes in a trauma room under the stands. Still, encouragement wafted through the exhausted huddle of players. *We've worked too hard to get here. We're not going to let this team ruin our dreams. This is ours. This is what we've been working for the last six months. No way we're going to let anyone take it away from us. We deserve it. Have confidence when you walk up there. Believe it, believe it.*

Sun Wen, the Chinese captain, exhorted her teammates, "Cheer up, cheer up." "I really thought we would win," she said. "The Americans were more nervous than the Chinese." But Overbeck believed the Americans had the advantage after two hours in the pitiless sun. The running was over now, the exhausting back and forth, and it had become a game of the mind, not the legs. Victory was inexorable, Overbeck believed, because the Americans wanted it more, because they had trained harder in the Florida swamp heat and because they competed more fiercely among teammates who turned pumpkin carving and card games and scavenger hunts into blood sport, because they had survived the lean years of backpack travel and diets of candy bars and queasy soup steeping with the heads of chickens, because they had ridden the coal trains until their faces were black with soot, because they had lived in rickety hotels with one hour of hot water out of 24, because they had led each other blindfolded down steep cliffs and harnessed themselves to ropes 30 feet above the ground to forge a sense of team, because they had run sprints in hotel stairways and parking lots and abandoned fields, because they ignored the disbelievers, building their sport from nothing into a consuming moment, a galvanizing instant, that would make people remember where they were and what they were doing and legions without tickets would swear they were present in the shadowless heat, girls wearing the Betsy Ross faces and the gender-equity tattoos, boys screaming in girls' jerseys, shirtless teenagers professing their love for Mia Hamm with greasepaint valentines and star-spangled boxer shorts. The billowing crowd and the final pep-talk squeeze of huddled players would bring a psychological inevitability, Overbeck believed. The Americans would win because they refused to consider losing.

"They were different people out there when PK's were going to start," said Tiffeny Milbrett, out of the game, her shoes off, walking around in barefoot anticipation. "Different people than I've ever seen. They turned into confident, no-fear people."

Briana Scurry took two hits off of her asthma inhaler. She had been standing in the sun for two hours, wearing a long-sleeve jersey, and it was 105 degrees, and she had begun to feel a little anxious. "I didn't want an asthma attack to be the thing that prevented me from making a save," she said.

Lauren Gregg, the assistant coach, read the list of shooters and Hamm did not want to be on the list, but Gregg told her it was too late. "We chose you," Gregg said. "You have to take it." She had turned in the names.

"Truth be told, I didn't want to take it," Hamm said. "I probably wouldn't have if Michelle had still been in the game. I had been struggling with them in practice, and I don't usually take them at all."

She didn't want the kick, but she didn't expect to have a choice, either.

"Maybe Lauren saw something I didn't see," Hamm said. "I don't expect coaches to come up and ask the players. Then what happens, you start second-guessing yourself. They are coaches for a reason. They picked five of us that they had confidence in. That gives you confidence walking out there."

For the fifth kicker, Gregg said she could have gone either way, Chastain or Foudy. Tony DiCicco remembered Gregg leaning toward Foudy and that he said, "Flip-flop them." He wanted Chastain fifth if she would shoot with her left leg. Of course she would, Chastain said. For months afterward, DiCicco would be driving, or he would be stopped at a light, and he would think to himself, "She took it with her different foot." It seemed more amazing in retrospect than it had at the moment. He could not think of many men or women who would be comfortable switching feet in the final of a World Cup. Chastain had become predictable with her right leg, and she had missed more than half of her penalty kicks during the year, by his calculation, but she was a performer and the fifth spot was a performer's spot. There was no one better prepared for the moment and all that it offered, the burden and obligation and the possibility of unrestrained exult.

"Brandi wants the spotlight and to have the responsibility on her," DiCicco said. "The ability to play with both feet, someone who normally takes the kick right footed and feels totally confident switching to her left foot, that's unique in my mind. Amazing confidence. Some players are afraid of failure, they don't want the role. Brandi wants it. She wants the spotlight. That's the type of player you want in penalty kicks."

As she walked toward the middle of the field, Overbeck waved her arms and pumped her fist, arousing the crowd, every gesture one of assuredness and dependability. Hamm was the goal scorer and Akers was the leonine presence, but Overbeck was the leader of the team. Frequently, in photographs, her index finger was extended on one hand, the sign for No. 1, the signal of victory. "Just like in practice," she told her teammates, clapping her hands. *Choose the side you usually choose. Don't change anything.* "Just like in practice."

Hamm walked toward the center circle, trying to calm herself, questioning whether she should be taking the kick, *I hate these situations,* telling herself and her teammates, "We're going to make these. Try to be as confident as you've ever been in your life. Know that everyone is behind you." The team gathered into a football huddle, and she said, "We deserve to be here. We're not going to lose this now." Later, she told teammates, she had been trying to convince herself as much as she was trying to convince them.

"In a way," Hamm said, "I think I was saying to myself that everything is okay."

Tisha Venturini said that someone told her to look around, or she said it to herself, and she took in the sweep of the red, white and blue audience, the standing and cheering and greasepaint faces and rippling of flags. Tears came to her eyes. *Look at this experience we're in. No matter what happens we're champions. We showed the world what soccer is like. Win or lose, we have proved ourselves, although winning would be better.* She was wound up, having expended her energy only in the last five minutes of overtime, but around her the veteran players seemed so calm. Overbeck, Foudy, Fawcett, Lilly. "Against Norway in 1995, I had a feeling that it wasn't going to be right," Venturini said. "It was a feeling, but there was nothing you could do. This time, the way my teammates acted, I had a feeling it would be all right."

Still, it was a horrible way to end a game, no place for nuance and gray-area interpretation, just the cold black-and-white of winning and losing, and she wondered what it would be like if penalty kicks went to a seventh shooter and the World Cup came to rest on her shoulders.

"Either you are a hero, or a loser," Venturini said. "It's a terrible thing. If you make the kick, you're a hero, if you miss you're an idiot." *I didn't play the whole game. If I lose this game for these players who have played their hearts out for 120 minutes, it would be the most horrible thing.* "When you're not in the game a whole lot, you're not in rhythm," Venturini said. "You're sort of cold. I was so thankful. I knew they were going to make it. I'm sure if I had gotten an opportunity, I would have been more positive. It happened just perfect."

Sara Whalen and Kate Sobrero, the ninth and tenth kickers, stood holding hands, awaiting China's first shooter. China had won the toss and would go first. The shootout would take place on the western side of the stadium, opposite the side of the 1994 men's World Cup, partly because ABC television had requested that side, partly because organizers wanted to escape any residual voodoo from the heartbreaking miss of Roberto Baggio of Italy. Baggio had ballooned his penalty kick and while the Brazilian players had danced and hugged in victory, he hung his head, motionless, as if the merciless conclusion had left him paralyzed with grief, unable to move a muscle. Sobrero was the only American player who had never scored a goal, and she did not want the responsibility of having to deliver her first in the penalty-kick shootout of the World Cup. She had been so nervous in practice and had punched a kick so high, DiCicco said, that it would not have found the net if one goal had been stacked on another.

"I didn't want to take one," she said. "I was hoping to God I wouldn't have to take one." *Please God, make them.* "Both of us were freaked out," Sobrero said of herself and Whalen. "I haven't made one in practice and I didn't want the World Cup to come down to my shoulders." *Please, God, no, no.*

Xie Huilin was up first for China. She had played only one minute of the final overtime. Her speciality was penalty kicks. Xie walked leisurely to the white spot on the field, 12 yards from the goal, and set the ball down. Her Chinese teammates stood like cancan dancers with arms around their shoulders. Whalen and Sobrero held hands, hoping this superstition would make Scurry inviolable, anything to bring her luck, to make the nervousness go away. *Come on, come on.* Scurry talking to herself in the goal, crouched, bouncing up and down like a downhill skier ready to leave the gate. Xie approached the ball and Scurry came forward several steps, but her feet were never set and Xie scored easily into the upper left corner. DiCicco thought he saw the referee flinch, and begin to signal a foul on his goalkeeper, but the kick was good and she did not raise her arm.

"I don't feel bad about this, I never really did," Scurry said about moving forward before the ball was kicked. "The referee was standing right there. Soccer is the only sport that is all up to the referee's discretion, right down to when the game ends. I'm thinking to myself, 'I'm going to do the best I can to make my team win and if it's not within the realm of the rules, the referee will tell me.' I've seen numerous men's shootouts, and they're all over the place, before the guy starts running up to the ball, practically."

Overbeck was up first for the Americans. Scurry went to the corner and turned her back. She could not watch. She had tried to watch in high school and college, but her teams usually lost in penalty kicks, and now it was too stressful to look and to know that it could end in failure. She turned her back and looked down at the ground and waited for the referee's whistle and the crowd reaction. Sandra Werden, Overbeck's mother, could not watch, either. When everyone else stood up, she remained in her seat. The crowd would let her know. Greg Overbeck, Carla's husband, was reasonably confident the Americans would win, but when he saw his wife jogging forward for the first kick, his jaw dropped. *What?* "I'm not real religious," he said, "but in that situation, you tend to find religion." *Whatever power is up there, I don't care if we win or lose, just please let Carla make the PK.* The first kick was the most important. It set a tone. If the captain missed the first kick, the Americans would be in a deep psychological hole. Carla would never forgive herself. "For the rest of her life, I didn't want her to feel she had let the team down," Greg Overbeck said. Before the game, he had also asked for divine intervention. *I know how responsible she feels for the team. Don't let her have a bad game, let in the winning goal. Don't let her make a crucial mistake.* And now he was asking again. *Can we have an addendum to our agreement?*

Carla Overbeck jogged to the penalty spot, chewing gum, licking her lips, and she blithely chipped the ball with her shoe. It backspun up and into her hands. Was there ever a more confident shooter? On the bench, her teammates were standing and kneeling, performing the small rituals of hope and superstitious influence. Christie Pearce put the pearl from a lucky necklace in her mouth. Overbeck rolled the ball in her hands, like a pitcher searching for the seams, then she squeezed it and set it down. She had never expected the game to reach this point, believing someone would score a goal in regulation or overtime. She was surprised to be one of the first five Americans, but she had scored a penalty kick in the 1995 World Cup and when Gregg had called her name again, she thought to herself, "All right!"

She knew that Gao Hong would try to stare her down, so she avoided the eyes of the Chinese goalkeeper. *Don't look at her. You know where you are going. Stick it.* She talked to herself, then everything went blank. Her breathing was slow and deep, her perception narrow, the thinking brain shutting down, the adrenaline surge, the blood-pump to her large muscles. The stadium went silent, 90,185 people in the bleachers, but she did not see them on their feet or hear the bulging applause. Everything silent, as if she were underwater. She did not remember running up to the ball or kicking it. She could not recall opening her hips at the last instant, and pushing the ball with the inside of her right foot and Gao diving, the goalkeeper's mouth wide open, the thigh muscles dimpling in explosive assertion, her hair in spiky tendrils, guessing about Overbeck, but guessing wrong and diving right while the ball went left. As Overbeck struck the ball, the index finger on her left hand extended outward, as if by reflex, *We're No. 1,* and the shot sailed unimpeded into the net. The tension relaxed in Greg Overbeck like an unknotted muscle, and tears rolled down his cheeks. "I didn't care if we won or not," he said. "I had everything I asked for. If we won, it was just gravy."

Exploding celebration, and Sandra Werden stood up and her

daughter was running back toward her teammates, flapping her arms, and jumping and cocking her arm and pumping her fist and jabbing her index finger. Her teammates hugged her and Julie Foudy told her, "Awesome," and kissed Overbeck on the cheek.

"That was the pivotal penalty kick," said Colleen Hacker, the team's sports psychologist. "A rock dropped in a pond, a ripple of confidence, her teammates could relax, bask in it. To score the PK and come running back the way she did, Carla is the Chris Evert of soccer. The ice maiden."

Qiu Haiyan to shoot second for China. Sobrero and Whalen locked arms in the center circle. Holding hands did not prevent the first kick, so they locked arms, hoping for telepathic interference with the second. Gao unable to watch her teammate, jogging up and down the sideline. Scurry in her downhill tuck, Qiu coming forward, and Scurry guessing correctly but unable to get her hands on the ball and the shot slamming into the upper left corner.

"The first two, I wasn't quite ready," Scurry said.

Joy Fawcett's turn for the Americans. Overbeck had been so confident in taking her own kick, but now she was nervous and she could not look. What a gripping, terrible way to end a game. She crouched at the edge of the center circle and she put her hands over her face, and she tried to look through her fingers, but mostly she relied on the reaction of the crowd. "Carla was on her knees the whole time," Hamm said. "She looked like she was going to be sick."

Scurry went to the corner and turned her back and Pearce put her lucky pearl in her mouth and Fawcett walked toward the ball, feeling her legs shake. *I hope no one can see my knees. They're knocking right now.* She did not like to take penalty kicks in practice, believing that her brittle confidence would be shaken if she missed. She was so nervous that, until a reporter told her differently three months later, she thought she had been the third kicker and not the second. "I was just trying to be positive, imagining myself taking a kick, which corner I'm going to, and scoring," Fawcett said. She preferred the right side of the net, using the inside of her foot to guide the ball. She placed the ball down and peaked at the right corner, but she avoided looking at the Chinese goalkeeper. Then she backed up directly behind the ball, not wanting the angle of her approach to give away the direction of her shot. She came forward slowly, chopping her steps as if running through a set of tires, afraid that her left foot would be planted too close to the ball if she took long strides. If the stutter-step approach was hesitant, it was also maddening for goalkeepers, who rely on the fluid rhythm of the shooter to time their own movements forward and laterally. "It's annoying as hell," Scurry said.

The rules say that a kicker can slow down, but not stop, during her approach. Gao bounced up and down on the goal line, trying to rattle Fawcett with her jumping, but Fawcett did not look. Gao said she never heard the referee's whistle, which signals the start of each kick. All of a sudden Fawcett was coming forward, slicing her steps but never stopping, and Gao was not ready and her anticipation abandoned her. She took one tentative step with her right foot, but it was all wrong, she was frozen to the line, and Fawcett put the ball easily into the other corner. Gao threw up her hands and turned toward the referee with a look of disgust and befuddlement.

"I was wondering why the whistle was not blowing," Gao said in Beijing three months later. "I didn't hear the whistle. I am still wondering whether I missed the whistle or the referee didn't blow it."

Something else was disturbing Gao. The American players were avoiding her stare. In the past, she would smile and they would smile and she might distract them or discover some nervous vulnerability. Now everything was changed. She was staring at them, but they were not returning her gaze. How could she intimidate them if they were not looking? Some sort of reversal was taking place. She could not unnerve the Americans and now she became unsettled herself. "I lost my judgment," she said. "I didn't know anymore if they were going right or left."

Two goals apiece. The midfielder Liu Ying was next for China, the first starter to take a penalty kick. Like many of her teammates, Liu had loved the movie *Titanic* and the music of Celine Dion. Unlike many of the Chinese players, Liu, 25, had begun to play soccer in elementary school. She lived in Beijing, and on weekends she frequently declined to visit with friends, preferring to spend time with her mother. Early on the morning of the match, when it was night in Beijing, 12 hours ahead,

Liu had phoned her mother. The *China Women's News*, a Beijing news-paper, had invited families of the players to watch the match in a local hotel. Liu phoned and asked why the newspaper had not sent someone for her yet. "They probably couldn't find my address," her mother had replied. "Definitely they will come."

The day before the final, Liu had aimed for the left corner while rehearsing penalty kicks. But that was practice, and now Scurry had dived that way on the two previous kicks and Liu began to hesitate. Should she go right or left? "I didn't have a plan," Liu said.

On her way into the goal, Scurry looked at Liu as she walked to the penalty spot. Scurry had not looked at the other two Chinese kickers and did not know who they were. This player, she knew, was No. 13. Liu's head was down and her shoulders drooped, and it seemed to Scurry that she did not want the burden of the kick. How few athletes ever relish these pressured instants of singular triumph or torturous mis-carriage? A batter with the bases loaded in the bottom of the ninth, a shooter of free throws in overtime, a kicker of field goals with the clock dying and the wind kicking up. Who could really want this oppressive freight? Scurry looked at Liu, and what she felt she could only describe in terms of the spiritual. Twice before she had sensed these moments that seemed predetermined, a complete absence of guessing and doubt. *This is the one*, Scurry said to herself. Whalen and Sobrero bent over, hands on their knees. Maybe this position would bring Scurry some luck. Scurry tucked into her downhill crouch, bouncing lightly, arms bent and slightly wider than her hips, staring her death-look stare, and everything was certain. "If I had had my eyes closed, I probably could have saved it," she said. "That's how sure I was."

Liu set the ball down, backed up at a sharp angle, and began her approach with a tentative jog. Only while she was running did she decide to place her kick to Scurry's left. Her intention became obvious, and her hips rotated in a way that gave the shot away. Scurry lunged with an explosive step, then planted her feet wide and dived to her left with such propulsive force that for three months she thought she had torn a muscle in her abdomen or ripped a piece of bone from her hip. Her body was parallel to the ground, her cleats kicking up turf, her arms extended like a diver's, and she pushed the ball away with both gloved hands. The shot by Norway had eluded her hands by inches in 1995 but this time everything was clear and inevitable and she almost felt as if she could have caught the ball instead of punching it away.

"The ball was huge, and if she had hit it in the corner, I probably still would have gotten it, that's how sure I was," Scurry said. "It was me and her and no one else was there. I didn't even hear the whistle blow, I didn't hear the crowd, I didn't see my teammates, nothing. Just her. That's all there was, her and the ball. It was just huge. It was like I had a string attached to the ball and I was pulling it and the ball was coming to me no matter where she shot it."

Jumping to her feet, Scurry pumped her arms once, twice, three, four, five times, *I'm a big badass*, still pumping, screaming at her teammates, *Make your kick, I set it up for you*, pounding the air, Overbeck off her knees, pointing her index finger upward, the Fourth-of-July picnic of waving flags in the stands, a man pumping his fist with a flag around his neck like a Superman cape. If the Americans made all five kicks, they would win. Liu threw her head back dejectedly and began walking toward her teammates at mid-field. "She hesitated, she changed her mind at the last minute," said Sun Wen, the Chinese captain. "In penalty kicks, the most undesirable thing is hesitation." Liu made the long walk back to midfield and Sun realized later that she had not given her teammate a hug before the kick. "I regretted it all the more when she failed to score," Sun said. Watching in a Beijing hotel, Liu's mother began to cry, Chinese journalists said, and she murmured to herself, "The championship was kicked away."

No one complained at the time, or lodged any objection, but Scurry would later be accused of impropriety for leaving the goal line before Liu kicked the ball. "There is no questioning the appeal of the U.S. team, nor the giant strides, both real and symbolic, made on behalf of the women's movement and women's sports in this country," wrote Bill Dwyre, sports editor of the *Los Angeles Times*. "There is also no questioning the fact that the U.S. cheated to win."

Donna Lopiano, the executive director of the Women's Sports Foundation who formerly taught ethics at the University of Texas, said, "It was cheating. If you knowingly violate a rule, you intentionally do it, you intend to cheat, period, end of story. She intentionally committed a foul. That makes it unethical. Ultimately the sacred nature of any game depends on players acknowledging the outcome must be a fair comparison of skills. What fouls do is prevent other players from using their skills to win fairly."

Wrote Phil Hersh of the *Chicago Tribune*: "Now that is gender equity. Women athletes have learned to blur ethical lines with gamesmanship as well as the men."

However, Joseph "Sepp" Blatter, the president of FIFA, soccer's world governing body, said that the problem was not with Scurry but with the rule limiting a goalkeeper's mobility. He was seeking to have the prohibitive rule amended to afford a more equitable chance at stopping penalty kicks.

"Even a fly does not sit there waiting to be killed," Blatter said.

The accusation of cheating seemed a harsh assessment of Scurry's violation, considering that it was an acceptable breach of a long-ignored rule. Cheating implies a deceptive transgression punishable by a fine, a forfeiture or an expulsion. What Scurry did was to commit a purposeful foul, where the infringement simply calls for a replay, such as happens in basketball when a player steps into the free-throw lane prematurely, or when a team that has a three-point lead late in the game grabs a player on the opposing team to prevent a three-point shot. In coming forward to test the referee's boundaries, Scurry did what a crafty pitcher does in throwing the ball two or three inches off the plate, hoping to get the umpire to call a strike on the edge of acceptance.

"She did not cheat, she created a foul which the referee missed," said Jerry Smith, coach of the powerful Santa Clara University women's soccer team and the husband of Brandi Chastain. "It's not Briana's fault. If the referees called it consistently, they wouldn't do it. When Michael Jordan takes two-and-a-half steps to make a layup, or Jerry Rice stiff-arms the cornerback or pulls his jersey, they're not cheating. They're doing their best to help their teams. It's up to the referee to decide what's foul or fair. Cheating is point-shaving or using drugs. If you want to criticize anyone, criticize the official. The official blew it, if you want to look at it that way." He added: "To some degree it's sexist to say that women aren't capable of thinking at that crafty level of gamesmanship."

The referee, Nicole Mouidi-Petignat of Switzerland, said that she was watching the shooters, not the goalkeepers, during the penalty-kick phase. "I cannot watch both players at the same time," she said. "I am not perfect. I am one woman, I am not a computer." After seeing television replays of the penalty kicks, though, she said that she believed her calls had been correct. "I see the same with the goalkeeper from China," Mouidi-Petignat said. "She came forward before the U.S.A. shot the ball. I give the correct decision," she said. "Ninety-thousand people say it's not a goal. If I say repeat, I have a problem. But I don't see that. I was correct. No one complained."

The Chinese media later objected to the call, and Gao, the Chinese goalkeeper, said that Scurry "took her dishonesty as her wisdom." But most players and coaches remained gracious. Sun Wen, the captain, said that she believed the referee was hesitant to call a foul on Scurry on the first two Chinese kicks because they were good. Had the referee called for a replay, she would have risked negating the kicks. And once Mouidi-Petignat did not call a foul early, she could not call one later, Sun said.

"She acted against the rules," Sun said of Scurry, "but I asked many Chinese referees and they said they usually wouldn't say that the goalkeeper had broken the rules." She added: "Because this was a world-class match, it was difficult for the referee to overturn a decision she had made already."

Liu, who had the kick saved, said "it was not important" that Scurry had moved prematurely.

"We told the players they should strictly obey the decision of the referee," said Ma Yuanan, the Chinese coach. "When the referee said nothing was against the rules, it was okay. We should remember that, even if the keeper moved forward, we still scored on the other four kicks."

Scurry's biggest mistake may have been in what she said—"It's only cheating if you get caught"—not in what she did. "I don't necessarily regret it," she said. "I was being honest. I guess I could have phrased it differently. That would have been helpful." In fact, she had done what she was coached to do. "It's just part of the game," Scurry said. "I don't know why people made such a big deal out of it. If you know soccer, that's just what you do as a goalkeeper on a penalty kick, because you almost have no chance, anyway. Most likely a great kick is going to score no matter what you do. Don't blame me because she didn't get a great hit on it, or I got close to it. I'm just doing my job. It's up to the referee's discretion. She could have called it back if she wanted."

The referee did not call it back, and Scurry went to the corner and turned away and Kristine Lilly walked up to shoot for the Americans. If she scored, the United States would be ahead 3–2. Lilly had stood at the center circle with Mia Hamm and she had noticed that Gao was diving toward the left corner. Lilly was left footed and the left corner was her preferred target. *Her movement is to my strong side. Do I change? No. I'm going to my strong side. It doesn't matter. That's where I'm going to put it. She can try to save it.*

She put the ball down and peeked at both corners of the net, but did not look at Gao. Steve Lilly was sitting in the stands along the goal line. When he saw his daughter walk up to the ball, he put his head between his legs and listened for the crowd. "I'm having a heart attack," he said. "The life of failure would have devastated me." Scott Lilly, Kristine's brother, sat behind the American bench. He had played collegiate soccer, and when Kristine hit the ball, a mild panic shot through him. *She mis-hit it.* She had meant to shoot low into the corner, but the ball had risen and Gao had guessed correctly, diving to her right, but it did not matter. Because she had aimed low, Lilly had a comfortable margin of error and her shot went beyond Gao's reach. Steve Lilly heard the crowd erupt and he jumped up and landed on his brother. Kristine ran back to her teammates, no demonstrative celebration, just as easy jog after another moment of fundamental reliability. *I did my part. We're going to win this.*

In the trauma room beneath the stands, doctors had stabilized Akers, and someone rolled in a television so she could watch the remaining penalty kicks. Zhang Ouying slotted a kick under Scurry and it was Mia Hamm's turn for the Americans. If she scored, the United States would be up 4–3 and China would be in deep trouble.

Hamm had noticed that Gao was moving to her right each time. That meant one of two things. Either Gao was guessing incorrectly, or she did not feel comfortable diving to her left, the side that Hamm preferred. As she walked toward the ball, Hamm kept trying to calm herself, to rid her mind of negative thoughts. *Nice, easy stroke. Don't try to complicate it. Believe in yourself. The pressure is not on you. Go up there with as much confidence as you've ever had.*

Later, when watching videotape of the final, Hamm would realize that she had not run up to hug her teammates after each penalty kick. Instead she had hung back, wrestling with the emotion that had always been the best and worst part of her game.

"It had nothing to do with 90,000 people watching," Hamm said. "It had to do with the fact that this was the World Cup final. This was something we worked extremely hard for. You don't want to let these guys down. The odds are with the kickers. If you miss, it's bad enough. If you miss the goal, it's even worse. I just didn't want to let the team down."

She had not seemed really confident to DiCicco the whole year. "A .350 hitter who hit .275," he said. The difference with Hamm now was that she was willing to take responsibility in these taut moments. He remembered the preparatory games for the 1995 World Cup, when Hamm scored two goals in a victory over Denmark, then seemed like a different player in the rematch. Overbeck had called out, "Don't pass to Mia," because Hamm was frustrated and was not chasing balls played into open space. "She wasn't lazy, she was frustrated and it was affecting her play," DiCicco said. "She worked through that. Now, no question, she wants the ball. She never prided herself on being a good penalty-kick taker. But she realized, 'I want the responsibility of winning and losing here.' In the 1991 World Cup she took a penalty kick and hit the post. When she missed, that was the end of her scoring. That's how fragile she was. But I'm proud of how she stepped up this time. It was very courageous of her to take that penalty kick."

Hamm tried to summon a confidence that bordered on arrogance, a certitude that she would succeed, then she took the ball and put it down and moved a lock of hair out of her face and she did not remember again until the ball was in the net.

"You hear all the excitement, but as you walk up there, you don't really hear it anymore," she said. "It's like it's far away. It's like the most focused you ever are. Everything kind of tunnels into what you have to do. The goalkeeper's not even part of the equation. It's just you and the ball. In your mind, you're picturing a successful kick, one you want to take. I think I hit a pretty good one. I can't even tell you where it went."

Gao moved to her right, but Hamm placed a low hard shot the other way. She pumped her fist and screamed, "Yeaaah," and ran back to her teammates and jumped into Shannon MacMillan's arms, but she did not smile. Her teammates hugged her joyously, and still there was no celebrative relaxing in her face. She looked at Tisha Venturini and let out an animal scream. Her face stayed hard and her eyes intense and her jaw clenched and it was a look not so much of relief as of fear confronted. "I ran back like I didn't want them to make me take that kick again," Hamm said.

China was down to its last chance now. Scurry walked into the net, punched one of the goalposts and said, "Let's go." Sun Wen, the captain, pulled up her socks over her shin guards, took the ball and kissed it, then set it down. Confusion on the American bench, a blur of possibility. *What's the score?* Some players standing, some kneeling, some sitting, a collective unknowing in the heat and the tension. Aaron Heifetz, the team's spokesman, was keeping a list of the shooters. "If Sun Wen misses, it's over," he said to the bench players. Scurry went into her crouch, *Come on, come on,* knowing that Sun would shoot to her right, but the American goalkeeper did not get a good jump on the ball and the Chinese captain scored to tie the penalty kicks at 4–4. Later, Heifetz said, Scurry told him that she felt something pull in her hip and she could not make an explosive lunge off of the goal line.

What if penalty kicks extended beyond five shooters? Could Scurry have been effective with an injured hip? It was a question that would not have to be answered if Brandi Chastain made her kick. The Americans would win 5–4. Chastain set the ball down and did not give Gao another chance to intimidate her with a wink or a smile. *Don't look at her. Don't look at her.* Until Hamm took the fourth kick, Chastain did not realize that she was number five. "I was getting nervous," she said. "I could be the last kicker." Her legs had cramped in the second overtime, and before penalty kicks she had kept admonishing herself, "You need to relax, there's a kick left," and she felt so tired that she did not seem to have control of her body. But her adrenaline was in overdrive now and she was not thinking about whether her muscles would seize. She set the ball down and, in the 100-degree heat, everything seemed to grow muffled as a snowfall. Scurry turned her back and Pearce put the lucky pearl in her mouth. "It was the most quiet, still moment of my life," Chastain said. "Nobody was moving in the stands. I don't think anyone was breathing. I don't think I took a breath."

Her husband, Jerry Smith, sat in the stands. He was the coach of a high-powered college team and he felt a coach's detachment. *All these people in the Rose Bowl, all the things that can happen, and my wife is in the spotlight in a defining moment. Not a lot of people have an opportunity in life to go through something like this.* He felt certain that Brandi would make the kick precisely because she had missed one against China four months earlier. "Everyone is affected differently by adversity," Smith said. "Brandi is the type of person, that if she missed a penalty kick, bet heavily she'll make the next one. Brandi has not always escaped blunders, but she has always found a way to make up for them." After putting a ball into her own goal against Germany in the quarterfinals, she had scored the tying goal in the second half. If she did not actively search for these decisive moments, she was prepared in case they arose. "Brandi has always found a way to come through in big moments," Smith said.

She pushed her hair behind her ears, and tapped her left foot into the ground, making her toes into a fist, and she drove the ball with the laces of her shoe. An instep drive, the shot is called, and it is designed more for power than accuracy. It would have been a mistake, Smith said, to aim where Chastain put the ball, into the side paneling of net, just inside the right post, too risky and hard to be that precise. To miss the goal entirely on a penalty kick would have been devastating. But if a shot is placed where Chastain placed hers, so close to the post as to startle her when she first saw a newspaper photograph, that shot is unstoppable by any goalkeeper in the world.

"Brandi goes for things a lot of people won't go for," her husband said. Gao knew where the shot was going, and she took a step off the goal line, but the ball was struck so hard and wide that it was almost in the net before the goalkeeper could extend her hands. Chastain hit the shot and she looked up and the ball was in the net and it seemed like there was no traveling time in between. The Chinese goalkeeper barrel-rolled several times in futility, and the Americans had won the World Cup and confetti cannons exploded and Chastain took off her jersey and twirled it over her head like a lariat. "Brandi wanted this more than anyone, and she knew what to do with it," Sobrero said.

She swung her jersey and she became a cultural Rorschach test. Some people saw the black sports bra, some saw the muscular definition and some saw the commercial conspiracy of Nike. She swung her jersey and her abdomen was as striated and symmetrical as a tray of ice cubes, and she had the oblong swell of biceps, and she fell to her knees with the look of sleek muscular rapture, eyes closed, her blond ponytail a triumphant exclamation point, her shoulders and arms flexed and ridged and channeled in the contractions of power and victory.

"Temporary insanity," she called the removal of her jersey. "I just thought, 'My God, that's the greatest moment of my life in soccer.' I just lost control, I guess." Later, she said, "I don't know what I did." Perhaps it was a symbolic unburdening of obligation, pressure, uncertainty, she said. "We had been carrying the weight of the World Cup on our shoulders, and this was a release of that weight," she said.

Her teammates ran at her, arms raised in ecstatic sprint, and they hugged her and she began windmilling her jersey, and Julie Foudy tackled her and they rolled on the ground, and Chastain kissed Carla Overbeck and she hugged Kristine Lilly and said, "I love you." Teammates gathering in victorious clumps, some running toward Chastain, others toward Scurry, pronging leaps onto each other's backs, Hamm crying at the jumble of exhilaration and fulfillment and relief and exhaustion, collapsing into Lilly's arms and telling Sobrero, "Are you kidding me? Are you kidding me?" as if the outcome were somehow still in doubt. She hugged DiCicco and she was sobbing. "That was total relief and release of a lot of baggage she carried," he said. Shannon MacMillan

279

and Joy Fawcett hugged and all the emotions came rushing forward and, MacMillan said, "We wanted to cry, we wanted to scream, we wanted to sit down and be quiet for five minutes."

Cindy Parlow looked into the crowd for the first time, she had been in her own little shell during the match, and she could not believe how many people were there, how they had painted their faces and stood in their seats and made a noise so loud that there were no individual voices, just one roaring voice. "All that hard work and our dreams had finally come true," she said. People were running up to Chastain, spectators on the field, a woman in white shorts whose bra was painted onto her breasts, another woman who seemed to be wearing little more than Saran Wrap. The coach, Tony DiCicco, felt an odd conflict, elation at winning the world championship, disappointment at not winning the match outright. "It would have been a beautiful game if a goal had been scored," he said. "I knew there would still be questions."

Questions about his coaching, questions about Scurry's save, questions about the removal of Chastain's jersey. A month after the World Cup, DiCicco said that the referee "may have choked" on the saved penalty kick. But he later amended his feeling, saying, "I'm not saying the ref should have called it. I'm saying Bri stretched it to about the breaking point of what's going to be allowed and what isn't. Obviously she kept it on the side of what was going to be allowed. I wouldn't say the referee choked. Nine of the 10 penalty kicks went in. It wasn't like there was an incredible advantage for the goalkeepers. One was saved. I'd like to think of it as a great save, versus a referee missing a call."

He said he believed that the shedding of Chastain's jersey was a sign that "women can be confident, strong, defiant. The day of the subservient woman is over." Funny, how the American team appealed to so many people because it was unsullied by money and selfishness and corporate fingerprints, and yet when Chastain removed her shirt the old cynicism returned immediately. Surely, many thought and wrote, she had a deal with Nike to flash her bra and to make her body a living, breathing mannequin. "Chastain changed her value both with the public and in the marketplace, because who can resist a vision of triumph with peerless pecs?" wrote Rebecca Mead of the *New Yorker* magazine.

"No one since the ancient Greeks, who piously depicted the goddess Victory with a breast bared. Her name, of course, was Nike."

There was great suspicion of involvement with Nike, but all the suspicion lacked any evidence of collaboration. Nike could not have known that Chastain would be fifth in the lineup and that her penalty kick would be the game's decisive moment. Chastain said she had sweated so much by halftime that she changed her clothes and did not pay attention to what bra she was wearing. "Nike makes a sports bra with a huge swoosh across the whole front," said Jerry Smith, her husband. "If they were involved in a promotion, they would have gone for a swoosh a lot bigger than the little one-inch one that Brandi wore."

What she revealed was not sexy lingerie, but a supportive piece of athletic equipment. After the consolation match that preceded the championship game, both Brazilian and Norwegian players removed their jerseys and exchanged them on the floor of the Rose Bowl. Chastain had previously removed her jersey after regulation to air it out. While training in Florida, the players frequently doffed their shirts after practice in the smothering heat, and they sometimes gave interviews in their sports bras, which were items of utility, not titillation. Chastain "has brought instant attention to a piece of clothing that is humble and practical, not a traditional bra of shine and lace and cleavage, but a sturdy compression garment," wrote Ann Gerhart of the *Washington Post*. "The sports bra is the cloth symbol of Title IX's success."

Was Chastain's celebration premeditated or spontaneous? The answer, most likely, is both. Premeditated in the sense that in soccer, where goals are so rare, all scores call for some exuberant display, especially one that decides a world championship. Spontaneous in the sense that Chastain did not live a rehearsed, calculating life and was not likely to have schemed a celebration the morning of the final or the night before. "Brandi takes her shirt off all the time," Sobrero said. "She took her shirt off after regulation; it's just that no one happened to see it. The girl takes off her shirt. She recruits in her bikini. It's just Brandi. That's why we love her. There's no one quite like her." She was a theatrical person who thrived in theatrical moments. "The team exhibitionist," Akers wrote on her Web site. "Every team needs one."

Linda Medalen of Norway and Sissi of Brazil had both raised their jerseys over their heads after scoring in earlier rounds of the Women's World Cup. And, in men's international soccer, removing jerseys after a goal was as commonplace as spiking the football after a touchdown. In April of 2000, an Iranian player named Mohsen Rassuli scored in a match and was so exultant that he removed both his shirt and his shorts.

"Brandi is a soccer junkie," Smith, her husband, said. "And she did what she had seen men do hundreds of times."

Why didn't anyone complain when the tennis player Patrick Rafter ripped his shirt off after winning a tournament? Chastain wanted to know. Or when Dennis Rodman frequently tossed his jersey into the crowd when he played for the Chicago Bulls? Despite what DiCicco believed, Chastain said the seed of removal had not been planted when she watched Medalen's unsheathed sprint in the first round of the World Cup.

"Everything exploded," she said of her celebration. "As soon as the ball hit the net, it all exploded. All the emotion, all the work that had gone into that moment, everyone's anticipation of what the World Cup could be, our satisfaction, it all came together. It was like fireworks. It came out of nowhere. It's hard to explain to people if they never had a moment that was the best moment you've ever had, times 100, in the most important situation. I don't think people can predict what's going to happen in that situation. The idea of making something up before and then doing it, it's not real."

18

"We Did It for Each Other"

T HE GAME WAS OVER, and the death look had left Briana
Scurry's face. She was smiling and her teammates surrounded
her and then she ran toward the stands to hug a friend. At the
moment of the saved penalty kick, she realized that she had reached
some sort of pinnacle, that she had experienced a moment of elation
so pure and consuming that it may never be experienced again. She
had felt in that high moment, or shortly after, a twinge of regret, and
she sensed, like Gatsby's Tom Buchanan, that she might be a person
who has accomplished so much by a tender age that the rest of her
life "savors of anticlimax." "That was the single most exciting
moment of my entire life," Scurry would say several months later, sitting on a couch in a hotel lobby, thinking back to the time when she
was pumping her fists and everything was certain and she knew she

could not be beaten. "I sometimes wish I could be there again and feel that again. I doubt if I ever will, feel that elation."

She was still on the floor of the Rose Bowl now, arms around her teammates, and all across the country editors in sports departments had begun a debate about what photograph to give the most prominent display in the next day's newspapers. A photograph of Scurry making a diving save of Liu's kick, her body parallel to the ground? Or Brandi Chastain in shirtless rejoice? Was it appropriate to display a woman in a bra, even if it was a sports bra, on the front page of a sports section, or on page one, of a newspaper? More papers chose the photograph of Chastain, but many chose Scurry, said Tim Burke, executive sports editor of the *Palm Beach* (Florida) *Post*, who edited a newsletter that discussed the photo displays.

"Some people were saying, 'There's a woman in a bra here.' Most of us came to our senses and said, 'This is a sports brassiere, this is harmless,'" Burke said, adding that his newspaper featured Chastain on the front of the sports section and Scurry inside. "We had never seen anything like that before," Burke said of the Chastain photograph. "From a content standpoint, it was an excellent photo, sheer joy and emotion. After the fact, our photo editor said, 'We dropped the ball, this was a great photo of Scurry, I can't believe we didn't run it on the front page.' His point was that Scurry should have been on the front in some fashion, not in lieu of Chastain, but in addition to. I couldn't argue. You could make the argument that it was the defining moment of the match."

The issue took on a racial meaning with many people, especially when ABC television cut away from Scurry just as she was about to receive her gold medal on the victory stand. Instead, ABC cut to a shot of Mia Hamm, who was next in line. Viewers did not see the medal being placed around Scurry's neck by Joseph "Sepp" Blatter, president of FIFA, soccer's world governing body.

"Our job is to document what is going on, and we feel we adequately showed all key members of the team," said Mark Mandel, a spokesman for ABC. "Because Mia had been given the star billing for the team all along, the director had decided he needed a picture of her. It wasn't a slight of Briana that he switched to Mia at that moment. Every director's decision is a personal call. There are probably hundreds of decisions going through his mind at any given moment, hundreds of variables. I doubt that the director could tell you why, at that moment, he felt it was the most important picture."

Among those who felt slighted when she saw a replay of the match was Scurry's mother, Robbie. "I know prejudice when I see it," she said. "I know black athletes, girls, are denied things, whether anybody wants to admit it or not. When they took the camera off, they shouldn't have done it. It wasn't fair. Without Briana stopping the ball, it's doubtful who would have won it."

Harry Edwards, a professor of sociology at the University of California at Berkeley, said that, intentional or not, the snub of Scurry projected a sense that she "did not fit the wholesome all-American image they were trying to project."

"I don't care what they were trying to do, they did it," Edwards said. "Don't expect us to play the fool. The fact that she was black cut to the quick. She just didn't fit in."

Twice, ABC's cameras did return to Scurry after she received her medal. The goalkeeper sought to defuse the issue, saying first on the *Tonight Show with Jay Leno,* and later in interviews, that she did not believe that the cameras had ignored her. "I watched a videotape and the camera was on me an awful lot," Scurry said. "Maybe it wasn't on me when they put the medal over my head, but it was on me after the game, when the celebration was going on. People watched the games and noticed one African-American on the team. They don't understand that field players and scorers get most of the attention anyway. It's the way the game is. I've gotten my fair share. Some nice things have come my way. I just wanted a little piece of the pie. I think I got my share."

As Chastain scored the winning goal, Michelle Akers sat up in the medical room under the Rose Bowl stands and she hugged Mark Adams, the team doctor. "Both of us were crying too much to talk," Adams said. Akers wanted to attend the victory celebration, and so the intravenous tubes were removed from her arms, and she was helped back onto the field by Adams and Dainis Kalnins, the team's equipment manager. Still wobbly, exhausted, not fully coherent, Akers thought she was walking alone. The crowd began chanting, "A-kers,

A-kers, A-kers," and her teammates hugged her and she took a small victory lap and waved and received her medal, then she headed inside to the American locker room, where she began cramping again. "She looked liked one convulsing muscle," said Donna de Varona, chairwoman of the World Cup organizing committee. Later, President Clinton came into the locker room and hugged Akers, and told her, "You're my favorite because you can take a punch, and I know something about that." She was given more intravenous fluids and eventually she recovered sufficiently to eat a burger and fries and to attend the team's victory party. She had looked into the mirror before the game and she had wondered who she would be when she returned, what would be revealed. Now she knew. She felt a contentment, a restful assuredness. "I had given everything," she said. "I had stepped out to the very edges of my faith, looked over the edge and jumped headlong and God had been there, holding me up." A day after the final, she wrote in her diary, "I looked in the mirror last night and saw the weary face of a battleworn soldier-warrior. But the eyes said it all. Exhausted, but fulfilled, satisfied. We did it."

Still, each advance in her career was tempered by the setback of injury. In April of 2000, following a training accident, Akers underwent shoulder surgery that was to keep her out of the lineup until as late as July.

The locker room was hot and full of people and someone was shaving the head of Brian Fleming, the team's general manager, and Arsenio Hall was pumping his fist and doing his dog-pound woof, a B-list actor having crashed an A-list party. "We had accomplished our goals, and it felt like a big weight was off our shoulders," Kristine Lilly said. "I felt lighter." Cindy Parlow went to pop the cork on a bottle of champagne, she said, and someone who looked like a Secret Service agent told her, "No, you can't do that." He mentioned something about a cork sounding like a gunshot, she said, and told her that she could not open the champagne while the president was in the room. "Get him out," Parlow said that she replied. "I'm opening it," she told the man, and she uncorked the bottle and champagne was spraying everywhere. Tiffeny Milbrett said that President Clinton hugged her so hard, "I swear he could have broken my back."

Julie Foudy sat next to Carla Overbeck in the locker room, the two exhausted captains talking, and Foudy began to laugh. Everyone was spraying champagne, even spraying it on the President, she said, and she was so dehydrated that all she could drink was water. The governor of California, Gray Davis, was standing next to her and she was so tired that she didn't even recognize him. "I can't move," Foudy told Overbeck. "I would love to go over there and celebrate, but I can't move." They sat there for a long time and people were chatting and she couldn't move. In March of 2000, a sense of lethargy would persist in Overbeck, and she would be diagnosed with Graves disease, a thyroid condition that was not expected to interfere with her ability to play.

Parlow left the locker room for a news conference, but she felt so drained physically and emotionally that words were skidding out of her mouth like cars without brakes. She did a radio interview, then television cameras pressed in and she caught herself in the middle of a sentence. "I had no idea what I had just said or what I was talking about," she said. "Complete exhaustion. So much had built up and so much had been expended. Everything was this blur."

She was talking and words were coming out, but her brain was not following. She stood up and said, "Thanks, guys" and walked away. "It was too weird," Parlow said. "To this day, I have no idea what I was saying."

President Clinton visited both locker rooms, diplomacy as much a part of this afternoon as sport. First, he visited the Chinese and said, "I want to say to the whole team how much we admire your performance in the whole World Cup. You were magnificent today. And we were very honored to have you in our country. You will win many more games." Then he visited the Americans and said, "First of all, I think everybody in the whole stadium was weeping with joy. It was the most exciting sports event I believe I've ever seen." And he added: "We learned a lot today about soccer, about women athletes, about courage and endurance and about genuine sportsmanship."

A group of American players visited China's locker room and exchanged jerseys with the Chinese players. The mood was somber, but an interpreter was in the room and the players traded subdued greetings and congratulations. Mia Hamm and Sun Wen, both having worn

No. 9, swapped jerseys, and Hamm told her, "You were the best player in the World Cup." Tiffeny Milbrett had known Liu Ailing, the Chinese playmaker, from their days in Japan's professional league. She hugged Liu and said, "You did good." The Chinese were devastated, but they were welcoming, Milbrett said. Liu hugged her back. "We weren't competitors anymore," Milbrett said. "We weren't evil opponents. It wasn't about going in there and saying, 'We kicked your butts.' They saw that we felt compassion and respected them. It was sisterly."

During the awards ceremony, Saskia Webber, the backup American goalkeeper, had looked down from the podium and she had seen that Liu Ying was crying. Of the 10 penalty kicks, nine had been good. Only Liu's kick was saved. After receiving her second-place medal, Liu had stood with her Chinese teammates and she had nervously run her hand through her short hair, and she had buried her strong chin in her chest, her head down in inconsolable sorrow. She did not blame Scurry for leaving the goal line to block her kick. "It is my fault," she said. "We have not won the world championship. It is no use to say anything."

Now the Americans were receiving their gold medals and Webber could see that Liu was crying. "I remembered knowing how that felt from being on the 1995 team," Webber said. "All the emotions. Her head was down. I remember pausing for a second. My mom is a person who always feels something for the others. She always makes a comment, 'You won, but they worked so hard, too.' I remembered how incredibly upset I was in 1995. That's why I wanted to go into the Chinese locker room. In '95, Norway did that little march in front of us and they walked away. There was no real respect there. For us to be able to communicate with the Chinese, even though they spoke little English, I thought was great. I wanted to go in there, to show them some respect."

Later that night, at the team hotel, Liu was cooking noodles when she was visited by Ying Wu, a professor of physical education at Millersville University in Pennsylvania, who had befriended the team several months earlier. The night before the final, Wu said, Liu had been relaxed and smiling and confident, writing postcards and autographing T-shirts and soccer balls. Now, she was melancholy, doleful, and Wu grabbed her shoulder and tried to comfort her, saying it was not her fault, that anybody could have missed a penalty kick.

"I was very concerned, not in the sense that she might do anything to herself, but the Chinese people are very reserved, not very good at expressing emotions," said Wu, a native of Shanghai and a former soccer player. "I believe it is healthy to express it. She started crying, I started sobbing. We were hugging each other and crying. I knew it was good. I knew that's all she needed, comfort, understanding."

Upon returning to Beijing, the Chinese team was received by President Jiang Zemin, who told the players, "You didn't disappoint the wishes of the masses. You showed on the playing field the self-reliance and confidence of Chinese women." In a reception at the Great Hall of the People, Jiang spoke with Liu and told her that he had studied mathematics in high school, that he knew about probabilities and that no one could be successful 100 percent of the time.

"It doesn't matter that you failed to score," Liu said that Jiang told her. "There are always winners and losers in battles. It was great that you had the courage to take the kick."

Three months later, Liu sat at the team's training camp in the hills above Beijing, and when she spoke of the penalty kick, she leaned her head on a window and looked far away.

"I blamed myself," she said. "After a while I came to realize it can happen to anyone."

She had collected herself and she had scored 14 goals to lead all players in China's fall league. Her Beijing team had won the championship.

"I'll never forget it," Liu said of the missed penalty kick. "Perhaps it will give me more pressure in the future. I'll try to get rid of the psychological barriers as quickly as possible."

Perhaps, a visitor said, she would have another chance to take a penalty kick against the Americans at the 2000 Summer Olympics in Sydney, Australia. "We are going all out in preparation for the Olympics," Liu said. "As a team, we are capable of getting the upper hand. If it ends in another draw against the Americans, I am confident enough to face them on a penalty kick." Then she smiled impishly. "But I hope China will defeat America in 90 minutes."

After the president and the media had cleared out of the American locker room, the team gathered for a final meeting. "We proved to the world that we are the best," Carla Overbeck told her teammates. "We did it because we believed in each other." The players and staff were huddled close, some standing, some sitting. Julie Foudy picked up on the theme of team achievement. "Forever, it's been about us, what we can do for each other," she said. The players thanked the coaches and the staff, and Tony DiCicco remembered telling his team, "You took this event, you put it on your shoulders and you made it a big event. You went out and promoted it for two years, then you had to win. Otherwise, it would have all fizzled away. Then you accomplished that. The stakes were very high. Not only did you win, you won over America. It changed our lives."

Mia Hamm was dehydrated after running back and forth for two hours, playing urgent defense when her offense was not there, all effort for 120 minutes, and she had nothing left. "Once my adrenaline was gone, my body shut down," she said. The pressure was gone, she had carried the sport and her team had won and everything was fulfilled, and she could feel herself letting go. "I don't feel well," she told Dr. Mark Adams, and he laid her on the floor of the locker room and began to run intravenous tubes into her arms. She remained in the locker room for two hours after the game, and she was unable to attend the team's victory party. Adams took her back to the team hotel and by 8 in the evening, she was asleep.

"Physically, it was the most uncomfortable I've ever been," Hamm said. "If it was even a tenth of what Michelle feels like, I don't know how she does it. I was hungry, but I couldn't eat. I was nauseous but I couldn't get sick. My eyes hurt open, they hurt closed. I was hot, I was cold. Anything I tried to do to get comfortable made it worse. I think you just invest everything, all your concentration, all your emotions, in running down a ball, encouraging your teammates, diving at a ball, saving them off the line, sideballing them out of the penalty box. There is always a level of commitment and in this environment it goes up. I think it went up in that game. I was crying at the end. It's physically exhausting and emotionally exhausting. I couldn't even talk."

The next morning, Hamm woke up and she felt as if she had been on a binge. She had not touched a drop of alcohol but she felt the dehydration of a hangover. She had slept for nearly 12 hours, but she felt she had hardly closed her eyes at all.

*   *   *

Briana Scurry's wakeup call did not come on the morning after the game. When she did awaken, the first thing she noticed was the absence of anguish. That had been the worst part about losing to Norway in 1995, waking up the next morning to the grogginess of defeat. "We won," she told herself. In the ensuing days, she would notice the absence of another constant reminder. For four years, she had thought about Norway continually, the winning goal playing on an endless reel in her head, the taunting celebration burned into her memory. She thought about the goal at night when she went to sleep. Every time she walked into a weight room, it was like a light went on in her head. But the Americans were World Cup champions now, and when she went to lift weights, she thought about other things and she never thought about Norway.

The morning after the final, officials of the United States Soccer Federation opened the sports pages of the *Los Angeles Times* to find the banner headline, "America the Bootiful," set above a large photograph of Scurry's penalty-kick save. On page 5 of the sports section, they saw another headline that stunned and disturbed them. It was an advertisement announcing an indoor victory tour by the players, who proposed to call themselves the All-American Soccer Stars. The federation's contract stipulated that five or more players could not appear as anything else but the women's national team. Its corporate sponsors would be incensed.

"It was a shock," said Hank Steinbrecher, then the executive director of the soccer federation.

It shouldn't have been.

Three months earlier, Steinbrecher had given the players permission to plan an indoor tour. Although he said he raised some "red flags," Steinbrecher also gave the players the go-ahead, saying the federation did not conduct indoor tours.

Four days before the World Cup began, John Langel, the Philadelphia-based attorney representing the players, wrote a letter to Steinbrecher, saying that plans for an indoor tour were proceeding and that the team was negotiating with the SFX marketing group. Steinbrecher did not respond. Langel sent Steinbrecher another letter on June 29, 1999, during the World Cup, stating that planning for the victory tour, to be held from October through December, was in the final stages. A day later, Steinbrecher replied, saying that there may be some conflicting dates with an outdoor world tour the federation was planning and that he wanted to discuss the matter after the World Cup. Nowhere in his response did he say that he was opposed to the indoor tour. The players took that as a sign to proceed.

When Steinbrecher and Dr. Robert Contigulia, the president of the national soccer federation, picked up the *Los Angeles Times*, they were livid. "It was very unprofessional," Contigulia said. "How can you embrace the women's team when they are not totally honest with you? This SFX thing was done surreptitiously." Actually, it was not. Clearly, the mishandling was done by the federation. This was yet another example of the amateurish, neglectful, myopic manner in which the soccer federation operated as the sport's national governing body. In larger sense, it was symptomatic of the archaic way that sports aligned with the Olympic movement were being run in the United States. Federation officials acted like jilted parents. Egos superceded any sense of public relations and fair business dealings with the players. It would have been so easy and correct and progressive to embrace the women's success. Instead the federation lashed out and appeared resentful, jealous. It soured the sweetest moment in the history of American soccer.

The fallout from this bungled episode was poisonous: The federation threatened to sue its own players over the indoor tour that it had agreed to let them explore. Instead of congratulating Tony DiCicco, who won more games than any American coach, man or woman, the federation criticized him and his leadership style. Eventually, he resigned his position. Bitter, the national governing body also declined to begin negotiating a new contract with the players for five months. Then it made a lowball offer, which the players rejected. The team boycotted a tournament in Australia in January of 2000.

"I do think U.S. Soccer grossly underestimated the value of this team and what the World Cup would do," said Marla Messing, the president of the Women's World Cup organizing committee. "To be fair, who didn't underestimate it? But they so underestimated it, and had such a vested interest in it that they got whiplashed the hardest. It's disappointing that after investing the most of anyone in the women's national team, the federation didn't get the chance to reap the immediate benefits of the World Cup."

The federation has no women in position of authority, except for a glorified traveling secretary with the men's team. It has always lacked vision in promoting the women's team. It has never had a grand plan to cultivate the women's game. After the Americans won the 1996 Olympic gold medal, another match was not scheduled for seven months. The team had played before 76,000 fans in the gold-medal game. There was obviously huge interest in the American women, and the potential for millions in gate receipts, but the federation lacked the foresight or hindsight to plan a victory tour. This time, the women planned their own.

In retrospect, Steinbrecher said, he should have said no to the players when they proposed an indoor tour. Better yet, said Donna de Varona, the chairwoman of the World Cup organizing committee, the federation should have consulted with the players before the world championship and devised a post-tournament tour that would have satisfied and benefited both parties. Instead, the federation threatened to file an injunction against the team to protect its marketing rights, and in a panic move, it offered the players $2 million to go on a nebulous international tour of Egypt and South Africa, the dates of which were never firm. The players declined, taking the $2 million offer from SFX for the indoor tour, wanting to let their fans see them close up and believing that the marketing group had shown them respect that the federation had not. "They don't understand what we are about," Mia Hamm said of the federation. The indoor tour proceeded after an agreement not to ambush the federation's corporate sponsors, and each of the players made about $100,000 from participating against a team of world all-stars.

"A deal should have been done ahead of time," de Varona said of the federation. "They didn't take the indoor tour seriously. They weren't prepared for the next thing."

The soccer federation's outmoded business practices reflected a systematic problem among sports governing bodies in the United States. Like the federations that govern track and field and figure skating, sports that were formerly amateur and have gone professional, the United States Soccer Federation has struggled to adjust to the shifting economic realities. Unlike, say, the National Football League, which concerned itself only with elite professionals, the soccer federation governed every aspect of the sport from the grassroots youth level to the professional men's and women's national teams. These various interests ground against each other like tectonic plates. Because there was no professional league for women, the federation also served as the employer of the World Cup players.

Although its budget had grown from $1 million to $40 million annually over the past decade, and it employed a paid staff, the federation was still volunteer-based. It operated more on protecting turf than providing a grand vision for an evolving sport. And it was not run by full-time corporate executives, as were the NFL and the National Basketball Association. Contigulia, the soccer federation president, was an unpaid volunteer, a kidney specialist who lived in Denver, while the federation offices were located in Chicago. And while he was supportive of the women's team, he could devote only part-time attention to the sport. That attention was often distracted by the need to shore up his own political base for reelection, to fight political skirmishes among competing interests that operated as petty, warring fiefdoms. It would be the equivalent of Paul Tagliabue, the commissioner of the NFL, having to spend considerable time fending off the political faction of Pop Warner football.

Communications between the federation and the women's team was poor, Contigulia and Steinbrecher conceded. Prior to the World Cup, federation officials showed up only once to see the American women's team train during its six-month residency camp in Orlando, Florida.

The disparity in treatment of the men's and women's national teams was evident in ways large and small. The top American women received about $40,000 in salary for the 1999 World Cup training camp, compared with as much as $135,000 for the top American men before the 1994 World Cup. Paychecks to the women were sometimes late, and bonuses from tournament victories were sometimes withheld or delayed. Until training for the 1999 World Cup, the women's team even had to chip in for its own fruit and bagels after practice.

Through the years, there had been a protracted waging for things like upgraded salaries, medical insurance and a more nutritious training table. In the fall of 1995, members of the women's national team walked out on strike when the soccer federation proposed bonuses only for the gold medal at the 1996 Atlanta Olympics. The federation later relented and offered bonuses for any medal-winning performance.

"Their argument was, 'We don't reward mediocrity,'" said Carla Overbeck, the American captain. "All these silver and bronze medalists wrote to the federation and said, 'You think my medal is mediocre?'"

In 1997, Steve Sampson, the coach of the men's national team who had won no important tournaments, was paid $370,000, while DiCicco, who had won the 1996 Olympic gold medal, was paid $99,600. In 1998, DiCicco felt insulted when his wife accompanied the team to a tournament in Japan and the federation handed her a food bill worth $1,500. When the federation listed its accomplishments for 1999, it placed a third-place finish by the men's team in a regional tournament over the women's world championship. And when it announced its 1999 player-of-the-year awards, it showed a highlight reel of greatest moments that did not include the women. In May of 1998, the federation announced Project 2010, a plan to win the men's World Cup by that year, but there were no specifics offered for the continuing success of the women. The women's coaches had to devise their own program.

"There is an old boys network in place, an underlying lack of interest in what the women are doing, almost to the point that they wish the team would go away," DiCicco said. "By all objectives, they measure themselves in what they can accomplish in the men's game. That's what the rest of the world is measuring them on. They're not measuring them on what they accomplish in the women's game, because in many parts of the world the women's game is considered a joke."

"Go away is too strong, but there are clearly those who wanted the men to have success before the women," said Marty Mankamyer, a woman who was a driving force to get women's soccer into the 1996 Summer Olympics and who is an executive assistant to Contigulia.

The federation did not resent the women's team, Contigulia said. Just the opposite. "The gals totally helped us get rid of the disaster in France [at the 1998 men's World Cup] and helped put soccer on the map," he said. "How could we resent them? I firmly believe in my heart that the U.S. must lead women's soccer and create change on the field and socially." But, referring to American coaches, he said, "The whole men's side doesn't respect the women's game," believing it to be on a level of teenage boys. "There may be some jealousy," he said, adding that the men's national team was competing against 200 other countries, most with superior soccer cultures, while the American women were competing "against five other countries."

This was a frequently made, but entirely specious, argument against the American women. First of all, only seven countries have ever won a men's World Cup, and only 11 have ever reached the finals in 70 years of competition. The power in the men's game is just as concentrated as it is in the women's game. A lack of competition was used to diminish the achievements of the American women, but of course it was a double standard. No one complained about the weak tournament fields when UCLA began its basketball dynasty or when the San Francisco 49ers won a handful of Super Bowls after playing against execrable regular-season competition in the NFC West division.

"There is another way to look at this—we beat the world at its game," said Anson Dorrance, the former coach of the women's national team. "This is the equivalent of Brazil winning the world championship in American football."

The American women did not deserve to be paid as much as the American men because the men account for most of the federation's revenue, while the women have never earned a surplus, Contigulia said. This is the argument that college football often uses against sharing the wealth, but it runs counter to the argument of Title IX, which states that money should be shared proportionately or women's sport will not fully develop.

"Their premise is that the effect of worldwide discrimination means the U.S. women will make less money," Langel said. "That should be unacceptable. This is a country built on equality."

Tom King, the chief operating officer of U.S. Soccer, said that the federation invested $4.4 million on the women's team in 1999 and lost $2.7 million. The federation receives about $3 million from FIFA, soccer's world governing body, for qualifying for the men's World Cup, and $700,000 to $1 million per game, American officials said. The federation receives no money from FIFA for qualifying for the Women's World Cup. The men's team also receives guarantees from other countries when it travels of up to $140,000, King said, compared with zero for the women.

"I don't see the WNBA players asking for the same salaries as the NBA players," Contigulia said.

In the case of soccer, however, the women are the NBA.

It is the women's team that is more popular and higher achieving. And to suggest the men's team is a cash cow is incorrect. The men's team didn't pay for itself either in 1999, King said, losing $700,000 on a budget of $5.9 million. An argument could be made that the American women deserve more money than the men, not just equal pay. They have won two world championships and an Olympic gold medal, while the men have won nothing. The biggest men's home crowds often come at matches where the ethnic population is cheering for the other team. While attempting to qualify for the 1998 World Cup, the American men played Mexico in suburban Boston rather than Los Angeles, because the Latino fan base would have been pro-Mexico. In January of 2000, the American men played Iran at the Rose Bowl, and there appeared to be only several hundred spectators rooting for the United States in a crowd of 50,000 Iranian-Americans. Sam's Army, the official U.S.A. fan club, resembled a sad platoon.

"We need to start getting behind soccer in this country," Bruce Arena, the coach of the men's national team, said after the Iran game.

Enraged by the indoor tour, and apparently disorganized, the federation did not offer a contract to the women's national team until December of 1999. Its behavior in the meantime was petulant and bizarre. Langel, the players' attorney, wrote a letter to the federation on September 22, seeking to begin negotiations. On September 29, he received a letter from John Collins, the federation attorney, who said that U.S. Soccer had not yet determined the number of games and training camps, "if any," that would involve the women's national team before the Sydney Olympics.

"Similarly," Collins wrote, "U.S. Soccer has not determined whether or not it will be offering contracts to any individuals to play on the women's national team."

The Americans had just won the World Cup and the federation didn't know whether it would be offering contracts to any of the players?

"I had no idea what that meant," Langel said. "If it was a shot across the bow, I didn't hear it."

The federation's behavior toward DiCicco, the women's coach, was equally perplexing. He had the best record in the history of American coaching—103-8-8—yet the national governing body reacted coolly toward him. A month after the World Cup, he met with Contigulia and Steinbrecher and was criticized for his leadership, told that his team lacked discipline. While his inclusive style of leadership was widely appreciated within the team, he was essentially told that his coaching method was too deferential.

"It was a very strong team and operated differently than most teams I understand," Steinbrecher said.

This was code-speak, DiCicco believed, for not keeping his players in line when they wanted to participate in the indoor victory tour. Contigulia would later apologize, according to DiCicco and say, "We were looking for someone to blame and we blamed you."

Even though DiCicco had won an Olympic gold medal and a World Cup, the federation had never fully respected him. In 1999, he was paid $167,166, about a third of the $482,852 paid to Arena, the men's national coach. Contigulia took two months after the World Cup deciding whether he wanted DiCicco to return as coach. He consulted numerous coaches, he said, who told him that China was the better team, that the Americans had won only because they were playing at home, that Mia Hamm had not been given sufficient freedom to attack, that the American play had been too predictable, that the defenders were getting old. It was another public relations disaster for the federation. DiCicco was the first to admit that his team did not play its best in the World Cup, and that some change may be needed, but the timing of the criticism could not have been worse. His team had just given soccer its most visible presence ever in the United States.

"They were waiting for us to lose, so they could get rid of all of us," DiCicco said. "We won and they were still trying to get rid of us. I'm not the only one who can win with this team. But none of us should be put through the criticism I went through. I wouldn't say they forced me out, but they didn't do much to try to keep me."

Who could say for sure that China was the better team? It didn't win. It has never defeated the Americans in an important tournament. While the Chinese may have been more skilled technically, there is more to a team than technical skill. DiCicco had built a side that was fitter and psychologically stronger. Defensively, it completely smothered a team that had defeated Norway, the defending champion, 5–0 in the semifinals. A strong argument can be made that it was more difficult, not less, to win in the United States with all the pressure the American team felt to succeed. China had hosted a World Cup in 1991 and had not even reached the finals.

"They did not give Tony enough credit," Messing said of the federation. "They believed the players were making all the calls and that Tony did not exercise enough authority. The fact is, he managed a veteran team of strong personalities, and he got the best out of them on the field. He won. The guy won. What more could you ask of him? If they had thrown their arms around him and told him he was great, I believe he may have made things work for the Olympics. I assume he wasn't ready to make any more sacrifices for people who were not grateful for what had been accomplished."

DiCicco was leaning toward retirement after the World Cup. The extended time away from his wife and four sons was troubling him. But when the federation did not give him a vote of confidence, or immediately offer to extend his contract, he changed his mind and decided to pursue the job. "That got my dander up," he said. "I didn't think there was sufficient acknowledgment or congratulation for what we had achieved."

Eventually, Contigulia decided that DiCicco should coach the Americans through the 2000 Summer Olympics. The federation was reportedly prepared to pay him up to $200,000 to coach through the

Games in Sydney, Australia, but DiCicco declined. He would grow exhausted during a grinding fall schedule after the Cup and his eight-year-old son, Nicholas, would finally ask the crucial question, "Are you going to coach, or are you going to be my dad?"

Facing 250 or 300 days on the road in preparing for the Olympics, DiCicco said, "I thought it was more important to be a dad." Who could blame him? It was a perfect time to leave, on top, victory in his final game. Women's soccer would not likely again experience that same consuming shiver. An Olympic gold medal would be a proud accomplishment, but he already had one, and what if he lost to the Chinese this time, or the Brazilians? Why take a chance on a final tarnish? Some of his players, though, were convinced that DiCicco would have remained head coach if the federation had been more solicitous and supportive of the women's team.

"I believe Tony just got tired of fighting for what he thought we should have," said Overbeck, the team captain.

In losing DiCicco, the federation lost the one person who most appreciated what it had done for the women's team. He realized that, despite its shortcomings, the national governing body had treated the American women better than any other federation or professional league in the world. U.S. Soccer had held the World Cup in huge stadiums, had spent $2.5 million on a training camp and had provided a nanny, a sports psychologist, and a chartered plane for a coast-to-coast flight between the quarterfinals and semifinals.

"There has been a tense relationship between U.S. Soccer and the women, and they both have to feel responsible for that," DiCicco said. "U.S. Soccer has never fully, in my mind, respected the women's side of the game. And the women have never fully acknowledged what U.S. Soccer has done for them. Mia Hamm wouldn't have a building named after her at Nike if it wasn't for U.S. Soccer. It wasn't going to happen because she had a great career at North Carolina. It's because of what she accomplished with the national team, before any other marketing group was interested and only U.S. Soccer was providing the funding."

As DiCicco's successor, the federation chose April Heinrichs, the former star forward on the women's team who had fierce competitiveness and motivational skills. But her teams at the University of Virginia had not been exceptional, and questions persisted about whether she was ready for the job now. DiCicco had endorsed Lauren Gregg, his longtime assistant who had won two unofficial world championships as head coach of the under-21 American women. No one knew more about the women's game, or had been more loyal or devoted in developing the sport.

Gregg had sustained her career through tremendous hardship, suffering from lupus and, in March of 1992, from a broken back that kept her in a wheelchair for more than a year. Still, she kept coaching. She was at the University of Virginia then, and she would be driven to practice each day, where she would view training from a golf cart. Doctors told her she may never walk again, she said, but "that never entered my mind."

"Why couldn't I coach?" she said. "I was determined to show that you could do it and be treated with the same respect whether you were standing or sitting."

In 1995, Gregg resigned from Virginia to devote her full-time attention to the women's national team as it prepared for the 1996 Summer Olympics. She fought indefatiguably for respect for the women's game, spent 200 days a year or more on the road, wrote a coaching book, did the job of two coaches on the men's side. And, as often happens to assertive women, the men in the federation considered her abrasive, overbearing. They whispered privately that she was "emotionally volatile" and did not have a "second gear" in her public manner. Strong men are considered fiery, strong women are volatile. In typically clumsy fashion, the federation informed her that she did not get the job after she had won a tournament with the national team in Australia and had flown directly to a coaching convention in Baltimore.

"I feel bad for Lauren," said Julie Foudy, the American co-captain. "She really pushed hard for us."

The World Cup team boycotted the tournament in Australia in January of 2000. After declining to negotiate for months, the federation had offered a stopgap contract from 1996 that the players rejected. Later that month, though, the federation's stance began to soften dramatically. It had been hammered in the national media, referred to as a Federation of Dunces in *Sports Illustrated*. And the women's position had solidified when the youth players who went to the Australian tournament agreed to play no more until a new contract was signed. Also, Scott M. Reid of the *Orange County* (California) *Register* described in detail the financial disparity between the men's and women's teams, revealing that the federation had paid three men a total of $686,677 to coach the men's national team in 1998, although only Steve Sampson actually coached the team and two others were essentially coaches in waiting. One of those men, Carlos Queiroz, was paid $271,662 to write a report on the state of soccer in the United States. It was also reported that Steinbrecher's salary had risen 84 percent over five years to reach $271,662 in 1998, along with $51,500 in benefits and deferred compensation. This severely undercut the federation's claim that it would be fiscally irresponsible to meet the $250,000 difference between what the women were asking in salary and what the governing body was willing to pay.

The federation's position became even more untenable when Michelle Akers was invited to the White House for the announcement of a $27 million equal-pay initiative, and Foudy sat with Hillary Rodham Clinton in the gallery during President Clinton's State of the Union address. It was clear that the team had support and popularity so broad that it reached the highest levels of the American government. After the State of the Union address, Foudy said, Clinton had told her, "We've had all of you here this week. The federation must think I'm getting involved."

Finally, on February 1, 2000, nearly seven months after the World Cup, the American women announced that they had accepted a new contract that would pay them a guarantee of $5,000 per month, up from $3,150, and would put them on equal terms with the American men by paying them $2,000 per match in appearance fees, an increase from $150 per match. The players said they were grateful for the raise and the chance to play again, but they were also weary and numb from the negotiating process, disappointed that the goodwill of a world championship had degenerated into a bitter contract dispute. Steinbrecher eventually resigned in the aftermath of the contentious negotiations.

"I have been on the team for 12 years and during that time we have had to have outside jobs to make a living," Overbeck said. "Women have to be treated equally as men."

Five days after Brandi Chastain scored the winning goal, Santa Clara University spent $10,000 on a full-page congratulatory ad in the *San Jose* (California) *Mercury-News*. The ad pictured Chastain in her sports bra and the headline said, "You Go Girl." Chastain had graduated from Santa Clara in 1990, and she was currently an assistant soccer coach at the school. If others had problems with the removal of her jersey, the Jesuit priests who ran Santa Clara did not.

"What's the big deal?" said Marlene Bjornsrud, Santa Clara's assistant athletic director, noting that the school's tennis and cross-country teams practiced in sports bras. "We chose to make a statement that may have been considered risky by some in the Catholic church. But those of us at Santa Clara, especially in the athletic department, celebrate all of who Brandi is and with no doubt or hesitation about anything she's ever done."

Father Paul Locatelli, the president of Santa Clara, was in Ireland during the Women's World Cup and did not have access to a television. He said he found a newspaper a couple of days later that carried the now famous picture of Chastain on her knees in rapturous celebration.

"I didn't think anything of it," he said. "We don't have a problem with what she did on the field. I think people who have reacted negatively don't understand the exhilaration of the moment. Brandi wasn't trying to make a statement. She was excited and proud and rightfully enthusiastic about winning the game. Men pull off their jerseys all the time. No one ever thinks anything if a man does it."

However, Nike's trumpeting of Chastain as a spokesperson for its Inner Actives bra, and the prurient fascination by mostly male sportswriters, signaled that women were still being viewed from the angle of gender instead of athletic performance, said Harry Edwards, the sociology professor who taught Chastain during her freshman year at California-Berkeley.

"The bra was the focus, it wasn't leg strength, speed, hand-eye coordination, or her ability to defend," Edwards said. "It was her bra size. It would be like focusing not on the distance of Mark McGwire's home runs, but on his cup size. It's the equivalent of him getting the jock-strap endorsement."

Stephon Marbury, point guard for the New Jersey Nets, served as honorary coach of the American women's soccer team during one leg of its indoor victory tour. Asked what he most remembered about the Women's World Cup, Marbury said simply, "The shirt." Chastain took a visitor to a Mexican restaurant near the Santa Clara campus a month after the championship match, and when she left, a curious pantomime occurred. Patrons stood in line for lunch and explained to their friends who she was. When the friends didn't know, the patrons motioned as if they were lifting their shirts. Of course. Then everybody knew.

Women on the network morning shows had seem troubled by her celebration, but the public overwhelmingly supported her, Chastain said. A nine-year-old girl from Phoenix told her that she wore her sports bra everywhere. A man wrote to say, "Brandi, Brandi, Brandi, why did you have to go and take your shirt off and show us those shoulders and biceps and those abs? I can never take my shirt off again. I'm totally embarrassed in front of my wife."

At an exhibition football game, Chastain wore a San Francisco 49ers jersey with her No. 6, and she led the team onto the field during the usual pregame stampede. One of the 49ers officials had asked her to remove her jersey when she reached midfield.

"Are you going to kneel down and take it off?" the official asked.

"No," she said.

"Come on. The place would go nuts."

"They're trying to turn it into a novelty," Chastain said later, sitting in the owner's box at 3Com Stadium. "It wasn't a novelty. That wasn't the intent. The intent was to celebrate the moment."

Television newscasters took off their own shirts in front of her, and corporate types wanted her to remove her jersey to pitch their goods. She declined. Each time, she said no. She scored a foosball goal on the NBA star Kevin Garnett in a Nike commercial, and she held her ground as Garnett said, "What's up with the shirt?"

"I'm not going to do it again," Chastain said. "I always say no. It was a spontaneous reaction. It's not something you think about before."

In October of 1999, Santa Clara proclaimed Brandi Chastain Day during a home match against Notre Dame. Twenty alums of the Santa Clara soccer team were invited for the occasion. Father Locatelli, the university president, handed a rose to each of the alums, and they formed a sort of tunnel for Chastain to run through. When she emerged from the tunnel, Chastain whipped off her T-shirt on a dare from the school's sports marketing director.

"You haven't changed," Father Locatelli told her, his face bright red.

"Oops, sorry, Father," Chastain said, and she put her shirt back on.

On a rainy day a month later, Father Locatelli was handing out trophies to members of the Santa Clara team for their first-place finish in the West Coast Conference. Looking around, he could not find Chastain. Finally, he spotted her wearing a black, hooded coat in the drizzle.

"I didn't recognize you with all the clothes on," he said.

The afterglow of the World Cup, along with an undefeated soccer season by the Santa Clara women's team and Chastain's presence as an assistant coach, had brought a lively feeling to the campus in the fall, said Bjornsrud, the assistant athletic director.

Santa Clara had dropped football in 1993. Women's soccer was the biggest sports draw in the fall of 1999. It outdrew men's soccer by more than 2–1. A total of 15,716 spectators had come to see the top-ranked women's team, compared to 6,256 to see the men's team, which would unexpectedly reach the national championship game. A crowd of 4,000, the size of the Santa Clara student body, had seen an early season match against Stanford. Attendance increased 50 percent overall, gate receipts had doubled. There was something else, too. Bjornsrud was getting more calls from women in their thirties and forties, interested in careers in sports administration. Doors seemed to be opening, roles seemed to be reversing. Male athletes were approaching her, asking why the women were getting all the attention.

"I don't know if I'm answering out of hope or reality, but I want to believe the World Cup has had a big effect," Bjornsrud said. "There is a different air of confidence from crew to cross-country to basketball to soccer. Women carry themselves differently. They feel they have something to contribute. They no longer feel they're being viewed as something we have to provide because of Title IX."

The old resistance is not gone, though. Even with an undefeated top-ranked women's soccer team, even with twice the attendance and twice the media coverage, corporate sponsors still had more interest in the men's team, she said. The corporate gatekeepers are still men, looking to put money into men's sports. One client called her, offering to sponsor a game for $5,000, and said, "I should be doing this for the women, but I've got to go with the men."

"It's a different market niche," Bjornsrud said of women's sports. "We haven't discovered it yet, how to get the gatekeepers of corporate dollars to actually put up big bucks for a women's sports team. Years of tradition fly in the face of that."

Still, there was a sense, in her 47th year, that a major corner had been turned by the World Cup, Bjornsrud said.

"I'd like to go to sleep for 10 years and wake up and see the impact," she said.

Two weeks after the final, Julie Foudy flew home to Southern California, listening to the airline headphones. First she heard Ricky Martin's "Living La Vida Loca," then "We Like to Party" by Venga Boys. The American women had danced to these songs in the locker room before each game. A flood of emotions surged in her and Foudy began sobbing. She had been too exhausted and drained after the match to feel any real sentiment. Then she and her teammates had spent two weeks celebrating, appearing with David Letterman, visiting the White House. Now she was alone on a plane and for the first time she began to consider what the American women had accomplished. She tried to write an e-mail to each of her teammates but she began crying. Once, twice, three times she tried, but the tears kept coming and she had to stop. Finally, at home that evening, she finished her letter.

Winning the World Cup was a wonderful thing, Foudy wrote, but it did not compare to the camaraderie of winning, to the locker room dance parties, the chest-bumping warm-ups, the Scrabble games and movies in the players' lounge, the pregame huddles and the fist-pumping speeches by Carla Overbeck.

"The thought of what we accomplished together makes me so

damn proud," Foudy wrote. "Even with all of the pressure of the tournament on our shoulders, we kicked ass. After all the chaos dies down, when we are old and cranky, don't ever forget the most important element of this whole tournament. We did it for each other. All the tough practices in Orlando, all the fitness when no one else was watching, all the miles traveled. We pushed each other, we encouraged each other. We believed in each other."

They believed in the invisible days, when no one came to see them but their parents, when they lived on candy bars in China and did not have running water in Haiti. They believed when the doubters told them they could never fill giant stadiums for the World Cup. They believed when Michelle Akers went out and the final distilled itself to penalty kicks. They believed when the American soccer federation told them they did not deserve to be paid as much as the men. They believed and they stuck together and they won because they would not accept anything less than victory.

SOURCES

I covered the 1999 Women's World Cup for *The New York Times*, spending nearly every day with the American players from May through the conclusion of the tournament in mid-July. I also traveled extensively with the American team during autumn matches after the World Cup, and visited Beijing to speak with the Chinese players, coaches, and officials. My primary sources for reconstructing the match were these extensive personal interviews, along with repeated viewings of the final on videotape and photographs of decisive moments. I have also included a short history of women's sports, which I gathered over the past six-plus years covering international events as the chief Olympics correspondent of the *Times*.

Chapter 1. Interviews with the American players and coaches. Eduardo Galeano, the Uruguayan author, wrote a poetic history of soccer, which included the record for penalty kicks, in his book, *Soccer in Sun and Shadow*.

Chapter 2. Interviews. Statistical information was provided by the National Collegiate Athletic Association and the Soccer Industry

Council of America. Bonnie DeSimone's story on the American women working together appeared on July 12, 1999.

Chapter 3. Interviews. Ann Killion's column on the appeal of the World Cup appeared on July 12, 1999. Mitch Albom's comments on the tournament appeared in *USA Today* on July 12, 1999. Larry Rohter of *The New York Times* wrote a story from Rio on July 4, 1999, describing the cultural nuances of women's soccer in Brazil. Galeano's book also discussed this subject. An article on lesbians in Australian soccer appeared in the *Sydney Morning Herald* on September 17, 1999. Rick Reilly's column on the women's soccer team appeared in *Sports Illustrated* on June 29, 1999. An article by Gary Smith concerning the Australian soccer team's nude calendar appeared in *Sports Illustrated* on December 13, 1999. A story on genital mutilation of African women, written by Celia W. Dugger, appeared in *The New York Times* on October 5, 1996. Amnesty International issued a report on female genital mutilation in 1997. A magazine article on Amy Love, written by Tracie Cone, appeared in the *San Jose Mercury News* on April 12, 1998. Clay Berling wrote about Love in *Soccer America* magazine on October 18, 1999. Holly Brubach's article on female athletes appeared in *The New York Times Magazine* on June 23, 1996.

Chapter 4. Interviews with the American players, coaches, trainers, doctors, and equipment manager.

Chapter 5. Interviews.

Chapter 6. Interviews. A series of essays titled *China for Women*, published by the Feminist Press at the City University of New York, addresses the complicated cultural facets of female life in China. The New York–based human rights group, Human Rights in China, published in 1995 a report on discrimination against women in China. A story on the scorning of female babies, written by Nicholas D. Kristof, appeared in *The New York Times* on July 21, 1993. A story by John Pomfret on the reaction in Beijing to the final match appeared in the *Washington Post* on July 11, 1999.

Chapter 7. Interviews. David Wallechinsky's *The Complete Book of the Summer Olympics* contains a detailed history of the modern Games. Information for a short section on sports for women in Iran was gathered during a trip I made to Tehran for the *Times* in the spring of 1998, and during subsequent telephone interviews for the book.

Chapter 8. Interviews. Statistical information was provided by the National Collegiate Athletic Association, the Women's Sports Foundation, and the National Federation of High School Associations. Curt A. Levey's op-ed piece on Title IX appeared in *USA Today* on July 12, 1999. A story describing a Title IX case in Lake George appeared in the *Albany* (New York) *Times Union* on September 4, 1999. A helpful reference for a history of Title IX cases can be found on a website maintained by the University of Iowa at bailiwick.lib.uiowa.edu/ge. Mia Hamm's autobiography is called *Go for the Goal.*

Chapter 9. Interviews. *The Complete Book of the Summer Olympics.*

Chapter 10. Interviews. An arresting account of Michelle Akers' struggles with chronic fatigue syndrome is contained in her autobiography, *Standing Fast.* She also maintains a Web site at michelleakers.com.

Chapter 11. Interviews. An article about the sexual harassment suit filed by former Oklahoma University soccer player Kathleen Peay written by the Associated Press appeared on October 7, 1999. An article about a hunting accident involving Bob Knight, written by Tom Vanden Brook, appeared in the *Milwaukee Journal Sentinel* on October 22, 1999. Debbie Keller's lawsuit against Anson Dorrance was filed on July 19, 1999, in United States District Court in Greensboro, North Carolina, as case No. 1:99CV400. An article by S. L. Price concerning the suit appeared in *Sports Illustrated* on Dec. 7, 1998. Another article concerning the suit by Martha Brant appeared in *Newsweek* on March 1, 1999.

Chapter 12. Interviews.

Chapter 13. Interviews. Kristine Lilly's description of soccer as a balm to soothe personal difficulties appeared in an authorized biography of the players, written by Marla Miller and titled *All-American Girls.*

Chapter 14. Interviews.

Chapter 15. Interviews. Amy Shipley's story appeared in the *Washington Post* on December 25, 1999. A story on potential marketing of the U.S. team appeared in *USA Today* on July 9, 1999.

Chapter 16. Interviews. Shep Messing described head games played by goalkeepers in his autobiography, *The Education of an American Soccer Player.*

Chapter 17. Interviews. Bill Dwyre's article on Briana Scurry appeared in the *Los Angeles Times* on July 15, 1999. Phil Hersh's article on Scurry appeared in the *Chicago Tribune* on December 13, 1999. Ann Gerhart's column on Brandi Chastain appeared in the *Washington Post* on July 14, 1999. Rebecca Mead's column on Brandi Chastain appeared in the *New Yorker* magazine in July, 1999.

Chapter 18. Interviews. Correspondence between the United States soccer federation and the players' attorney, John Langel. An article by Scott M. Reid on salaries of federation officials appeared in the *Orange County Register* on January 24, 2000. Outtake from Michelle Akers' diary first appeared in *Sports Illustrated,* December 20, 1999.

BIBLIOGRAPHY

Akers, Michelle with Tim Nash. *Standing Fast*. Apex, N.C.: JTC Sports, 1997.

Blais, Madeleine. *In These Girls, Hope is a Muscle*. New York: Warner Books, 1995.

Burton Nelson, Mariah. *The Stronger Women Get, the More Men Love Football: Sexism and the American Culture of Sports*. New York: Avon Books, 1994.

Dorrance, Anson, with Tim Nash. *Training Soccer Champions*. Apex, N.C.: JTC Sports, 1996.

Galeano, Eduardo. *Soccer in Sun and Shadow*, trans. Mark Fried. London: Verso, 1998.

Gardner, Paul. *The Simplest Game*. New York: Collier Books, 1994.

Glanville, Brian. *The Story of the World Cup*. London: Faber and Faber, 1997.

Gregg, Lauren, with Tim Nash. *The Champion Within*. Burlington, N.C.: JTC Sports, 1999.

Guttmann, Allen. *Women's Sports: A History*. New York: Columbia University Press, 1991.

Hamm, Mia, with Aaron Heifetz. *Go for the Goal*. New York: Harper-Collins, 1999.

Hey, Kenneth, and Peter Moore. *The Caterpillar Doesn't Know.* New York: The Free Press, 1998.

Howe, Florence and Susannah Driver, eds. *China for Women.* New York: The Feminist Press at the City University of New York, 1995.

McPhee, John. *Levels of the Game.* New York: The Noonday Press, 1969.

Messing, Shep, with David Hirshey. *The Education of an American Soccer Player.* New York: Bantam Books, 1981.

Miller, Marla. *All-American Girls.* New York: Pocket Books, 1999.

Okrent, Daniel. *Nine Innings.* New York: Houghton, Mifflin Company, 1985.

Savage, Jeff. *Julie Foudy, Soccer Superstar.* Minneapolis: Lerner Publications, 1999.

Schum, Tim. *Coaching Soccer.* Indianapolis: Masters Press, 1996.

Wallechinsky, David. *The Complete Book of the Summer Olympics.* New York: Little, Brown and Company, 1996.

ACKNOWLEDGMENTS

T HOSE WHO DISMISS SOCCER often do so with the complaint that too many matches end without scoring or inherent drama. My rebuttal was that a 0–0 match was not only worthy of viewing, but was worthy of an entire book.

I would like to thank Neil Amdur, sports editor of *The New York Times*, for giving me the time and encouragement to write this book. I would also like to thank Erik Eckholm, Elisabeth Rosenthal, and Yan Ping of the *Times*' Beijing Bureau for their assistance, insight and hospitality.

I'm grateful to Tony DiCicco, head coach of the American team, and to Lauren Gregg, his top assistant, for countless hours of patient explanation. Without the diligence and enthusiasm of Aaron Heifetz, the team spokesman, in setting up interviews, this book would not have been possible. It should be acknowledged also that Aaron broke the world sprinting record for a man in a vest as he raced toward Brandi Chastain after her famous penalty kick. I would like to thank Marla Messing and Donna de Varona, the two chief organizers of the Women's World Cup, for their extensive interviews and unfailing candor.

Andreas Herren, a spokesman for FIFA, soccer's world governing body, generously wrote a letter to the Chinese soccer federation on my behalf. Once the visit was approved, Chinese officials, coaches, and players could not have been more receptive. Harold Xu was my lifeline in Beijing, with his translating, appointment-making, and perceptiveness. Elliott Almond of the *San Jose* (California) *Mercury News*, who wrote extensively about the Chinese team during the World Cup, was kind enough to offer his help and to put me in touch with Liu Jing, sports editor of the *China Youth Daily* newspaper. Ling Cao, a graduate student at Claremont University in California, graciously agreed to translate Chinese Web sites for news regarding the soccer team. Jun Shen, a college player at Iowa State University and a close friend of the Chinese captain, Sun Wen, provided valuable information about life as a female soccer player in China, as did two college professors who befriended the team, Stephen Tsih of San Jose City College, and Ying Wu of Millersville (Pennsylvania) University.

I would like to thank my friends Phil Hersh and Christine Brennan for their advice and support. Other reporters who realized the value of the Women's World Cup and gave it thorough, professional coverage deserve special mention. Among them were George Vecsey, Bonnie DeSimone, Skip Bayless, Amy Shipley, Grant Wahl, Grahame Jones, Mike Penner, Randy Harvey, Mark Starr, Martha Brant, Diane Pucin, Mark Zeigler, Scott Reid, Ann Killion, Jody Meacham, Peter Brewington, Jill Lieber, David Leon Moore, John Powers, Shira Springer, Mike Jensen, Liz Robbins, Steve Davis, Michelle Kaufman, Mechelle Voepel, Barry Wilner, Liz Robbins, Filip Bondy, Michael Lewis, Kelly Whiteside, Ursula Reel, Gwen Knapp, Steve Goff, Dan Giesin and Abby Haight.

David Hirshey at HarperCollins could not have been more ebullient and supportive as an editor who is unsurpassed in his knowledge and love of soccer. Thanks to his soccer-literate assistant, Jesse Gerstein, for his discerning eye regarding the manuscript and accompanying photographs. And special thanks to my agent, Elyse Cheney, for her guidance and willingness to take a chance.

My greatest thanks go to my wife, Deborah Longman, for understanding the peripatetic life of sportswriting, and to my daughter, Julie-Ann, a soccer player who knew immediately why the American women were so popular. "Because they're good," she said.

Insert One

p. 7: "Gao Hong . . ." —J. Brett Whitesell, International Sports Images

"The graceful Joy Fawcett . . ." —J. Brett Whitesell, International Sports Images

p. 8: "Sara Whalen . . ." —J. Brett Whitesell, International Sports Images

"Kate Sobrero . . ." —Phil Stephens Photography

Insert Two

p. 1: "Michelle Akers . . ." —Phil Stephens Photography

"Balanced with her left hand . . ." —Robert Beck, *Sports Illustrated*

p. 2: "Michelle Akers . . ." —J. Brett Whitesell, International Sports Images

"Michelle Akers . . ." —Peter Read Miller, *Sports Illustrated*

p. 3: "Akers lies like a boxer . . ." —John McDonough, *Sports Illustrated*

p. 4: "Mia Hamm gets . . ." —Phil Stephens Photography

"U.S. captain Carla Overbeck . . ." —Michael Stahlschmdt/Sideline Sports Photography

p. 5: "Briana Scurry . . ." —Michael Stahlschmidt/Sideline Sports Photography

"Mia Hamm . . ." —John McDonough, *Sports Illustrated*

p. 6: "The American players . . ." —J. Brett Whitesell, International Sports Images

"Chastain . . ." —Robert Beck, *Sports Illustrated*

p. 7: "Brandi Chastain . . ." —Robert Beck, *Sports Illustrated*

"The goalkeeper . . ." —Robert Beck, *Sports Illustrated*

p. 8: "We proved to the world . . ." —J. Brett Whitesell, International Sports Images

"Brandi Chastain . . ." —Phil Stephens Photography